Praise for Music to My Years: Life and Love Between the Notes

"Artie Kane is unique … uniquely intelligent, brilliant, and in spite of his struggles with himself … uniquely lovable. Also, for anyone interested in the inner byways of the Hollywood musical scene, his book is a highly recommended read." — *John Williams*

"Coming from a music-loving, humorous, and glamorous Hollywood family, I found this book encompasses all those things, and more. A wonderful read …" — *Joan Benny*

"Artie Kane's personal story is by turns amusing, depressing, uplifting, disastrous, and hilarious … but always fascinating. While fostering an early prodigious talent and evolving into the highly developed artist he is today, he has used his years (and his ears!!) to learn and absorb all the aspects of music and life that have confronted him. I feel blessed to have known him, and continue to be astounded by his constantly evolving perspectives. Prepare to be amazed! (and amused!!)" — *Dave Grusin*

"Artie Kane is a beloved friend and a world-class musician with quite a story to tell. Reading his book was like discovering a new classic movie on TCM, one where John Garfield plays piano instead of the violin, dates every hard-boiled dame on the lot (and I mean EVERY dame) and then ends up in paradise with Doris Day. A page turner, a music lesson, a love story and a thousand laughs, this is both a man and a book well worth spending time with, and I am honored and thankful for the good fortune to have done both." — *Marc Shaiman*

Music to My Years
Life and Love Between the Notes

Music to My Years
Life and Love Between the Notes

as told by

Artie Kane

to

MARIAN BLUE

AND

JOANN KANE

edited by Candace Allen

AMPHORA
EDITIONS
Venice CA

Music to My Years copyright © 2017 by Artie Kane and JoAnn Kane.

All rights reserved. No part of this book may be used, reproduced or transmitted in any manner without written permission except in the case of brief quotations in the context of reviews and articles.

ISBN 978-0-9836550-3-9 (Hardcover Edition)

Library of Congress Control Number: 2017946460

Cover Photo: *Phil Teele, Bass Trombonist/Photographer*
Photo Restoration: *Michael Stadler*
Dust Jacket and Book Design: *Morgan Bondelid*
Frontispiece & Back Cover Photo: *Joel Franklin*
Recording Engineer: *David Malony*
Archivist: *Bob Richardson*

Additional credits and permissions are listed on page 349 and are considered a continuation of the copyright page.

Printed on acid-free paper in China by P. Chan & Edward, Inc.

Published by Amphora Editions
P.O. Box 212
Venice, CA, 90294 USA
www.AmphoraEditions.com

Text set in Garamond

For my mother and Uncle Joe

Artie's Family Tree

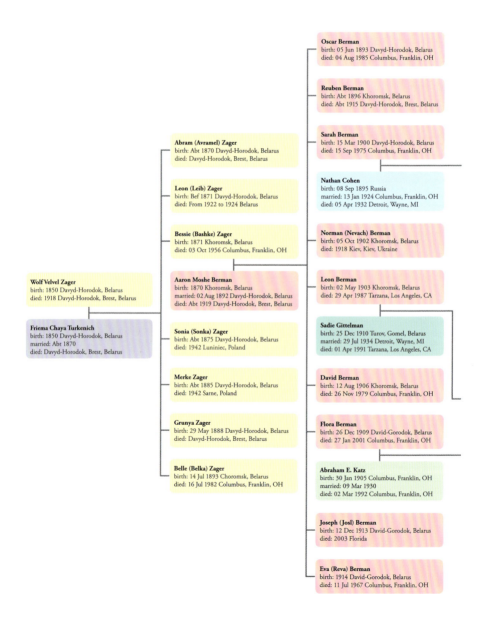

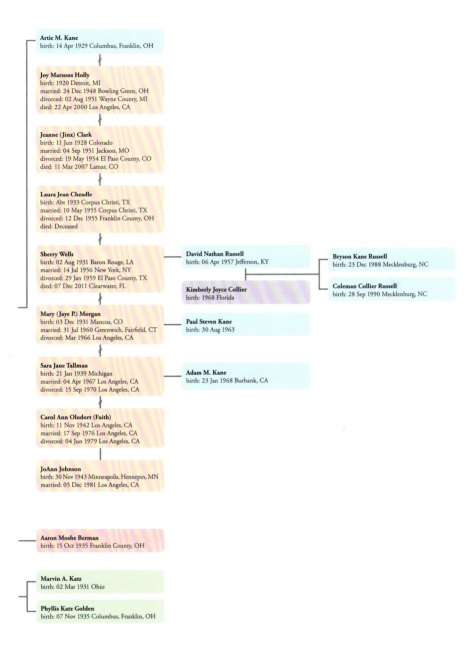

CONTENTS

ONE: *Straighten Up and Fly Right*	1
TWO: *America the Beautiful*	5
THREE: *This Could Be the Start of Something Big*	11
FOUR: *You've Got a Friend*	25
FIVE: *Music, Music, Music*	34
SIX: *Got a Lot of Livin' to Do*	49
SEVEN: *Skater's Waltz*	64
EIGHT: *You're in the Army Now*	82
NINE: *The Second Time Around*	91
TEN: *Short People*	104
ELEVEN: *Brother, Can You Spare a Dime?*	110
TWELVE: *New York, New York*	131
THIRTEEN: *The Party's Over*	136
FOURTEEN: *California Here I Come*	141
FIFTEEN: *Charade*	174
SIXTEEN: *Love in Bloom*	198
SEVENTEEN: *High Society*	219
EIGHTEEN: *Tradition*	229
NINETEEN: *What Kind of Fool Am I?*	244
TWENTY: *Strike Up the Band*	257
TWENTY-ONE: *A Time for Love*	265
TWENTY-TWO: *Blue Hawaii*	279
TWENTY-THREE: *Take the "AA" Train*	292
TWENTY-FOUR: *It's a New World*	306
TWENTY-FIVE: *Our Love Is Here to Stay*	328
ACKNOWLEDGEMENTS	346
INDEX	351

A piano lives at the center of my world.
My mother, eight wives, four girlfriends and three sons
elbow their way into the space around it.

ONE

Straighten Up and Fly Right

The walls slide in and out like a kaleidoscope. Cigarette smoke swirls around my head. I grab the edge of the conference table and focus on a notepad to stop the motion. I feel a hand on my shoulder. My lawyer, David, leans toward me and asks if I'm okay. I nod. He hands me three deposition notices from the plaintiff, calling musicians from my orchestra for questioning. I breathe faster but can't get enough air. I'm sure it's another panic attack.

Peering over her horn-rimmed glasses, my ex-girlfriend's attorney announces she intends to take this case before a judge. Her threat hangs heavy in the cramped conference room.

My collar's too tight. I loosen it. Sweat slides down my neck in rivulets. No settlement has emerged in fifteen months of accusations and investigations in a palimony suit against me based on my two-year cohabitation with an orchestra contractor—a migraine-afflicted chain smoker. Now I'm headed to court—maybe even bankruptcy—considering attorneys' fees.

I shudder. I want to scream, "Take it all: the house, the car, furniture, whatever. Just get the hell out of my life."

Instead, I bolt upright. My chair crashes behind me. Patti and her lawyer look at me. A slight grin pulls at the corner of the attorney's mouth as she turns to her client and whispers, her eyes fixed on me. I lunge for the door and stumble out of the airless room, down the hall, and to the parking lot. I stop; I can't remember where I parked. "Where's my goddamn car?"

Minutes later, I spot it and head that direction. Punching the unlock button, I fling the door open and reach for a brown paper bag from the supply I keep under the seat. I blow into the bag. It inflates. I take in a breath. The bag deflates. I repeat the process several times until I catch my breath, relax and stop hyperventilating.

I stand. My head spins. I lean against the car, steady myself and wait for the panic to pass. Questions swarm through my mind. Will my colleagues side with Patti because she provides them with work? She says I promised to marry her. I didn't. No one knows anything. Too embarrassed about the relationship, I've never spoken about it except to my shrink.

Something's wrong with my brain. I can't think. I feel weak, unable to cope. I'm losing control and allowing this woman and her lawsuit to overwhelm me. Why? I have everything to live for: the love of my life and a successful career—which I fear I'm about to ruin.

The lawsuit triggers my feelings of dread; the settlement conferences and depositions bring on panic. My tranquilizers stop working, so I take more, but my nerves are stripped raw.

I get in my car and grip the wheel to stop my hands from shaking. I can't clear my head. I notice my lawyer watching me from the open doorway. I drive over and say, "I can't go back in that room. I can't face those women snickering and plotting my demise." I tell him I'm sick and unsteady and promise to go see my doctor.

David must think I'm crazy, but in a caring tone, he asks if I'm able to drive. Tears well up in my eyes. I tell him yes. Truthfully, I need something to calm me down, take the edge off. My heart is racing. My doctors argued for a month about my condition. Take the pills;

don't take the pills. Sixteen years I've taken my prescribed concoction of Valium and Dilantin, but last week my internist cut out the Valium cold turkey. Ever since, I feel anxious, my skin crawls and I itch all over, my head is on fire, or I'm freezing cold. Anguish and despair crush my spirit.

I'm afraid I'll destroy my last chance at happiness—that I'll lose my career, my music and the girl I'm so sure I can love forever. Just when all of life's paths were converging into one happy journey, Patti surfaced like a great white shark, gripping a lawsuit between her teeth.

I feel drained. I change my mind about the doctor and head for home, realizing I haven't slept in a week. I'm thinner; my pants sag around my hips and drag along the ground. Everything I eat backs up. My throat burns. My ears ring. At home, I go to my desk and look over the music editor's notes on a new show. I watch a video of the opening sequence. I don't have a clue what to write. My thoughts are jumbled; not one musical idea that fits the scene comes to mind. I'm incapable of creating music for the films I was hired to score. The blank page of manuscript paper stares back at me; my pencil stops midair. I know I can't meet the deadline and must pass up another job.

I rush to my piano; it's always been my solace. Quivering and twitching, my hands hover inches above the keyboard, unable to settle on a musical goal. Tears stream through my beard, my shoulders shake. Without music, I have nothing; I am nothing.

Aaron and his fiddle

TWO

AMERICA THE BEAUTIFUL

Fifty years before Valium took control of my life, my uncle Joe called to my mother, "Look Sarah, Aaron runs to the piano and plays his violin notes on the keyboard. Maybe we should switch him to piano lessons instead of teaching him music on a pint-size fiddle."

Mother agreed. "I told you, Joe, he likes the piano better. He's always at it, trying to reach the keys. I put him on the bench the other day, and I think he would have stayed for hours if I hadn't had two customers waiting for comb-outs in my shop. Aaron doesn't bang on the keys like other children; he uses his fingers and listens to each note."

With that, Joe and my mother convinced Agnes Wright, who taught piano in our neighborhood, to take me as a student. And so, at age three and a half, I began my life in music.

As a child, I listened to this story and others about my family's emigration from Davyd-Horodok in

The piano feels better

Belarus to the United States. They were part of the second generation of Jews who had begun their exodus from Eastern Europe to escape the pogroms and anti-Semitism of the Russian czars. The accounts of their journey and determination, especially my mother's and Uncle Joe's, influenced my life and helped shape my attitudes about family, discrimination, love and music.

In 1909 my great uncle Leib Zager, a blacksmith, secured two visas and took his youngest sister, Belle, to New York and on to Columbus, Ohio, where a friend of hers had settled. Before returning to Belarus, he also sent a visa to my uncle Oscar who had saved money for his passage to New York by making and selling cheese on a relative's farm. Leib had made connections in Columbus and persuaded Jewish businessmen to vouch that Oscar had the means to support himself. As the first family member in the United States to set up a business, Oscar relied on his marketing experience to purchase goods cheaply and sell them at a profit. He opened a shop in a narrow building squeezed between two warehouses, and in a small window, he displayed trinkets and shiny objects that attracted customers.

Life in the United States was challenging, but gradually, those first to arrive built up businesses from meager savings and sent for other members of the family. My mother, Sarah, fourteen at the time, begged her brother Oscar to arrange for her passage to America and threatened to drown herself if he didn't. She seemed even then to be what we now call a drama queen. I would learn about her histrionics soon enough, but not before I discovered her tenacity. When she arrived and saw the jewelry in Oscar's shop window, she put a ring on each of her fingers, a bracelet on both arms, and a gold-colored chain around her neck. Oscar told her it wasn't the kind of jewelry she should wear, but she insisted. After her skin turned green, she decided Oscar might have been right, and she returned the jewelry. People often mature with experience and age, and my mother was no exception. By the time she reached thirty-five, she was the family matriarch.

Mother quickly learned English, and Oscar found her a job as a seamstress at a department store called Reeser's. She earned three dollars a week. Later, the manager of Reeser's shoe department set Oscar up with three hundred pairs of shoes to sell at discount.

Yes, the family struggled, but unlike my great-grandfather Velvel Zager, who was bayonetted to death by Russian soldiers enforcing a curfew as he walked home from Shul, they were no longer afraid for their lives.

My pretty mother

My grandfather Aaron Moshe Berman died in Russia during the flu pandemic of 1919, and as a result, his youngest children, Joe, Flora and Eva, were considered orphans even though their mother was alive. Though scared, the children felt lucky to be among those sent to England in 1922. From there, they sailed to Ellis Island. They arrived aboard the *USS George Washington,* a ship of 2,500 orphans under the age of ten, and moved in with my mother.

The family's goal was to live in the United States, and Oscar paved their way, sending visas and money to his brothers and sisters. His brother Leon, however, arrived in Nova Scotia without papers. When he called the family in Columbus for help, my father, who was courting but not yet married to my mother, picked Leon up at the dock, took him to Windsor, Ontario, and smuggled him across the border to Detroit. From there, they went to Columbus where a Jewish organization re-created his naturalization papers.

Everybody worked; everybody contributed to the family. Uncle Oscar started Leon in the shoe business. Aunt Flora worked at a confectioner's shop after school, Uncle Joe sold apples and newspapers at the corner of Main and High, and Eva eventually helped in Leon's shoe store.

The last of the family left Russia in 1922 when Uncle Dave brought my grandmother Bessie and his cousin Max to the United States, landing at Ellis Island by way of Cuba. They traveled with an Irish family. To fit in, Uncle Dave and Max had dyed their hair red.

My parents married January 13, 1924, and moved to Detroit where my father worked as a tailor. He'd been born Nathan Chapneck, a name he changed, or immigration officials changed—to Cohen—upon his arrival at Ellis Island. His U.S. Army honorable discharge papers show that between 1917 and 1919 he served two years in the U.S. Army in France. According to Uncle Joe, the family liked my father because he was helpful to them and good to my mother.

Relatives on my father's side of the family were musicians in Russia. Perhaps some of my musical ability was a gift passed down from my father

Sarah and Nathan Cohen,
married January 13, 1924

Nathan, Aaron, and Sarah

to me. I wish I could remember him, but he died in 1932, a week before my third birthday and before I got to know him. In early photographs, my father is holding me in his arms and smiling at me. I look content and safe. He must be responsible for my having been a happy child. In another photo, I'm riding a wooden scooter in front of our Detroit house while he clicks the camera as I play.

My father with me at four months old

My first set of wheels

I owe my continued happiness in life to Uncle Joe who pushed me toward music and gave me purpose in life. He became my self-appointed music practice supervisor and told me about living in Davyd-Horodok as a child. "When the Russian troops stopped in town, we couldn't go to school because it wasn't safe to be out on the street. Flora and I sometimes hid in our cellar watching through peepholes as the soldiers marched past our house. We were frightened of them. If they came through while we were in school, we had to wait until the army left before it was safe to go home."

One day while he sat at the piano with me, I asked him if he had learned to play the violin at school in Russia.

"Flora learned music at a Russian girls' school, but I only learned reading and numbers at mine," he said. "One of our neighbors played in a small orchestra. He taught me to play on his violin like I tried to teach you."

"I like the piano better."

"I can see that. It's good we found a fine teacher like Miss Wright for you. You are a lucky boy that our family came to America and that you were born in the United States. In Russia, you wouldn't have had music lessons or a piano."

Reading at age four

Uncle Joe — the reason I'm a musician

THREE

This Could Be the Start of Something Big

I grew up as Aaron Cohen, a boy with my own room who took piano lessons, was spoiled by my grandmother and was pressed to succeed by my mother, Aunt Eva and Uncle Joe while Uncle Dave sat in *his* chair reading *Der Tog,* a Yiddish newspaper about anti-Semitism and the diaspora of Russian Jews. The only music Dave liked was sung by the cantors at temple Agudas Achim. Their loud voices sounded sad, out of tune, and hurt my ears. I was afraid of Dave, not just because he wouldn't let me play the piano when he was home, but because he was disagreeable. He was impatient with his mother and yelled at her when she'd fall asleep in a chair. He was unpredictable, and I never knew if I was in danger when his temper exploded.

Wearing my tallith

The awkward combination of these five adults—two unmarried uncles, one unmarried aunt and two widows—fouled up my feelings about affection. The brothers and sisters hollered a lot because Bubbe was hard of hearing, and because they often argued with each other. I don't recall any tenderness—any hugging or kissing between the single members of my family—and though they were attentive to me, I don't recall being cuddled by my mother or hugged or kissed by anyone. There were no examples of fondness or warmth between them.

Sarah and Aaron
Aunt Flora and cousin Marvin

In contrast, my mother's other sister, Aunt Flora, and her husband, Abe, adored each other. Abe couldn't keep his hands off Flora. She'd be in the kitchen dishing up dinner for their kids, Uncle Joe and me, and Abe would be kissing the back of her neck. Flora would say, "Not now, Abe," but I could tell she liked it. Aunt Flora was a good cook, unlike anyone in our house. Uncle Joe and I would go there to get a tasty meal whenever they'd invite us. Their oldest son, Marvin, was my pal even though he was two years younger. Marvin was smart and his schemes got us in trouble, but Mother always blamed me as the instigator.

Sometimes on the weekend, we'd all go for a ride on Sunday with Abe and Flora. Joe would sit in front, and Mother and Flora in the back with Marvin and me between them. Abe would turn around while he was driving and say, "Hi honey." He'd reach around to rub Flora's knee and she would again say, "Not now, Abe." I was lucky to have these examples of love and affection and lucky Uncle Abe kept control of the car.

Uncle Joe was my sponsor and champion. He would come home early from work to supervise my practicing—before Uncle Dave arrived—put a firm hand on my shoulder and say, "Time to practice, Aaron."

My hopeful mother

At four years old, I had to be lifted onto the bench, until Joe built a step for me. He'd sit in the chair next to the piano and say, "Take that section a little slower until you get it right, and watch your fingering." Years later, he told me how I'd work it out carefully until I learned the notes, and then I'd play it up to speed. He said I'd get mad if I stumbled and was petulant if he stopped me and said, "Do it again." Since Joe had played both the violin and the accordion, he knew what it took to learn music; he was strict and didn't let me get by with anything. He made sure I was well prepared for my lessons with Miss Wright. No kid could have had more encouragement than I received from my teacher and uncle with my mother cheering me on. Joe told me later he was amazed how quickly I learned, that I devoured music and could play pieces all the way through the first time I saw them. I always wanted more at each lesson, especially Bach and Mozart.

Comfortable at a keyboard

At my first competition, when I was five and a half years old, I won a statewide contest for six-to-twelve-year-old piano students, sponsored by The Ohio Federation of Music Clubs. I took first place and Mother read all the praise from newspaper articles to me. According to Joe, I had no fear, only concentration and a fierce determination that allowed no mistakes.

DURING GRADE SCHOOL, I wasn't always happy to practice. I liked playing games and marbles with other kids and didn't want to stop. On days when Mother was in charge of my practice time, I'd hear her holler "sonny boy" a block away and wish she'd leave me alone. Once I started playing the piano, though, I didn't want to stop until I'd learned and worked out the fingering of each piece and could play it perfectly. It didn't matter how much music Miss Wright assigned; I learned everything. I wanted to please her and Joe.

Competitions were easy for me to win until I was about nine, but as I got older, I began to hate them. With cold hands and an upset stomach, I felt scared and unsure of myself. Teachers smelling of strong perfume and judges who swarmed around to watch my fingering and hand positions made me uncomfortable. It was hard to concentrate. They talked while I played and didn't care if I heard them or if they crowded me at the piano. It must have been the start of my claustrophobia, that and being pinned in the back seat with Mother and Aunt Flora for car excursions. Before long, I felt lucky to get second place, which upset Mother.

School accompanist

After I had flawlessly performed the fiendish Mendelssohn Rondo Capriccioso on the *Major Bowes Amateur Hour* and lost to Tommy Smith, a towhead playing an elementary flute called a tonette, Miss Wright told me not to be concerned about contests anymore. She said I didn't need to prove to any judges that I could play. "They know you can play just like I know you can."

Practice time

I was progressing and loved the piano. No matter what went on in the family or at school, when I played the piano, everything in life was good. Joe bought tickets and took me to performances by every major pianist who played in Columbus, including Rudolph Serkin, Artur Rubinstein and Josef Hofmann. Inspired by artists who played with the Columbus Symphony, Miss Wright assigned me more difficult repertoire.

Through all the music lessons and performing commitments, I got good grades at Fairwood Elementary School. I could read quickly and did well in spelling bees. Arithmetic came easy for me, but I know that musicians often excel at math. In fifth grade, I played at school programs and accompanied for class singing. Mother wouldn't let me play sports for fear I'd injure my hands. Because of this, some of the boys, including Danny Peyton, called me a sissy piano player. Danny lived four blocks from me. He was a mean kid, a little beefier than most of my classmates, and he used to meet up with me as I walked to school. He wouldn't say anything, but he'd ball up his fist, stick out the knuckle of his third finger and hit me in my right arm just below my shoulder. Then he'd laugh and call me a sissy. I didn't want to be called anything worse, like tattletale, so I didn't tell my mother or Uncle Joe. I'd try to avoid Danny by leaving early or late, but he'd watch for me. My arm hurt and was always black and blue and yellow. I thought about defending myself, but I knew my mother would kill me if I hurt my hands. She never saw the bruises on my upper arm. I liked to believe I could beat up Danny, but instead, I hired Jack Hastings, a real big guy, to be my bodyguard. I stole money from my mother's pocketbook to pay Jack. It was worth it to watch Big Jack intimidate Danny.

One day when Jack was sick and had to stay home, Danny caught up with me and slammed me with a hard punch. I dropped my books in the snow, turned to my left, clasped my hands together, swung around with all my weight and caught Danny in the jaw and neck with both my hands. He went down, hard. I stood over him and thought: One of us is going to die. Danny lay there a while. I didn't move. I waited for the fight. When Danny got to his feet, he picked up his books and walked ahead of me to school. From that day on, he didn't hit me, and we became pretty good friends.

Mary Pryseski and Aaron Cohen prepare for concert

My mother, unaware of my achievements in self-defense, kept a scrapbook, including newspaper articles, about my musical accomplishments, competitions, honors and performances. When I was eleven, I won a scholarship to the Columbus Boychoir School, founded by Herbert Huffman, and now known as the American Boychoir School. In 1950 the organization moved to Princeton, but when I attended, it was a private school located on the grounds of the East Broad Street Presbyterian Church in Columbus, Ohio. The school didn't have a bus, and it was too far from my neighborhood for me to walk, so Uncle Joe would drop me off on his way to work at the Paradise Club, a bar he owned in the colored section of town. Uncle Dave also owned a bar, the Tivoli, in a poor white neighborhood.

MARY PRYSESKI TO JOIN PIANIST AARON COHEN, 9

An unusually precocious talent on the piano is Aaron Cohen, the 9 year-old Columbus lad who will be heard at 9 o'clock Easter Sunday night, Apr. 9, at the Hartman Theater in a program which he will share with a talented Bellaire coloratura soprano, Mary Pryseski.

There is a line of sympathy between the two musicians, Mary in her twenties and Aaron, aged 9. Miss Pryseski's parents came from Poland and she lost her father a few years ago. Aaron's ancestors came from Russia and he, too, has lost his father, though his mother has been at once his mentor and his inspiration.

Tickets will be on sale at Heaton's tomorrow morning and daily at a reasonable scale of prices. The complete program follows:

Ave Maria .... Schubert
Il Bacio .... Arditi
  Mary Pryseski.
Two Part Invitations .... J. S. Bach
  No. 4—Allegro.
  No. 13—Allegro.
  No. 8—Vivace Brilliante.
Sonata. Opus 49. No. 1 ..... Beethoven
  Andante.
  Allegro.
  Aaron Cohen.
Eili, Eili .... K. Schindler
Songs My Mother Taught Me . Dvorak
"Roberta, O Tu Che Adoro" from
  "Roberto Il Diavolo" .... Meyerbeer
  Mary Pryseski.
  Intermission.
Preludes .... Chopin
  Opus 28, No. 4.
  Opus 28, No. 20.
  Opus 28, No. 15.
  Opus 28, No. 6.
  Opus 28, No. 9.
  Aaron Cohen.
Fruhlingsglaube .... Schubert
Song of the Lark .... Grunn
  Mary Pryseski.
The Little Shepherd .... Debussy
Dr. Gradue Ad Parnassum ..... Debussy
  Aaron Cohen.

The school's music director, John Klein, was a gifted musician and teacher who wore stylish clothes and always looked suntanned. I was principal singer of the alto section and piano accompanist for performances. On special occasions when the group sang at the Presbyterian Church, Mr. Klein also had me play and accompany the Boychoir on the church's organ, a complicated instrument with so many settings and foot pedals that another student had to turn pages for me.

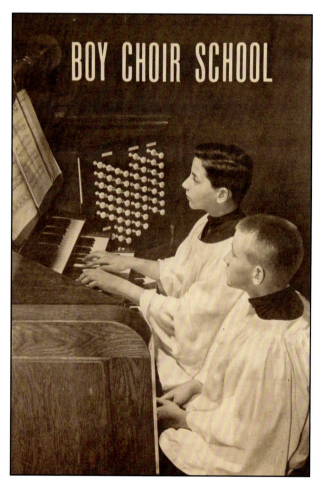

The pipe organ located in the sanctuary of the Broad Street Presbyterian Church in Columbus, Ohio, was originally built in 1937 by the M.P. Moller Company of Hagerstown, Maryland. It had four manuals with sixty-six ranks of pipes.

During the holiday season, my family had to wait for me to finish all the Christmas music programs at the church before we could leave on the train to Miami for our winter vacation. That was one of many sacrifices they made for my career. We never booked compartments on the train. Instead, we sat upright in assigned seats the entire trip, which took two days and one night. I couldn't sit still all that time, so I walked or ran through the cars. I sat in empty window seats, watched the towns and farms, and was fascinated by the maneuvering of the engines and tracks at stations along the way.

On one of our holidays, I met Matt Gilbert, a cartoonist for the *Cleveland Plain Dealer*. When I told him I was a pianist, he asked a lot of questions and said he'd heard of the Boychoir School. He recalled reading articles about me from the Columbus newspapers. I told him about the competition and scholarship to the Boychoir, and he asked if I had felt nervous at the contests. I told him about Major Bowes and my loss to the boy playing the tonette. I told him I was only winning second place now. Matt said I should change my name if I ever made it to the big time. Artie Kane was his suggestion. He said it was easy to remember and that I'd go further with that name than Aaron Cohen. Matt didn't say anything about Cohen being a Jewish name, but even at age eleven, I understood about prejudice. My mother often told me to keep to myself and not to talk about the family or what we did. Listening to Uncle Dave's rants was another clue.

AT THE BOYCHOIR SCHOOL, I had respect for Mr. Klein as a teacher. He taught me music theory and encouraged me to sing to improve my ear training. He seemed impressed with my ability to sight-read music by looking way ahead of what I was playing. My hands played the music I'd memorized seconds before while my mind absorbed where the piece

was going. One day, he invited me and another student, Lennie, to have dinner with him and his friend. I got permission from my mother, and they picked us up from school in a cool Pontiac convertible. Lennie sat up front with Klein's friend, a heavy, rosy-cheeked fellow who looked like Daddy Warbucks in *Little Orphan Annie*. I sat in back with Mr. Klein. I was on edge from the start, like before a competition. I didn't know how to act with my teachers outside of the classroom or when I wasn't performing.

We were supposed to go to a restaurant but ended up eating at his friend's house. On the way back, Mr. Klein notched up my discomfort by telling dirty jokes. I laughed but didn't really understand them.

On the drive back to our homes, we passed a park with swing sets. It wasn't dark yet, and Mr. Klein suggested we stop and try them out since there was still some daylight. I thought that was a dumb idea, and besides, I hated swings. Lenny thought it would be fun and got right on and started pumping his legs.

Mr. Klein kept saying, "Come on Aaron, try the swing." As soon as I got on, he put his hands on my lower back and pushed me to get going. I got right off and said I didn't like swings.

He sat on the swing and told another dirty joke. Then we got back in the car, and he said, "You like dirty jokes, don't you, Aaron?"

Choir's Soloist

This young pianist, Aaron Cohen, is a student at the Columbus Boys' Choir School, where he is instructed in the parts of speech and mathematics as well as the niceties of choral singing. An accomplished pianist, he is to be the soloist at the two concerts which this boys choir will give at Memorial Hall Thursday afternoon and night, May 8.

Aaron Cohen, 12, Doubles Thursday

One of the best juvenile pianists Columbus ever has known, Aaron Cohen, 12, is to be heard in the concert of the Columbus Boys Choir School. It will be given at two hours, 4 and 8:30 p. m., Thursday at Memorial Hall.

Developed by Agnes Wright, he now has a large repertoire of the classics; has played widely; has even been heard in a full-length concert program at the Hartman Theater—gave it, as a matter of fact, when suffering from fever. He will play a group of the classics in this concert.

He is a pupil of the choir school; takes his academic studies there; sings as a member of this organization which Herbert Huffman directs.

Tickets may be had now at Heaton's.

I hesitated but said yes. He told another joke. I felt queasy.

"Do these jokes excite you?"

I wasn't sure what he meant, so I said, "I don't know."

"Well, let's see." He reached over and put his hand on my crotch.

I threw up all over him. That was my answer. They drove me home immediately. For several days, I refused to speak, but Uncle Joe pried the story out of me. Joe left the house without a word, went to Mr. Huffman, the director of the school, and to Mr. Marshall, the headmaster.

He told them if John Klein was not gone from the school the next day, he would come back and kill him. Klein was dismissed. Over the next two years, I continued singing with the Boychoir and eventually became their staff accompanist.

There'd been talk of my accompanying summer music programs with the Boychoir School, but after my experience, the family decided to send me to Camp Wilson, the YMCA summer facility near Columbus. Though the camp originally boasted a militaristic bent, by the time I attended, it had evolved so that the emphasis was on crafts, dramatics and expressive arts such as music.

I didn't want to go to camp. I wanted to stay home, but Joe said I should have a change of scenery, let things settle and wait until after summer to go back to the Boychoir. Everyone needs an Uncle Joe.

Fifth from the left, Aaron Cohen at YMCA Camp outside Columbus, Ohio

FOUR

You've Got a Friend

When I was thirteen, Miss Wright had a meeting with Mother, Uncle Joe and me to say she'd taught me all she knew. She suggested we find another teacher who worked with more advanced students, and she gave us some names. I was very upset to lose her. No one could replace Miss Wright as a teacher. I craved her praise.

Uncle Joe found a highly regarded teacher at the Conservatory of Music in Cincinnati. He and Mother drove me on Sundays for lessons with Karin Dayas, who coached a few private students at her home. The long drive from Columbus made me carsick except when my cousin Marvin came along. He distracted me and talked about cars the whole way, naming each one that passed. When we arrived, I'd have to use the bathroom that was under the steps in the hallway. It reeked of disinfectant, which made me feel worse. Then I'd have my lesson. The teacher's teeth were stained yellow and brown from smoking, so I tried not to look at her when she talked. I looked at the keys and held my breath. In spite of these unpleasant circumstances, I learned a lot from her, but I never cared about pleasing her, nor did I feel the connection I had with Miss Wright.

Later that year, Miss Wright went to the hospital for an emergency appendectomy. She died during surgery because the anesthesiologist didn't know she had asthma. I was angry and inconsolable over her death and hated my piano lessons in Cincinnati even more. I still treasure the copy of Gershwin Preludes she gave me on my thirteenth birthday where she wrote, "For Aaron, with best birthday wishes, Agnes Wright."

On May 24, 1943, the Boychoir gave a well-publicized concert at Town Hall in New York that featured me playing several piano solos including Chopin's Scherzo in C# minor and Mendelssohn's Scherzo in B minor. From that performance, I won a year's scholarship to study piano with Madame Djane Lavoie-Herz, a prominent piano teacher in Manhattan.

By this time, both Uncle Joe and Uncle Dave had been drafted into the army to fight in World War II. With the tenacity of a bulldog, my tiny ninety-seven-pound mother took every opportunity to advance my career. She closed her beauty shop for the year and took us to New York that fall without any plan or financial support. We moved into the fourteen-story Greystone Hotel that had been built in 1923.

Greystone Hotel, NYC

We had a room with two studio couches, a table and two chairs, an upright piano and a bathroom. Sections of the hotel were being converted into apartments. The army occupied the first five floors. Every morning, several hundred soldiers exited the side entrance and marched up the street to a school for weathermen. The streets of New York looked like an army training camp.

My piano teacher in New York, Madame Herz, was a severe woman who wore long velvet European-styled gowns and had very short, cropped hair. She was an excellent pianist who came right to the point when speaking with my mother.

"You want this boy to be a concert pianist?" she asked. My mother nodded, yes.

"Stand up," Madame Herz said to me, continuing to talk to my mother.

"Do you know what that means? Practicing eight hours a day. He has to be strong. He should be playing baseball or football."

"But he'll hurt his hands," my mother protested.

"They'll heal." She put her hand on my chest and shoved me backwards across the room. "Weak," she declared, but she took me as her student anyway and set me up with three lessons each week.

My mother didn't send me out to play baseball or football, but she made sure I ate full meals at the cafeteria after her workday. She would eat only a small portion of cottage cheese. I think she would have starved herself to get me strong enough to please Madame Herz.

Madame Herz put me to work on scales, forcing me to use my fingers like hammers on the keys, over and over again, rarely allowing me to play piano pieces. I had been a pianist for eleven years, had appeared on radio shows and was something of a star in Columbus, so I resented the endless hours of retraining my hand position.

In the mornings, Mother and I would catch the subway. She went one direction to her all-day job at Arnold Constable Department Store. I went uptown to Broadway and 135th Street where I attended the High School of Music and Art. There, I took accelerated classes in music, such as ear training and harmony. I was ahead of most students at the music school because I had perfect pitch and could name all the notes and chords the teachers played. I could play in all the time signatures and could sight-read any music they put in front of me.

Even though I did well in the high school music classes, I hated New York. I felt uprooted—taken away from my friends and everything that was familiar and comfortable. The only person I hung out with was another student, Howard Kester. We'd skip classes regularly to go to the Paramount Theater on Broadway where the big bands and famous musicians performed. Those experiences provided a better education for me than any lessons or classes.

My mother worked long hours, and after school, I'd get into hot water with some of the hotel residents who thought I was smart-alecky. I remember being lonely and missing my family, strange group that it was.

After classes, I practiced the piano at the hotel, and then I had free time. The staff liked me. I was a smart kid and a quick study. They let me run the service elevator, deliver items to rooms and do odd jobs, giving me entrée everywhere but the bar. That's how I got to know Miriam Staniloff (Midge), a gorgeous, blonde model at the famous John Powers agency. I was fourteen. She was twenty-two.

We met on a Sunday in the lobby when I overheard two women complaining that they didn't have fresh towels and that the housekeeping staff was gone for the day.

"I can get you towels," I said walking toward them.

"How can you get them?"

"I know where they keep the key to the linen room."

That's how it started. I found two good friends, Midge and her roommate, Rose Pichinson, a formidable career woman with a funny sense of humor. After that, if I wasn't at a lesson, I was with Midge. Even Rose, who worked for McCann-Erickson, an advertising agency in New York, seemed to like talking with me. They were different from the women in my family and from my mother's customers.

An only child, I had grown up in a house dominated by women. Although my two uncles lived with us in the Columbus house, they worked every day, and during World War II, both were away in the army. My mother, aunt and grandmother were always in charge. The stench of permanent waves from Mother's beauty salon filled our house. Her customers wore thick makeup and bright red lipstick, like my mother, and like the clown Emmett Kelly. But, when I saw Midge come back from modeling, wearing all her makeup, she looked beautiful. She was also beautiful without it.

I think the friendship that developed between Midge and me gave me a connection to a good side of life and kept me out of trouble. I needed someone to like me—someone to impress. When Midge smiled at me, I felt appreciated, strong, rich and happy. She seemed interested in me for who I was, not for anything I could say or do for her. Our friendship was totally innocent. She never had any ulterior motives or hidden agendas. I believed that then and I believe it now.

She was a success, posing every day for magazine ads, in a business that devoured women like most people scarf down chocolate bars. In her case, though, the business didn't hurt her; my mother ruined her.

Midge and I took walks together. After work, she'd change into jeans and put her long blonde hair in pigtails. Then we'd walk along Broadway or Seventh Avenue and talk about the music I liked and my piano teacher who had died, whom I missed so much. Midge told me that her husband, Sheldon Staniloff, a captain in the army, had received orders for New Guinea soon after they were married. She was lonely and missed him. That's when she moved to New York to model.

One Sunday afternoon when the hotel bar was closed, Midge and I snuck into the bar, and I played the piano for her. I think she was impressed; I hoped she was. Mostly, though, it was such a change to have someone to talk with about my life.

In my family, no one wanted to listen to a kid. They'd say, "Go practice." Even though I could go to Joe about anything, it wasn't like talking to Midge. He would sit with me while I practiced. Joe knew about practicing. It was always, "Play that section over until you get it right, Aaron." But there was no real talking between us about serious things like I had with Midge, such as how we were both only children and how that felt.

I'll never know how she got permission from my mother to take me on the bus to her family home in Spring Valley one weekend. Mother must have thought her family could be helpful in my career because her father owned a small theater in the town about forty miles outside New York. The trip itself was short and not particularly memorable. What I remember is that I had to sleep in the same bed with her father and that Midge and I took walks in the woods and on the country roads around the town. I probably had a crush on her, but she told me I was like a younger brother to her, and I liked it that way.

Each morning, before school and before Rose and Midge went to work, I brought them coffee and Danish from Stark's Coffee Shop across the street from the Greystone. I'd come down from my Room 1007, go to the shop and come back to the sixth floor, knock at their door, Room 638, a number I remember more than sixty years later, which demonstrates how important some things can be, and hand off their breakfast. They must have given me money to pay for the food because I didn't have money of my own except for subway tokens. Then I'd go to school. Life was good.

Some nights at the hotel, Midge went out with her friends from work. Those times seemed empty and eternal. I'd hang out in the switchboard room with Dottie who plugged and unplugged all the calls in and out of the hotel. She was pretty and very tall, at least six feet, and I enjoyed being around her if I couldn't be with Midge. She was funny and liked to talk. One night when it was getting late, Dottie said to me, "You need to go to bed now."

I said, "I won't leave unless you kiss me." So she kissed me on the forehead. Typical of a fourteen-year-old, I didn't wash my face before I went to bed. Next morning, as usual, I got coffee and Danish, dropped it at Midge and Rose's room and went to school.

When I came home and looked for Midge, I couldn't find her. Not that day or the next. She didn't show up. I asked the desk clerk, "Is Midge here?"

"She checked out," the clerk said.

I panicked—a true panic as I'd never had before, worse than when I had to play a competition. I couldn't think. I ran down Broadway to the bus stop where the buses went to Spring Valley. I stood there with this huge hole in my heart, not knowing what to do. I had nothing to look forward to. I was afraid to get on the bus and I had no money.

Later, Dottie told me the gossip going around about Midge's relationship with me and that someone had told my mother I'd been seen returning from the sixth floor early in the morning with lipstick on my forehead. Instead of talking with me, my mother jumped to conclusions and threatened to go to the authorities and have Midge charged with corrupting the morals of a child. I don't know exactly what Mother said, but according to Rose, it was enough to make Midge quit the modeling agency and return to her parents' home.

If only my mother had talked with me, I could have told her all about Midge, that we were just friends, that I'd never kissed her or anything. Then my mother could have gotten to know both Rose and Midge, and we could all have been friends. Instead, my mother made untrue assumptions and ruined everything.

After Midge left, I was crushed and heartsick. I remember stifling tears in my pillow at night so Mother couldn't hear me. I hated New York more than ever, and I hated my mother. I didn't trust her, and I didn't think she liked me except when I was winning a prize or giving a performance. At my next piano lesson, I told Madame Herz it wasn't fair to her that I continue my lessons since I didn't want to practice anymore. Mother and I moved back to Columbus where she negotiated my return midyear into the ninth grade class at South High School. She made sure I didn't have to make up the time spent in New York. What I didn't know was the lengths my mother would go to control my life and career from then on.

RADIO NEWS
KID HATES NEW YORK

Aaron Cohen who plays piano each day at 1:30 p.m. on "Song Shop" with songstress Marilyn Day and announcer M. C. Marty De Victor had chance to study classical music in New York on scholarship under Madame Herz, who taught Rachmaninoff, but after a year of it announced he was going home—"couldn't stand New York—too many people and none of the friendly—not enough room—hated living in an apartment—but, most of all, hated classical music. At present Cohen is content to be a student at South High School, play in Snook Neal's band, on his radio show, and in private jam sessions. He loves to improvise with boogie-woogie. Although he hates New York he would return if offered a job with a band there.

Boy Pianist Prefers Swing Rhythms

South High Student Has Own Program on WBNS; Possible Concert Career Failed to Charm Him

By BEATRICE BUTTLER

Hep-cat, cocky and sophisticated one minute, shy, embarrassed and 16-year-old like the next, is the description of Aaron Cohen, the boy pianist featured Monday through Friday at 1:30 p. m. over WBNS.

Aaron, who lives at 1056 Lockbourne-rd, started the study of piano when he was three years old. At four he won the first prize in a state-wide contest, competing with children of seven and eight.

For 10 years Aaron studied under Agnes Wright. Each summer he went to New York to play for Prof. Silotti, Rachmanioff's teacher, who advised him as to his next season's study. Later he studied with the Columbus Boychoir and in Cincinnati. While a member of the Boychoir he went to New York and played a solo concert in Town Hall.

Discards Classics

As a result of this concert Aaron received a scholarship from Madame Merz. After a year of classical music he came home. He tossed aside a concert study to play the music he liked, sweet and lowdown.

At present Aaron is satisfied with being a junior at South High School and a member of the student council. When he isn't at the studio or playing with Snook Neal's orchestra for local dances, you may find him wtih his friends in a jam session.

Here is one home town boy who was on his way to making good in the classical music field, but just didn't like "long hair."

FIVE

Music, Music, Music

Back in Columbus, I started tenth grade at South High in the fall of '44. I was fifteen when Geer Parkinson called my mother to offer me an afternoon job playing piano at WBNS radio station in downtown Columbus. As the program director, Geer had kept track of my local concerts and the competitions I had won. He thought I might attract some young listeners to the station. Mother called Miss Alva Edwards, principal at South High, and asked if my class schedule could be arranged to accommodate the radio programs.

Miss Edwards said of course, and she scheduled all my classes in the morning. She always complimented me when I played at school functions. I respected her. She looked like a principal but she didn't flaunt it. Some teachers have to let you know they have power, but not Miss Edwards. She was the embodiment of it.

MISS ALVA EDWARDS

The Musicians' Union, Local 103, got into the act and told the station

I was too young to be in the union, but Mr. Parkinson advised them they'd better figure out a way because I would be playing programs with or without a union card. They worked it out and my mother ended up signing the union documents. All my paychecks were sent to her. Years later, I asked for my money, and she said, "You spent it all, sonny boy."

My radio job started with me playing classical piano music and evolved into a busy schedule of fifteen-minute solo piano segments with some popular music, plus I played with the Snook Neal band and accompanied a girl singer named Marilyn Daye. Because of these experiences, I got some classmates together and formed a band at school. We played for assemblies and school dances.

My neighborhood was mixed middle class with colored and white families who shopped at the same markets and at Cunningham's Drug Store, which had a soda fountain at the back. One day after rehearsing for one of the dances, Kenny, who was a terrific drummer, the trumpet player, the bass player and I sat in a booth across from the fountain where I ordered Cokes for everyone. Mr. Cunningham called me up to the front and said, "Aaron, I can't serve Kenny at the soda fountain."

"What do you mean?" I asked.

"He's a Negro. He can't sit back there, and I can't serve him at the fountain booths."

"Mr. Cunningham, Kenny's parents are customers in your store. I've seen them in here. What do you mean you can't serve him a Coke?"

"I'm sorry. You can take the drinks outside, but you can't sit in here with Kenny and drink them."

"We'll just leave, Mr. Cunningham."

Mr. Cunningham was a nice man. I don't think he was prejudiced. I think he had to follow the rules about segregation that existed in certain neighborhoods of Columbus. We all took the bus downtown to the big drugstore where we all got served. I began to understand a little about my family who used the word *schwartzer* in their discussions and complained about places where Jews were also unwelcome.

I LOVED MY JOB at the radio station. I'd take the streetcar to WBNS and start playing at one thirty. At the time, I didn't know what a brilliant education I was getting or how invaluable the experience would be in my career.

WBNS staff pianist, Aaron Cohen

Between programs, I'd run across the street to the music store, Summers & Son, order the latest popular music that had come in, and talk to Gloria Mertz who had been a popular cheerleader in school and graduated from South High School two years ahead of me. She lived at home with her family. I liked her because she had a great smile and was interested in music. We talked about the big bands and stage shows when we got together.

Summers & Son
Everything Musical

Gloria Mertz
Lens Yearbook 1945

After she finished work, we'd walk to the Palace Theater where traveling bands headlined the marquee: Frankie Carle, Stan Kenton, Woody Herman, Benny Goodman, Count Basie and Les Brown. I learned volumes from listening to these giants. I'd incorporate new band riffs and jazz harmonies into my piano arrangements for the radio programs. My exposure to these bands expanded my musical vocabulary as I took the leap from classical music into popular music and jazz.

Aaron Cohen & Frankie Carle

One day Gloria and I were walking near the music store holding hands when out of nowhere my mother and Aunt Eva appeared, yelling at Gloria and calling her a streetwalker. I froze. My mother had that effect on me. This wasn't the first time she had made false accusations when she thought the wrong girl was influencing my life. I thought of Midge and how that had turned out. Unable to defy my mother, I watched, mute, as she and my aunt insulted my girlfriend. Gloria stayed cool; my mother and aunt walked away. I apologized to Gloria and felt stupid for not defending her. I didn't speak to my mother at home. I came in late and left early to avoid her.

A few nights later, Gloria and I left the stage show at the Palace. I saw my Uncle Leon pull his car up across the street. My mother popped out of the passenger seat and rushed toward us. "Run," I yelled to Gloria. I ducked behind a parked car and watched. Gloria didn't run. My short, high-strung mother grabbed Gloria's arm and called her another bad name. Then she reached up and slapped Gloria across the face. I ran back, opening the knife I carried in my pocket, thinking I would kill my mother if she hit Gloria again. Strong and athletic, Gloria could have pushed my mother away or blocked her. Instead, she stepped to the side and walked past my mother to the bus stop. My mother scurried back to the car. I ran after Gloria and hailed a taxi. We went to her house and we told her mother and uncle what happened. I gave my house key to Gloria's uncle so he could confront my mother about slapping Gloria, and use the house key if she refused to answer the door. When he returned, he gave back my key. No one answered the door, he said, but he didn't want to use the key.

WITHIN THE WEEK, GLORIA AND I RECEIVE SUBPOENAS to appear in Juvenile Court. On the morning of the court date, I take a taxi from school and pick up Gloria at the radio station. We arrive at the detention center together. She tells me her uncle is meeting her later.

Inside, I see my mother and a family friend, Bill Broner, huddling in the corner of the courtroom. I know him as Uncle Broner, his wife as Tante Lil. Close friends of my aunts and uncles long before I was born, they have a litany of stories about the family—some funny—some mean. Uncle Joe doesn't have much to do with them. I don't think he likes them.

I'm convinced something sinister is going on between the judge, my mother, and the Broners, who own a big furniture store in Columbus. She's a calculating woman who sometimes drives Mother and me up to New York for my piano evaluations with Professor Siloti, or to Boston to see a fortune-teller. He, Bill Broner, has political connections and a way with women. I can tell he's sweet on my mother, but Lil puts up with him.

I'm certain Mother and Bill Broner have made some deal with Judge Taylor to scare me—all because of my girlfriend, Gloria. But detention?

They wouldn't go that far. Broner talks to a uniformed man and points at me. The man walks over and says, "Are you Aaron Cohen?" I nod. He ushers me to a seat at the front table and sends Gloria to another seat two rows back. I see her uncle come in and sit next to her. I feel better that she has someone with her.

Judge Genevieve Taylor glares down at me from her bench in juvenile court. "Stand up," she snaps. "Aaron Cohen, you are going to juvenile detention unless we get some things straightened out here, young man." She tells me to sit down again.

All I can think is this can't be happening to me. I'm not a criminal. I'm only sixteen. I haven't broken the law.

My mother sits at a table to my right. Gloria's behind me; I can't see her. People I don't know occupy other rows.

A small woman about five-foot-one, Mother has dark, flashing eyes and is no one to toy with. As the matriarch of the family, she was treated with respect by her brothers and sisters. I know she has good skills as a beautician because her clients call her at all hours to work her magic for their last minute events, but I'm unaware of her flair for drama until she clears her throat, stands and delivers a diatribe about how she has sacrificed everything for my career. I look straight ahead, but I can see her arms gesturing through her performance as she pleads her case: a poor suffering woman who works her hands to the bone to pay for her son's piano studies.

My mother finishes and Judge Taylor tells her, "You're a wonderful mother, Mrs. Cohen." She looks at me and changes her tone, "Stand up, Aaron!"

"First thing you should understand is you are a minor and therefore you have no rights in my court. Second, you are lucky to have a mother who gives up everything to support you and your musical talent. You don't seem to appreciate what she's doing for you."

She tells me how, before law school, she studied music in college and knows it's a very tough profession. "Maybe it's too difficult for you and you should give it up, go home and be a normal kid. Do what your mother tells you."

She stops, looks at my mother who shakes her head, and continues, "But your mother says you have a fine talent and music takes a lot of time and work. I can see this girl, Gloria, is too sophisticated and too old for you. She is a distraction to your studies. You are not to see her anymore. If I discover you are with Gloria again, you will go to the reformatory. Do you understand?" She leans forward on her desk like a crow ready to pounce on me. "Will you follow my ruling, Aaron?"

I'm not afraid of this judge or anyone. I feel angry, like the last time Danny Peyton hit me. "No. I won't stop seeing Gloria, ma'am." Judge Taylor leans back, her arms straight on her desk, her mouth open as if a scream is stuck in her throat.

I take a deep breath and cut her off. "First we need the truth about why we're here today. The only reason my mother doesn't like Gloria is because she's not Jewish."

The courtroom explodes. Judge Taylor stands, points at the door and yells to the bailiff, "Take him away. Lock him up." The bailiff puts his hand on my shoulder, walks me upstairs and books me. He takes my watch and money, checks my pockets and gives me jail clothes—jeans and a t-shirt—and marches me into a room to change. I ask him, "What's the charge?"

He looks at his clipboard. "Incorrigibility."

"What does that mean?" I ask.

He shrugs his shoulders. "I don't know."

JUVENILE DETENTION, unlike jail, didn't have metal bars and clanging cell doors, but it was confinement. Isolation rooms, with narrow windows in the doors, kept violent kids and those with venereal diseases separated from the rest of us. Locked in an area with bad, criminal kids, I was no longer angry. I was scared.

I felt sick. I wished I could take back what I had said to the judge. Neither my mother, nor any members of my family came to get me. I thought about killing myself, but there were no sharp objects, and I didn't know how to do it. In the past, playing the piano made me calm and always eased the tension in my stomach. I could lose my thoughts in my practice, but there was no piano for me in detention. There were only kids I didn't know—kids who looked mean, kids who had done bad things. My life had been sheltered from these kinds of kids. My mother investigated all my friends and wouldn't even let me go out for sports because she claimed, "Kids today play rough and you could get hurt." Obviously, she didn't know the kids in here were much rougher. I bet she hadn't thought about that when she cooked up this deal. I didn't know how to behave in lockup or what was expected of me. I didn't know whether I should try to act tough.

The boys occupied one side of the building; the girls stayed on the other side. I kept to myself and didn't talk to anyone. Nighttime was the worst. Silently, I curled myself into a ball on my assigned bunk and hoped the older, bully-type kids, lying nearby on their cots, wouldn't beat me up during the night. When I did drop into sleep, I'd jerk awake, really scared, hearing the whispers of other inmates. The next day was Thanksgiving. I wondered if I'd be alive to be thankful.

How could this have happened to me? The only thing I had done was date someone two years older and outside my religion. This country isn't supposed to lock up people for that; people came here for religious freedom. My family taught me that, and I think I learned it in

Uncle Joe in the Army, 1942

history class. Yet my mother had convinced a judge to threaten me. She must have gotten help from Broner; she wouldn't know how to do that on her own. Nothing like this would have happened if my father hadn't died, or if my Uncle Joe hadn't been away in the army. They would have protected me from my crazy mother.

The next day, a couple of strong guys came up to me and said, "We know who you are. You're the piano player on the radio, aren't you?"

I answered, "Yeah," trying to sound tough and disinterested.

"We want you to play during our Thanksgiving dinner with the girls today. Do you play boogie-woogie?"

"Yeah, but I'm not going to play here."

"Oh yes you are," they threatened. "There's a piano in there and we got permission for you to play."

Everyone filed in for dinner, the boys and the girls. I sat at the piano—the only place I felt safe. I played boogie-woogie. I played for all I was worth and they loved me. The girls kept calling me a celebrity. All the kids were nice to me and so were the guards. For the first time since I'd been locked up, I felt okay. Once again, the piano was my center, my grip on life.

I wasn't as scared that night in the dormitory room. The following morning, as I was marched down the stairway to the judge's chambers, I could see through the hall windows it was snowing. My mother was seated in there, quiet for a change. I found out later that Geer Parkinson, my boss at the radio station, had called her when I didn't show up for work. He had asked enough questions to figure out what was going on. He called the judge and told her I'd lose my job if I wasn't back at the radio station that same day. He also threatened to make problems if she didn't release me from detention.

My mother seemed smaller and more humble, slumped over, looking penitent in a straight-backed, wooden chair. I stood with the bailiff in front of the judge who addressed me in a softer tone than in her courtroom.

"Aaron, I want you to go home and mind your mother. Will you agree to do that?"

"Yes, ma'am," I said. Sometimes you have to do what you have to do; I didn't want to go back to Juvenile Lockup. I wanted out!

To save face, Judge Taylor put me on probation for a year. My probation officer, Miss Calhoun, was nice to me—really nice and understanding. I think she could tell something was wrong with the situation. She looked kind and smiled at me as she went through the rules for my provisional freedom period. By the time we finished the paperwork and got outside, I wanted to throw my arms around her right there on the courthouse steps.

Standing in the snow with my mother on one side and Miss Calhoun on the other, I said, "Mother, I want to make a deal with you. I'll obey Judge Taylor's ruling, but I want your permission to meet with Gloria and tell her that we can't see each other. You can even go with me." In my mind, I reasoned that was the decent thing to do.

Through clenched teeth, my mother said, "You heard what the judge said."

"The judge doesn't care if I see Gloria. She only cares about whether you give me permission, so I'm asking for your permission."

"No!"

I shrugged my shoulders, "Okay. See you later."

"Where are you going?" she demanded.

"To the radio station to play my programs and prepare the music for next week." She couldn't argue with that because it was my job. I had to turn in the music titles so the station could list and pay royalties for the music in advance. After that, I went to Gloria's house to tell her what I had promised.

Somehow, Gloria and I remained friends. We continued to see each other, which might not have happened if my mother had not made her my forbidden fruit. Gloria's uncle was on our side, unlike Uncle Dave who had returned from the army earlier than Joe and meaner than ever. Mother suspected I was seeing her and gave me another lecture, which she ended by insisting, "From now on, you bring your friends to the house for our approval. You have a nice home, with a record player, a radio, cheese and crackers, and peanut butter and jelly sandwiches. We want to see your friends—here in this house."

Uncle Dave

Of course, I never brought Gloria home, but I did bring my school friend Jerry Salem and his girlfriend home one day and introduced them to my mother and Uncle Dave. Since his discharge, Dave had become angrier than I remembered and spent even more time reading Yiddish publications such as *The Forward*, known in my family as *Der Forvitz*.

After Jerry and the girl left, I was reading the comics in the green, overstuffed chair where Uncle Joe used to oversee my practice sessions. I heard my mother and Dave discussing Jerry's girlfriend and the cross she wore around her neck. From behind my paper I said, "Don't tell me I have to ask someone's religion before I can bring them into the house."

Dave leapt from his chair, ripped the paper from my hands and started beating me with his fists. My mother cheered him on. "Teach him a lesson," she demanded. I felt my head snap back and forth. My nose was bleeding and I thought I might pass out. When he quit, he said, "You stay here. I'll be right back."

I had no idea where he was going, maybe to his bar for reinforcements where he often had to break up fights between angry drunks. As soon as Dave drove away, I got up and walked out the door, my mother yelling, "You come back here."

I made it to the payphone at the gas station on Livingston Avenue. I called Miss Calhoun and told her, no matter what the court said, I wasn't going home again. "My uncle is liable to kill me." Miss Calhoun explained how to get to her house by streetcar. She said to come right away. I pulled up my collar to hide my face and looked out the window the entire ride.

When I rang her doorbell, Miss Calhoun opened the door and gasped at the sight of my bloody nose and face. She phoned the detention center, drove me there and told them to clean me up and arrange for me to stay the night in a private room. She asked me if I had any relatives I could live with.

"Maybe Uncle Oscar and Aunt Fanny might take me in for a while." I gave her their address and phone number.

The court notified Uncle Dave that he was not my legal guardian and if he ever touched me again, he would be prosecuted.

I stayed with my aunt and uncle for a few weeks until my mother bought a small house and moved us out of the family home. I didn't have a choice but to go with her since I wasn't yet eighteen. Uncle Joe returned from the war surprised to find us gone, leaving my two uncles, their sister Eva and their mother to live in the house. Like before, my mother turned the garage of our new home into a beauty salon. We lived in that house the last year of my high school days.

After hearing about my encounter with Dave, Joe explained that Dave's experiences in the war had been bad and that he had come back different, but he seemed the same to me, just meaner.

DURING MY SENIOR YEAR, Miss Edwards continued to arrange my class schedule and supervise my selections. "Come into my office," she'd say. I'd sit down and wait. She knew I was salty and didn't care about school, but I respected her and her advice. She talked to me about my radio programs and figured out times when our band could play for school assemblies and did all she could to accommodate my music.

"Let's see. You're taking French next semester … oh, you'll never get along with him," she said, looking over my schedule and assigning me to another teacher whom she thought I'd like better. All my classes finished by noon so I could play the music programs in the afternoons. I had no extra-curricular activities and no study periods—only the core requirements. The rest of my time was spent working or trying to stay out of arguments with my mother.

Fortunately, I also got along with the music teacher, Miss Ruth Lippincott. She was cool and let me hang out in her office. Sometimes she talked with me about music. She knew I was already a professional musician, so she had me come to classes and demonstrate on piano whatever composer we were studying at the time. Those two women, Miss Edwards and Miss Lippincott, helped me survive school.

A few months after detention, and after my mother and I moved into the small house, I awoke one morning looking at Joan Schiff standing at the foot of my bed.

Joan was in my class and we'd gone to a movie together recently.

She was a nice girl. My mother approved of her because she was Jewish and because her family owned a string of shoe stores in Columbus. Eventually, the business became the United Shoe Corporation.

"What are you doing here?" I asked, grabbing the bed covers.

"Your mother told me to wake you up."

"Get out of here," I snarled. She ran out.

I dressed and flew down the stairs to confront my mother in her beauty shop.

"What the hell was that girl doing in my bedroom?" I said, interrupting a hair styling.

"Listen, sonny boy, everyone who marries into that family manages one of the family shoe stores. You should think about that." She resumed her comb out.

"Are you kidding?" I asked. "After all that money you've spent on my piano lessons, you want me to manage a shoe store?" I stormed out and could hear her complaining to her client, "I'll never understand that boy."

Meanwhile, my class was marching toward graduation. I was a C student with some Bs, which wasn't bad, I suppose, for a kid who never studied or turned in homework. I didn't have the time or the interest.

One day Miss Edwards called me into her office. She started by complimenting me on how well the band played at the last dance. Then she got to the problem. "Aaron, you haven't been to geometry or algebra class this semester or last, and your teacher won't let you graduate unless you can do the work he assigns."

"I don't care if I graduate. I can get a job anywhere with or without a diploma," I said.

She smiled. "I know you don't care, but your mother does. Here's what we're going to do. I have twenty problems that your teacher devised for you to work out. Take a look at them and tell me if you understand them."

I looked, but had no idea how to solve even one. "I can't do these,

Miss Edwards. I can add, subtract, multiply and divide faster than anybody, but I don't understand algebra or geometry. I never attended class."

She cut the problems in half and worked them out explaining them to me as she went along. "Do you understand what I'm doing?" she asked.

"No, not really, maybe a little," I answered, to make her feel better.

She finished all ten and handed them to me. "Take these problems home and copy the work in your own hand. Bring them in tomorrow and I'll turn them in."

I was too naive to realize what a risk she was taking. Looking back, I wish I had kept in touch with her and told her how much I appreciated what she did for me.

I turned eighteen. I graduated. My mother and Uncle Joe were happy. I got a steady job playing in the band at Club Gloria. I was happy because I could make my own decisions about the direction of my life. If only I had been able to predict the consequences of those choices.

Comedian Harry Jarkey at Club Gloria, Columbus, Ohio
left to right: Harry Jarkey, Aaron Cohen, Jimmy Midlick, Leo Dworkin,
Tug Morris, Richie DiCenzo and others.

SIX

GOT A LOT OF LIVIN' TO DO

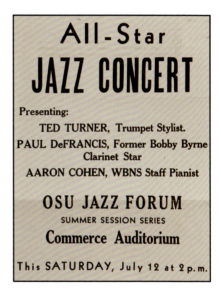

My FIRST SUMMER OUT OF HIGH SCHOOL centered on music. Thanks to Joe, who had supplemented my savings from the radio station, I'd been able to buy a used '37 Ford in my junior year to get around. I played jazz concerts with some notable musicians, and I kept my staff position at the radio station. The bosses expanded my schedule to include a weekly program called *Saturday's Rhythm*. I also continued as accompanist for the Columbus Boychoir driving back and forth between various rehearsals and concerts. On weekends, I played two shows a night, plus dance sets at the Club Gloria, which was out on the Scioto River northwest of the city on Riverside Drive. Bandleader Lou Posey hired me as the pianist for his local dance band. Lou staked out Columbus, driving from gig to gig, the same way the old territory bands staked out a region and traveled from town to town playing one-night stands. By the end of the summer, I'd made enough money to support myself and replace my Ford with a new Dodge convertible. I was beginning to stretch for my independence.

Betty Moon, a blonde knockout, frequented the club. She was a big tease and wore tight-fitting clothes. I was unsure of myself and felt outclassed, but on New Year's Eve, she needed a ride home at 2:00 a.m. She liked riding in my convertible.

When we arrived at her apartment, she took me upstairs, and before I knew what was happening we were on the couch doing it.

She whispered, "Be quiet, my mother's asleep in the next room."

"Oh, Jesus." Danger didn't turn me on. I knew not to tangle with anyone's mother and made my way downstairs, thoroughly shaken.

It bothered me how quickly Betty and I progressed to having sex. We were talking, getting to know each other and then she took her clothes off. I wondered who Betty had been with two hours earlier. My only reference was Gloria and we'd been friends for months before we even kissed. That was more exciting. Part of the thrill is the wanting and I wanted a relationship, some connection with the person. Friends told me I was a romantic. "You should get laid and move on," they said, "no commitment, no responsibilities." Not me, I wanted to be with a woman I could talk to, have dinner with, who liked me, not one who serviced me.

The next week, I called Betty and asked her to go out. I wanted to start over and get to know her. She was mad that I'd walked out on her, but finally she said yes. I parked near the airport landing strip so we could talk. It probably wasn't a good choice for talking. A lot of couples necked at that area. In no time we were at it again, no buildup, no romance, no talking. It turned me off. I drove her home. She never came back to the club, and I never saw her again.

At the end of February, the conductor of the Columbus Symphony, Izler Solomon, called. Because of my radio programs and write-ups in the local papers, he asked me to play Gershwin's *Rhapsody in Blue* for a Pops Concert on March 6. Despite my heavy work schedule, I agreed to learn and perform the piece. At the time, I didn't appreciate what an honor it was to perform Gershwin with the symphony. It was just an imposition to me because I had to find another pianist to fill in at Club Gloria on a Saturday night since I had to play Gershwin at Memorial Hall.

Aaron Cohen Is Soloist At Saturday Pop Concert

GEORGE GERSHWIN'S "Rhapsody in Blue" will be played by Aaron Cohen, pianist, at next Saturday's "Pop" concert of the Columbus Philharmonic Orchestra, Izler Solomon, conducting.

The 18-year-old pianist, who is now a member of the staff of the Columbus Boychoir, was a pupil of the late Agnes Wright and also studied in Cincinnati at the Conservatory and the College of Music and in New York City. When the Columbus Boychoir was formed, he was a member of the original choir and sang with the group for several years, later joining the music department of WBNS, where he played for four years.

Aaron Cohen prepares for *Rhapsody in Blue* concert

It took less than a week to learn the piece; I've always been a quick study. Music came easy. I didn't consciously memorize it. That happened as I learned it. I wanted to look good on stage with the symphony. People said I was pale and should get out in the sun. I bought a sunlamp, sat under it too long and cooked to a well-done, lobster red.

Adding to my discomfort, I had to rent tails, a cummerbund and one of those formal shirts where the collar stands up at the neck, right where my skin was burned. I don't think I ever looked forward to a concert, but I might have enjoyed this one more without the cinched clothes and stiff collar.

I only had one rehearsal with the orchestra. I'm sure Maestro Solomon had been pressured to call me because of my radio acclaim. He took the piece faster than normal, probably to get it over with. I could handle the tempo, though I'd have to prove it. To make matters worse, the musicians were not friendly, nor were they impressed. I was just a kid with a following.

It's Saturday night; Memorial Hall is packed. I walk to the piano, sit, adjust the chair, and Maestro Solomon cues the clarinet player. He starts the trill, which everybody recognizes as *Rhapsody in Blue;* then slurps up to high B-flat. With my ice cold hands on my knees, I wait through the clarinet rendition of the melody, then through the schmaltzy, muted-trumpet section where I play piano asides, then through the full orchestra blasting out the melody leading into my big piano solo—a series of progressions ascending the keyboard, gaining in tempo as it reaches the bombastic theme. Halfway through I lose my concentration and forget everything—I mean everything. The hall is silent, the orchestra is silent, the conductor's baton stops midair. The audience holds its breath. And I don't know what to do for what seems an eternity.

I start the whole passage over. I'm burning hot. My heart's pumping. Sweat rolls down my neck and stings my sunburn. I hold my breath, and I keep playing. It works. I get through that passage and the rest of the piece without a flaw.

The audience goes wild—probably from relief. Then I'm supposed to bow—something I've never done before. The conductor gestures to me and takes a small bow. I mimic him and bow. We stand there. I bow again and again. He bows again; we both bow again. We walk off stage. The conductor yells at me, "You've got to play an encore. They won't stop until you do."

"I don't have an encore," I say.

"You've got to play something, anything."

I wander out on stage. They're still clapping and hollering, "Encore." The only thing I can think of is Chopin's "Minute Waltz," so I play it fast—in less than a minute it seems. The audience goes nuts again and all I can do is bow some more.

I see I should end a performance by playing something slow, like "Liebestraum," to calm down the audience.

Backstage, Uncle Joe stands with me, beaming like I'm his son. People congratulate me, and each time I ask, "Didn't you hear the part where I got lost?"

Uncle Joe says, "Just say thank you. These people are sincere and want to compliment you. They probably don't even know you started over."

Joe is right. His advice is priceless.

Norman Nadel, a concert critic whose column "On the Aisle" ran in *The Columbus Dispatch,* wrote:
> The applause after the performance was out of this world. It shook the rafters with clapping, hollering and whistling. He [Aaron] was so flustered by the clamor for encores that he forgot concert etiquette and failed to recognize the efforts of the conductor, orchestra and concertmaster. This confusion had an element of charm which sent his audience into further ecstasies.

In my own defense, one doesn't learn to bow on the radio.

MY TICKET OUT OF COLUMBUS arrived in the spring of 1948 from comedian Harry Jarkey, who came through town and performed at

Harry Jarkey

Club Gloria. I'd been playing his shows for two years as a member of the club's band, so I got to know Harry and his wife Jennie, a classic Italian beauty who danced at the Fox Theater in Detroit. I remember she wore big hats and told me she liked the way I played Harry's material. They were crazy about each other, a real example of true love, which impressed me. I was sixteen and Harry was thirty-two when I met him. In 2012 Harry celebrated his one hundredth birthday with forty-five of us tearing up and cheering during his welcome routine. He's still got it.

The Delewese family owned the Club Gloria. Sam, the old man, carried a gun in a shoulder holster. His sons Nino, Dino, Aldo, Gino and Rocky were married to the waitresses, and the entire staff—like *The Sopranos*—were family by blood or by marriage. Starting a fight was a bad idea because there was no way you could win against the family.

Nevertheless, fights sometimes broke out. Bandleader Ray Cincione would cue the musicians to play "The Star Spangled Banner." Everyone would stand up, the fight would stop and the sons would throw out the instigators while the old man ran after them waving his gun. Today, scuffles might last longer because people won't stand for our national anthem.

Harry was taking his show on the road, heading to Wenona Beach Casino at Bay City, Michigan, and later to Tampa Bay, Florida, with a few clubs in between. He asked me to put a small band together and travel with him. The opportunity offered me a chance to learn about managing a band. It also gave me independence from my mother. I hired

The band

the best local players: Leo Dworkin, trumpet; Richie DiCenzo, sax; Tug Morris, drums; and Jimmy Midlick, bass.

Living conditions on the road shocked me. Small, crummy rooms with thin walls broadcast the slightest sound to the room next door. As Harry said, "The walls were so thin, I heard the girl in the next room change her mind."

Wenona Beach Casino

Wenona Beach Casino was better and had a group of cabins up in the hills for the performers. Separate buildings housed men and women's bathing facilities. I became friendly with the magician's assistant, Princess Nadia. I still wanted a relationship with a woman, but I was learning that companionship, especially on the road, was often better than spending the night alone. And companionship wasn't all that hard to get.

One night Nadia stayed in my room. The next day about noon, I was brushing my teeth in the kitchen sink when I looked out the window and saw my mother seated beside nasty Uncle Dave who was parking his Oldsmobile near the cabins. I couldn't fathom why they would come here except to check up on me and see that I wasn't living with a shiksa.

I locked the screen door, shut the inside door, woke up the princess, told her not to make a sound and to go back to her cabin as soon as I left. When Mother and Dave knocked, I only opened the inside door so they couldn't barge in. "What are you doing here?" I asked, irritated and groggy like I'd just woken up.

"We've come to see you," my mother announced like it was something I'd been waiting for. I sent them across the grounds to Wright's Café and said I'd join them after I showered. While I was gone the princess left, avoiding an ugly scene with my relatives.

Uncle Dave bought breakfast. We talked about the family back home, and I told them how great it was to play with the guys from Columbus. People strolled through the open pavilion restaurant as we ate; some waved and some stopped to say hello. After breakfast, the three of us walked around the rides, and I showed them the casino. When I offered to get them tickets to the show, they said they had to get back. Right, I thought; you're just out for an eight-hour drive to check up on me. I felt empty and hurt that they didn't care about seeing the show or hearing my band play. Uncle Joe would have stayed, but I was sure Mother and Dave were only interested in catching me doing something wrong. They left happy after concluding I was gainfully employed and living alone. My mother wouldn't have approved of the events that followed.

Harry booked the Holly Sisters' dance act into the casino. I'd played for them before at Club Gloria in Columbus, but just as a member of the band. At Wenona Beach, I had to rehearse their act with my band, so I got to know the girls. Joy was in her late twenties and dating Al Mack, a club comedian on the circuit, who visited her often. One day, his visits stopped and I stepped into the picture. Joy and I would go to dinner and she'd speculate that Al must have found someone else. She seemed sad but also angry that he would leave her. I could always get her laughing and distract her. We'd go to the stable to ride horses or to the beach to swim. Some of the band guys would hang out, too. If I had to write a homework assignment of what I did that summer, it would be titled *Summer Fun with the Boys in the Band plus Joy*. Richie, our sax player, showed Joy how to play his tenor sax. I have a photo of her in a bikini against a palm tree blowing on that instrument for all it's worth.

Joy Holly at Wenona Beach

Artie and Joy at Wenona Beach

Joy had dark curly hair and the lean body of a tap dancer. She was limber and could fold herself into amazing positions like a contortionist. We had fun together. With ten more years experience in lovemaking than I had, she slowly introduced me to all of it. I applied myself, proving to be as dedicated a student in copulation as I'd been in music.

After an eventful summer of sexual exploration, Joy invited me to her hometown, Detroit, for a couple months before we were due in Tampa, Florida, where Harry had booked us for the winter season. Joy's parents owned a huge apartment building that covered a city block at Dexter and Fullerton. They gave Joy and me a room in their palatial apartment, and I was so clueless that I didn't think anything of it. We were playing house, and I just thought, "Oh, how nice. What a convenience. You are giving me your daughter and a place to sleep with her."

While there, I got an interim job on weekends at a club in Toledo. Then in October I went back to Columbus to visit my mother and to change my name, a goal of mine since grade school when I had met Matt Gilbert on the train.

I never forgot Matt's advice, so on October 19, 1948, I persuaded my mother to go with me to probate court in Franklin County, Ohio. She changed her name from Sarah B. Cohen to Sally B. Kane. It wasn't hard to convince her. After all, Cohen wasn't my father's real name. Any reluctance she may have had was overshadowed by her desire for people to know she was my mother and for us to have the same last name. I became Artie Kane.

Except for a couple more visits to Columbus, I agreed to stay with Joy until the end of December when we were to leave for Florida. I didn't catch on that there was a scheme in play or that her father was a Polish gangster. I can't prove he was a gangster, but he didn't seem to have a real job, and I did notice his shoulder holster. One day, he said he wanted to have a meeting with me. I wasn't prepared for that meeting.

"Joy wants to marry you," he said.

"Oh, no, no, no," I said.

"Yeah, yeah, yeah," he said back.

That was not part of my plan at all. I hadn't considered that our living arrangement in her folks' apartment had meant anything other than what it was—a good time and easy sex. Joy and I had never spoken about marriage. Ten years younger than her, I thought I was just a passing fancy, same as her comedian lover had been.

I guess I never considered Joy's feelings or that she might have wanted us to have a future together. I'm not proud of it, but back then, relationships were like music jobs to me: When it was over, you moved on to another performance, another band, another club. Though Joy never talked to me about making plans together, her father, while wearing his gun, was very patient and clear as he explained it to me.

"Joy wants to marry you, so that's what's going to happen," he said smiling—the kind of smile that means trouble.

"I'm a minor. My mother would have to sign for me to get married and she won't. I'm only nineteen." I figured a threat about my mother would scare anyone.

"You won't be." His voice lost its smile. "Tomorrow, you will go with Joy and her mother to the AAA office in Bowling Green, Ohio, at noon. You will ask for Tom and apply for a driver's license."

"I already have one." He waved away my protest.

"You will put a five dollar bill in the application that you give Tom and tell him you are twenty-two. He'll put that on your new license."

That's how it happened December 24, 1948. Joy's mother, a sturdy, no-nonsense woman, marched us downstairs to the Justice of the Peace for the marriage ceremony, and when it was over, so was any physical attraction I had for Joy. I'll never understand why she had to trick me, force me, into marrying her.

We left for Tampa in the '49 Cadillac Joy's parents gave us as a wedding present. In the back seat, Lady, a beautiful, hyper-protective boxer Joy had adopted in October, became the subject of the only civil conversations between Joy and me. The dog liked me best. I'd wrestle

Artie and Joy married in Bowling Green, Ohio, December 24, 1948

Lady — my protector

with her, feed her and pay attention to her. After the meeting about the marriage, Lady was the only creature in Detroit I wanted a relationship with and the only reason I didn't end the marriage.

The twenty-hour trip to Florida wasn't the first, nor would it be the last time I'd travel when silence ruled the car and tension was palpable. It took three days and two overnights before we arrived at Larry Ford's Supper Club and found the motel that would be our battlefield for the next three months.

The rehearsals and shows were a welcome distraction, providing time away from Joy, who was jealous of any woman who said hello to me. Girl singers were the most difficult because they were touchy. Their music was never in good order, or marked correctly, so while I played rehearsal for them, they'd come over, put their hands on my shoulders and say, "Oh sweetheart, letter B needs to go slower," or, "Could we pick up the tempo the second time through?" Whatever it was, they always had to come close and get physical. This is where Lady came in handy. I bought a short, thick, leather leash and looped it around the leg of the piano, so if a singer or dancer sallied over to give me instructions, Lady would rear up as far as the leash allowed and growl. The singer would back up and holler out her wishes, sparing me the hugs and shoulder rubs and Joy's jealous rages.

We were near the end of our season in Florida, looking at unemployment for a few months, when one of the stagehands came up to tell me Gypsy Rose Lee was in the audience and wanted me to come to her table.

She was married to the well-known Spanish artist Julio De Diego. She complimented me on the band and my piano work and offered me a six-month train tour with strippers and a circus doing eight half-hour shows a day. She was a charming woman and the tour sounded like a good opportunity for the band and me since we didn't have another booking. I told her I'd talk it over with my musicians.

No one in the band wanted to go. The money wasn't terrific but adequate. However, they didn't see the efficacy in keeping the band together and earning six months' salary. They wanted to go back to Columbus where there were no steady jobs. I was disappointed. It was a huge loss to me. These musicians were good. They could cut a show quickly and they cooked. It was a blast to play with them. Still, back they went, and I can tell you, they all stayed there and were content to play gigs on the weekends for the rest of their lives. Breaking into the industry requires toughness, flexibility and courage, as Madame Herz showed me when she pushed me backwards into the wall. I would have had many regrets if I hadn't stretched out, reached for more and jumped higher to see what I could do.

I made calls trying to find other work in Florida, all the time fighting with Joy. Worse, someone poisoned Lady at a motel when we left her one night in the car with the windows cracked. I had to buy a box and shovel and bury her. I had such hatred for whoever did that. It made me sick and I cried and couldn't stop. Hurting a dog is like beating up a kid; such atrocities are less than human. Life with Joy was now completely unbearable. She was angry most of the time, and I couldn't forgive her for using her father to coerce me into marriage. Now, we'd lost our only connection, Lady.

A club called Ka-Sees in Toledo offered me a job as pianist and bandleader, but I had to find a pickup band. I called the Detroit musicians' union and came up with players for trumpet, sax, bass and drums.

Joy and I headed back to Ohio, still fighting. She was jealous of any woman I spoke to, even on the telephone.

Doris Rokiki and her brother, Junior, owned the club. I thought I'd try something new. I asked the stagehands to build a setup to raise the piano so the keyboard would be waist high and I could stand while playing. I'd seen Maurice Rocco, an entertainer, do this. It was exciting to an audience and it looked good on stage. I had to put my foot on the platform to reach the pedals. The position looked flashy and gave me more freedom with my arms.

The singer, actress Frances Langford, was booked at Ka-Sees the same time I played there. She was married to the tall and handsome actor Jon Hall. He starred with Dorothy Lamour in *The Hurricane* and in other films including *Arabian Nights* and *Ali Baba and the Forty Thieves*. I couldn't imagine why Frances wanted to sing in a club. She had to be making plenty of money from her films, but I heard she loved to sing.

Frances and Jon often stood in the wings and listened while I played my sets. One night, they took me aside, and Jon said, "Listen, you are really good. You're a fantastic pianist, but could you manage to smile a little when you're on stage?"

"Look," I said. "I can either play or I can smile. That's my choice. I don't think I can do both at the same time. I'm not a performer."

When I think back, I was kind of a smartass. They were nice people trying to help me. I should have been more appreciative.

I didn't know how to explain what I really meant. I wasn't a performer, not in the sense of Liberace. He was a great performer who happened to be a great musician. Liberace's career was just taking off. He loved people and would stay after a show for hours signing autographs. But there's a lot of pressure when you're a performer and that wasn't part of me. Sure, I had a little showmanship in me, but I was just trying to sell the music, not my personality.

Life took another turn when I had terrible stomach pains in the Toledo motel where Joy and I were staying. I was in trouble, so the front office sent me to a nearby doctor's office. The guy poked around all over my stomach, which really hurt in some places. He was rough and surly and didn't make a diagnosis. He told us to drive to the hospital emergency room. The ER doc pressed gently on my abdomen. I flinched. He did it one more time, and then said to the nurse, "Prepare him for surgery. Quickly. Appendectomy."

All I could think of was Miss Wright and that she had died during the same kind of surgery. I was scared and the pain was terrible. I was lucky and it was over quickly, but in 1948 you had to stay in the hospital four days after an appendectomy. While I was away, the new musicians I had hired from Detroit raised hell at the club, borrowing money and drinking. Junior called and told me I had to do something about them.

"For chrissake, I just had surgery. What do you want me to do?"

"Well, they're out of control. They're your guys."

The day the hospital released me, I went to the club slumped over and walking like Groucho Marx. I called the band together for a meeting and said, "You're fired."

"What do you mean? What's going on? What's wrong?" they clamored.

"Junior told me everything. Go pack up your instruments. You're fired."

That's when I decided to get out of the nightclub business. Both of my bands had disappointed me. The guys from Columbus were so talented, but they wouldn't break out and go on the road with Gypsy Rose Lee. It was a lost opportunity. And the Detroit musicians were more into raising hell than making music. I didn't want to be responsible for anyone but me. I sent Joy to her parents and told her I'd call for her when I found a job.

SEVEN

Skater's Waltz

I'd heard Holiday on Ice was rehearsing a new show at the Toledo Hockey Arena. They were looking for a pianist to rehearse and go on the road with the show. I drove from the nightclub to the arena and introduced myself to the big guy at the door.

"I know who you are," he said, and introduced himself. "I'm John Finley, general manager of the company."

"How do you know me?" I asked in my not-so-charming voice.

"After the shows in Toledo and in Tampa, some of the cast and crew would go to the night club and listen to you and your band."

Talk about good timing.

"So do you want the job as a pianist with us?"

"Yeah, that's why I came over here. What do I have to do?" I asked in a nicer tone.

"Nothing. You're hired."

Holiday on Ice, like the radio station job, was a gift. No audition required. During my childhood, my job was to win first place in competitions, often against older pianists. My nervous system would work overtime, my hands would get ice cold and my stomach would churn during auditions and competitions.

As a result, throughout my career, I'd say, "Put me on the job, and if you don't like me, don't use me again. Just don't ask me to audition."

After hiring me, John called in the conductor of the show, Carmen Nappo, and said, "Here's your new piano player." It was awkward. Carmen had never heard me play in the clubs, but he didn't have any say in the matter; John Finley was the manager. John didn't travel with the show, but he was around when the company put together new shows and practiced at the hockey rinks in Toledo, Ohio, and Sioux City, Iowa.

Artie Kane joins Holiday on Ice

"We have two choreographers," John explained, "one for the chorus and one for the principal skaters. You'll play for both at tomorrow's rehearsal, and then they'll decide who gets you. We'll hire another pianist for the other."

John Finley, General Manager, Holiday on Ice

It turned out both choreographers wanted me, so management offered me the entire rehearsal schedule: eight hours during the day with the chorus and four hours at night with the principals. The ice show paid union scale. I put in long hours, so the money was good.

My experience with dancers proved helpful working with skaters. I sight-read all the music and marked it up with the choreographic terminology of the skating routines; I knew them thoroughly. If the choreographers wanted to work from the skaters' cutbacks, I checked my markings, found the place and counted off eight beats, allowing them to start wherever they wished. I had learned this technique working with dancers, and it saved a lot of rehearsal time. With other pianists, rehearsals were endless because they had to go back to the beginning of a routine each time they stopped.

I loved the challenge of learning the skaters' vocabulary although a couple of years later it got me in hot water with film star and three-time Olympic Champion skater Sonja Henie; but I won't digress, not yet.

When I settled into the Willard Hotel, where the show booked rooms for skaters and show personnel, I faithfully sent for my jealous wife, Joy, who spent every hour at rehearsals knitting and watching me. At each break, she confronted, "I saw you talking to that little red-headed skater."

"Yeah, I work with her, and she has to give me changes and directions."

I had to defend myself every time some girl said hello. Joy would ask why the skater spoke to me. Why the waitress smiled at me. She'd remark that the assistant choreographer was cute. I'd agree and Joy would get angry.

By now, our physical relationship had dwindled to nothing. I wasn't interested in a forced commitment. She'd been back less than a month when I told her she should go back to her dancing career, and I asked for a divorce.

Joy returned to Detroit, but she refused to give me a divorce.

I stayed with the show, knowing the experience would further my career and enhance my musical knowledge. The redheaded skater Karen Knaack and I developed a friendship, something I couldn't have done around Joy. Over the years, I've had many platonic relationships, and I've heard many snide comments, reminiscent of my mother. I never had the chance to defend my friendship with Midge to my mother. She charged in like a dozer and leveled Midge and me both.

One night after rehearsal, Karen and I were talking in her room when the phone rang. "We have a problem here," the show manager, Bobby Johnson, said. He was a feisty guy you wouldn't want to tangle with, but we were pals.

"Joy is back in town," he said, "and because you're still married to her, we had to let her into your room." Bobby sounded like he was enjoying the conversation. "Unless you want to press charges, we're not going to throw her out."

"What are you saying?" I asked, confused.

"The front desk gave her a key. I'm in your room now. Joy has destroyed everything you own with a razor blade, and she cut herself in the process, so there's blood all over. She's on her way down the hall to find you."

Before I could hang up the phone, I heard pounding on Karen's door. Taking a breath, I pulled Karen back from the door, and when I opened it, Joy's voice cut like blades on ice. "I see you've made your choice about us," she said. Bobby stood behind her with his low-key smile.

"Yeah," I said, not thinking.

She lunged at me and hit me with her fist so hard I saw stars. Bobby grabbed her and pulled her back, yelling to me, "Shut the door." I did and then crumpled to the floor. When I came to, Karen was helping me up.

After Bobby and some others got rid of Joy, I went back to my room and to the aftermath of her anger. I'd spent a lot of money on nightclub clothes for performing—suits with matching suede shoes and such. Joy shredded everything and cut right through the centers of the shoes. Bobby said I was lucky I wasn't in my room when she arrived. Fortunately, my show jacket and pants were in the dressing room. They were all I had left to wear for performances.

Joy was as dangerous as her stepfather. I wanted a divorce, but I didn't know how to get it without her cooperation. As it turned out, friends were looking out for me.

The marvelously Italian Dolores Pallet, musical director of Holiday, was kind to me and appreciated my work. We enjoyed discussing everything from music to philosophy. Dolores had been a ballerina in her youth. A prodigy, she studied piano and was a fine musician. She was once the

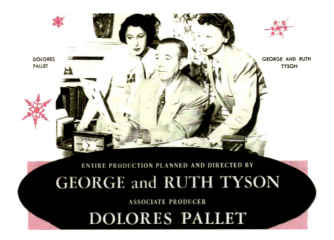

music assistant to producer Leon Leonidoff at Radio City Music Hall; now she was my friend and my boss.

Dolores found me a lawyer, Mr. Earl Boxell from the Toledo firm Zachman, Boxell, Bebout & Torbet. I laughed about the name, which sounded like a Dizzy Gillespie riff. I came to love the sound of it when Mr. Boxell got me out of my mis-marriage to Joy. I kept in touch with him, a dignified, silver-haired lawyer and used him later for another divorce. After a couple of years, I called to say hello and pave the way for a friend who needed help. When Mr. Boxell's secretary punched me through to his line, he answered, "Good morning, Artie. What is her name and home state?" It took me a few minutes to convince him I was calling for someone else.

In addition to everything else about Dolores, I liked working for her because I felt useful. She made the music selections, and I contributed ideas on the arrangements. If I didn't like a piece, I'd play it so it sounded terrible. She'd give me a look. Dolores was motherly toward me—I was only twenty—and tolerant of my personality, but sometimes she'd say, "Honey, I'm still your boss."

"Who are you trying to convince?" I'd retort. She put up with my arrogance, lucky for me.

Sometimes she'd get haughty and quiz me on my musical knowledge, "Do you know the theme of Rachmaninoff's second piano concerto?"

"No," I answered.

"Everybody plays this piece. I played it in Italy as a child."

I felt stupid and uneducated. "Let me see the music," I said, sight-reading it perfectly. Still, her comment felt like a put down.

The arranger for the show, Paul Summey, once said, "Don't let it bother you, Artie. Yeah, she can name them, but you can play them." That made me feel better.

In the music business, the ability to give and take criticism and make and receive suggestions is tricky. People have to learn not to let their egos overcome common sense. It's not easy, and experience doesn't always help. Most bosses, conductors and composers appreciate input from the orchestra or their staff, but not always. It's difficult to hear mistakes in a section of the orchestra especially if there is a lot of percussion or loud brass playing. Later in my career, during a recording session with the prolific film composer Elmer Bernstein, I sat quietly at the piano—TACET—for one cue while the rest of the orchestra recorded. I heard some wrong notes in the woodwind section. When they finished playing, I raised my hand and asked Elmer if there might be some mistakes in the winds about halfway through the cue.

Elmer, who had grown up in Brooklyn, had developed an English accent after working a few times in London. He looked over his glasses and said in a clipped British tone, "I believe you're tacet in this cue, Artie?"

I shrugged and answered yes. Elmer adjusted his glasses on his nose and called up the next cue. Too bad, because the mistake is still in the film's score.

I've had my share of mistakes, conducting and otherwise. There's a book of musical cartoons and jokes with a sign on a conductor's podium that says, "Wave your arms till the music stops. Then turn around and take a bow."

An orchestra colleague, Larry Bunker, had such good ears that he could hear a clam (what the players call a mistake) from the studio next door. Larry was a sensational percussionist. He and I often questioned anything that sounded wrong in the orchestra. During a rehearsal, Larry watched me struggling with a particularly difficult cue where there was a fast run up the keys I had to catch on the fly. To make it, I used the questionable Chico Marx technique of turning over my right hand to grab the top note with my index finger.

Larry came up behind me, cleared his throat and in his droll manner asked, "Wouldn't it be easier if you crossed your left hand over your right to play the top note?"

Of course, he was right, but I hadn't thought of it. He made me laugh, but I was grateful for his suggestion when we recorded the cue.

Morris Chalfen, Owner/President
Holiday on Ice

DURING THE 1930S AND 1940S, BEFORE HOLIDAY ON ICE, small traveling ice shows called *tank shows,* named for the portable system of pipes and compressors that made the ice, were popular. Hotels such as the New Yorker and St. Regis hosted these shows on postage stamp rinks big enough for only one or two skaters.

Holiday on Ice was a new kind of ice show. When it debuted in December 1943, with a troupe of skaters and musicians at the Toledo, Ohio, hockey arena, the show was immensely popular. Holiday on Ice returned the next year with an even bigger cast and played eight days to a full house. Meanwhile, brothers Emery and Calvin Gilbert, experts in ice and refrigeration, developed a large, portable ice system for rinks about 65-by-125 feet.

By the time I joined the show in 1949, entrepreneur and promoter Morris Chalfen teamed up with the Gilbert brothers to take Holiday on Ice on the road. They shipped the large, portable rink system ahead to the show's next destination while the rest of us stayed in Toledo to rehearse. This eliminated costly delays due to setup. Later, we traveled on the company's privately owned train cars, along with our costumes, instruments, spotlights and sets. By the time the cast and musicians arrived, the ice rink was ready, and it was show time.

Six months and a few towns later, the company decided to create a show for Europe. I got on well with the producer of the show, George Tyson, but was surprised when he asked me to be the musical director and conductor for the European tour. I thought Carmen Nappo, the stateside conductor and my boss, was the logical choice. He wanted to go to Europe and was hurt by what he perceived to be a snub. Carmen never spoke to me after the producers offered me the European show.

If Carmen had been sent to Europe, I would have taken over the stateside show. I'm not sure which venue the producers thought was the most prestigious or important. Was the Europe offer praise, or did it show doubt in my ability to handle the stateside show?

It didn't occur to me to ask. Some people might say I'm shortsighted because I seldom ask enough questions in business or personal relations, not even in hindsight. Luckily for me, Tyson's offer was a great professional opportunity, and I agreed to it readily. Shortly afterward, Mr. Tyson called me in for a meeting.

"Please sit down, Artie, and don't get excited. I want to discuss an idea with you."

"Okay," I answered, ready for trouble.

"We're concerned about your role with the European musicians because you look so young. Would you mind if we put some grey in your sideburns?"

"Look, if you don't think I can do the job, don't send me."

"Now Artie, I told you not to get excited."

Tyson was only thinking ahead to avoid problems. I said no to the grey. Not surprisingly, I wasn't always right. As Tyson anticipated, I had confrontations with musicians and personnel that might have been avoided if I'd looked older or were more mature.

Back then, I was a little pugnacious.

Tyson had received complaints about me from show personnel who took my frankness as an insult. I was inclined to say what I thought. My family always taught me I should be truthful; they didn't know about the fine points or the social skills of knowing when to be quiet.

One day, show director Annie Schmidt walked out of a staff meeting and said she had turned me in for overstepping my role in the company. Her job was to keep the show tight, so whenever I noticed things that were sloppy, I told her. I knew every bar of music, every move. I knew the names of every skating maneuver, what the costumes should look like and when lighting cues were missed. If skaters or singers didn't perform correctly, I told her. She thought I was a pain in the ass, a good description in retrospect.

Once I told the owner of the show, Morris Chalfen, "I don't want to do a good show just because you're in town. You don't even buy a ticket. I think the show should be good all the time, so I let people know when I notice flaws. You got the wrong guy if you just want a piano player. I take my job seriously."

"Well, Artie," he said, "we pay Annie to be the show director, and we pay you to play the piano for the show."

Chalfen was great. I cringe when I think of things I said to him. He could have fired me for talking to him that way, but I think he knew I was sincere and cared about the show.

Holiday on Ice was a training ground for my career. The experience

Jinx Clark — star of the European Tour

of working with different orchestras and dealing with musicians, talented performers and their personalities were learning opportunities that gave me insight and skills I used throughout my professional life.

Manager Bill Stine was one of many marvelous characters among our show staff. A crusty guy, he worked miracles moving and setting up the show's ice-making equipment from venue to venue. He worked nonstop, organizing the setup of the show and solving every problem that occurred. During a rehearsal in Sioux City, Iowa, I went to Bill's office to request a piano tuner. Bill wanted to know what was wrong. I explained that the rehearsal piano on the ice was missing its heater rod, so when I played, sometimes a key would stick and not come up. Bill looked at me and said, "Artie, give it time."

Meanwhile, my relationship with the star of the European tour, Jinx Clark, was developing into something wonderful. I didn't realize it at the time, but she looked a lot like Gloria—same dark hair pulled back up on her head so you could see her cheekbones and forehead. In rehearsals, she never missed her cues. She was a powerful skater, athletic and a dynamite performer. She never lost sight of the audience, and they responded with cheers. She had attitude.

She also had a mother who traveled with her and shared her room, making privacy scarce, but during rehearsals, Jinx and I talked. She would sit at the piano with me while I played for other principal skaters. Once, she confided that she tried to end her life after she'd lost a baby fathered by a married actor who dumped her. That explained why her mother, Louise, seldom allowed Jinx to be alone with men unless they were gay, and why after Jinx and I went to dinner a few times, Louise started to come along, too.

The signs were all there, but I wasn't paying attention: She was the worst example of a stage mother, with her nose in every corner of her daughter's professional and private life. Wherever we went, to dinner, shopping, she joined us. We were a threesome, walking along with Jinx in the middle, holding my hand on one side, her mother's on the other. If Jinx leaned over to kiss my cheek, she'd lean the other way to kiss her mother. I was so enthralled with Jinx that I didn't realize our relationship was ludicrous. I adored being with her and was proud to be seen with her on my arm.

After rehearsal one afternoon, we were alone, so just the two of us walked back to her room holding hands. We opened the door, and there sat Louise glaring at us. We dropped hands and blushed like we'd been caught kissing.

Louise said, "Tell me this, Jinx, is Artie prepared to give you a ring?"

Caught off guard and embarrassed, I snapped back, "You know it would have to be a friendship ring, Louise, because my divorce isn't final."

Jinx would have been a better name for the mother. That woman put me off. I accepted her, though, because I was crazy about her daughter and was convinced my feelings meant I was in love. My longing for her was night and day from what I had felt for Joy. And unlike Joy, no matter how many girl skaters I rehearsed, Jinx was never jealous.

Jinx and Artie in Brussels

HOLIDAY ON ICE TOOK THE SHOW TO BRUSSELS where I celebrated my twenty-first birthday. My relationship with Jinx (and Louise) was becoming more intense and difficult to manage, and my responsibilities as the show conductor were piling up.

My first night, I had dinner with the contractor of the orchestra, Roland Durselen, at the Metropole Hotel where I stayed. He advised me that the band was good, so I had better be up to the job. It was my responsibility to lead the musicians, to answer their questions and to give the correct cues to start and end each segment of the show. The show wasn't new, but the band and town were. I was prepared. I knew the music and skating routines cold. Previous bands had played the music many times, and all questions had been resolved. No mistakes existed in the orchestra parts. Still, I had nerves before the first dress rehearsal in Brussels.

The company had sent me over a week ahead of the skaters to make sure the setup was fine for the band, and to play through the music and to acquaint the musicians with the show. One night, I ventured out for dinner at a restaurant down the block from the hotel. Seated at a table, I was making notes in my music about the next day's rehearsal when I noticed two women watching me from a booth. Eventually, they sauntered over and asked to join me for a drink. I said okay. They asked where I was from and what I was doing in Brussels. I told them about the show. When they finished their drinks, we walked out together. They asked if I'd like to come with them. I said no—that I had a girlfriend traveling over with the show.

One of them said, "Well she's not here now."

"No, but she will be soon," I said.

The other woman remarked, "You are a very strange American."

The show opened with "The Skater's Waltz" in cut time at march tempo (a significant variation from the original piece). The orchestra sight-read it perfectly up to tempo. It was exhilarating, and I was thrilled with my new job, nerves and all. It was the best feeling in the world, later surpassed only by the ecstasy of conducting an orchestra playing my own compositions in Hollywood.

At the end of the Brussels run, the band gave me an engraved cigarette case. I didn't realize at the time what an honor that was coming from the players. The show was a success, and Jinx was the star. We left for the next venue, Geneva, where the trombone player, Frando, knew a diamond cutter. We had a ring designed—we being Jinx, her mother and me. My divorce from Joy had not yet come through, so we called it a friendship ring, just like I had told Louise.

The best musicians in Europe were in Brussels and Paris. By the time we played Milan, five key musicians had joined the show, including a French drummer and an Italian trumpet player. The trumpet player was pretty good, but he played as if he were apologizing for having a loud instrument. The company had hired an interpreter from Brooklyn who spoke five languages, so after the first couple numbers, I asked him to tell the trumpet player to play out a little more. I needed more guts from the brass. When the conversation with the player was over, I asked the interpreter what the trumpet player said.

"He wants to know if you think he's going to blow his brains out for this kind of money."

Perhaps grey sideburns would have provided me a little more respect, but I was glad for the laugh.

I missed American food. After several months in Europe, I was so hungry for a cheeseburger or something familiar that I called a friend in Columbus and asked him to send me a case of Spam. My mother would have screamed because it was definitely not kosher. The box arrived at the Duomo Hotel in Milan. Staff delivered the package to my suite, which had a picture window that overlooked the Milan Cathedral and framed a giant Coca-Cola sign. At least they had Coke. Jinx and her mother stopped in after rehearsal so we could argue more about whatever subject her mother could think up.

I opened the shipment and took out one of the cans with the rounded corners. Turning it repeatedly, I tried to figure how to open it.

Louise said, "Give that to me. I'll open it."

I wasn't about to take one more put down or order from that woman. Finding the special key soldered to the bottom of the can, I began unrolling the metal strip that sealed those tasty little pig parts molded into the gelatin-greased can. When the metal snapped off, I tried to pry it open. It wasn't budging, so I worked at it. Again, Louise put her hand out, "You don't know how to do it. Give it to me before you hurt yourself."

Not a chance, I thought. The Spam can was my place to take a stand. I grabbed hold of the top with my right hand and yanked it up, slashing off parts of my third and fourth finger pads, which dangled like earlobes from my fingers. Blood flowed freely over the Spam. Jinx screamed and Louise called the front desk for a doctor who arrived shortly, followed by several skaters who'd heard about the disaster. The doctor poured antiseptic and applied pressure, and then pulled out special pliers for clamping on metal staples to close the wounds. After bandaging my fingers and hand together, he put my arm in a sling and strapped my forearm to my chest to inhibit the bleeding.

My mother would have killed me on the spot if she'd seen my hand bleeding. The skaters worried about my well-being and hoped my career as a pianist was not over. Jinx hovered and rubbed my back.

When the show manager, Al Grant, walked in, he asked, "Hey Artie, can you work tonight?"

"Yeah, I can work." There wasn't really a choice. He couldn't exactly fly someone over from the States for the show that night. The only thing I couldn't do was play the piano solo in the Entr'acte, but I conducted the show for the next two weeks with my left arm. To the band and skaters, I looked like a fifth grader, right hand over my heart, forever pledging allegiance to the flag. The worst consequence was that my stand against Louise had failed to improve my position. It may even have made it worse.

Throughout the tour, many of the logistics of our day-to-day operations needed improvement. For instance, the show manager, Bobby Johnson, hired a bus to drive the company from the Hotel Duomo to the show venue. Per Johnson's rule, the American company boarded the bus first while the musicians, all Europeans except me, waited outside. I thought this was rude and demeaning to my musicians. The next day, I paid another bus to arrive a half-hour earlier for the musicians. When the regular bus—Johnson's bus—arrived, it had no place to park. Bobby groused and shouted. The show owner, Mr. Chalfen, came out of the hotel and wanted to know what was going on. When I told him, he asked if he and his wife could ride to the show on my bus. That resolved the problem to one bus and no discrimination.

Setting up the stage was always complex. The band played on a ten-foot tall platform. Our drummer, Bob Thomas, was at the top. In order for the musicians to see me, I conducted using a lighted baton, which I plugged into the alto sax player's stand light. The wire ran up my tuxedo coat and down my sleeve to the baton.

Besides being a great show drummer, Bob was a good-looking Frenchman. He flirted every chance he got, often missing cues when he turned to talk with the line skaters assembling for the next number. I had a frank exchange with him.

"Bob, you need to watch me for cues, so don't turn around to talk to the skaters during the show, okay?"

"Sure," he said. Nonetheless, he did it again and missed another cue on the next show.

That time I embarrassed him in front of the band. "If you do that again, Bob, I'm coming for you," I warned.

On the next show, he did it again, so I started up the steps, angry and intent on knocking him off the platform. In the process, I pulled over the saxophone music stand, broke the light and tripped. I had forgotten I was tethered. While picking myself up off the floor, I counted off the next number. I didn't reach Bob, but he never did that again.

Most of the European orchestras were very good. They sight-read the music as if they'd played it for years. If there was a problem, I could fix it musically. I took every note seriously, maybe too seriously. I wasn't a patient leader. I don't think I finished the tour any smarter or as a better person, nor did I rise to the challenges that could have made me a better conductor. However, the experience ultimately paid off as I matured and later discovered that talent alone wasn't enough to get a job. I needed humility and an attitude adjustment. Political savvy and perseverance were important, too; I had daily lessons in both.

I hadn't wised up about relationships either. I continued to compete with Louise for Jinx's affection. In hindsight, I came to recognize the codependency between mother and daughter that left little room for me.

Other people weren't as blind as I was. Doc Carlin, a clever comic skater in the troupe, tried to warn me: "If a guy marries Jinx, he marries her mother."

I slammed him into the wall and threatened to kill him because I took it as an insult to my beautiful girlfriend. I've always been protective of the women I dated, but I wasn't always smart. In frustration, I told Jinx one of the rumors floating around the company. "You know, Jinx, people think you and your mother are lesbians." The remark made her angry, but she must have discussed it because her mother's reins loosened slightly.

At the end of the tour, I returned to New York alone on the Cunard ship: *RMS Caronia*. A ferocious storm with forty-foot waves kept most of the passengers in their rooms taking pills for seasickness. I spent most of the voyage in the empty bar moping about Jinx. She and her mother had flown back.

In the States, I conducted and played for the smaller show, Ice Vogues, and courted Jinx through months of rehearsals and performances. Her mother went home at times. Jinx and I enjoyed the freedom. My divorce from Joy came through. In September 1951 I married Jinx, and of course, her mother.

RMS departed La Havre 10th October, 1950 … arrived port of New York 17th October, 1950. Cunard line, nickname Green Goddess. Photo by Oscar J. Johanson

EIGHT

You're in the Army Now

Before the Holiday on Ice European tour ended, I had suffered an asthma attack in Bern, Switzerland, that was so severe I was unable to climb stairs or do anything strenuous. We were in Basel, Switzerland, near the German border. I had to seek medical help, and I could barely get through the shows until I got used to the air. A few months later, after I'd returned to the States, the military ordered me to report to Fort Hayes, Columbus, Ohio, for induction. I filled out papers stating I had asthma. The army requested additional papers verifying my condition.

It was fall of 1952. The U.S. was battling the Soviet and Chinese invasion of South Korea. Jinx and I were touring with the ice show in Salt Lake City, so I went to a local asthma clinic and submitted to scratch tests—twenty in each arm for five days. After two hundred tests, the clinic drew up papers showing results that I had reacted to 95 percent of the tests. The doctor told me I was allergic to my own saliva. I took all the papers back to Fort Hayes and went through the induction process expecting the army to reject me.

When I handed the wad of papers to the doctor there, he said, "Thank you. Next."

The next line was for the hearing test, where, naked, we stood in a corner, one at a time, with our backs to a sergeant at a desk. He called out numbers for us to repeat. My turn. He spoke softer and softer until I heard nothing, so I was silent.

The sergeant yelled out, "You're in the army. Next."

Stunned, I followed orders and showed up at the Columbus train station for a twelve-hour overnight trip to Fort Meade, Baltimore, Maryland. Waiting to board the dark green Pullman car with the gold labeling, I heard groups of inductees who I guessed from their nearly incomprehensible accents were from West Virginia. On board, I watched two musclemen with shaved heads smuggle on cases of beer and stash them under the last berth in my assigned car. They yelled as if they were at a sporting event, slapped each other on the back and slugged each other's arms. A few of these guys couldn't even read and had never been on a train before. Someone hollered, "What's that sign say?" Someone else answered, "Don't flush the toilet."

They treated our black porter with contempt, constantly calling him to open their drinks or insisting he give up his church keys. They addressed him using racial slurs and ordered him to clean up spilled drinks and food. Drunk on beer and liquor, one idiot used the bed curtains to swing down from a top bunk to join a free-for-all, breaking the rod and tearing the curtain, and then he demanded the porter fix it. Another threw an empty beer can at a porter's back to get his attention.

Racism was rampant in West Virginia. I wasn't sure how they felt about Jews, but I was pretty sure I was unacceptable. I clutched the curtains of my berth, hoping these animals would leave me alone so I would survive the night. Reminiscent of juvenile detention, I spent the night hyperventilating, trapped and incarcerated once again.

At Fort Meade, the army gave me a number and issued me a duffel bag as tall as I was. I couldn't pick it up, so I dragged it. They took my personal items away and shaved my head. Ah ha, I finally had the haircut my mother had refused to allow, except now I didn't want it. My only hope was to be assigned to a band, but I'd still have to go through basic training, and that terrified me. I wasn't athletic. My mother's obsession with the protection of my hands had kept me from participating in sports. I wasn't a quick responder and I had never handled a gun. My only skills and quickness were on a keyboard. Hell, I could get killed during training.

As if to reinforce my fear, the sergeant filling out my paperwork asked, "What are you?"

"What do you mean?" I asked.

"What are you?" he repeated without clarification.

"An American? I'm from Ohio, a Buckeye?" What was he driving at, I wondered.

"No, we want to know who to call if you get injured."

So that was it, the army wanted to know my ethnicity or religion.

"How about calling a doctor?" I suggested.

That first day, we lined up in front of our bunks, and an officer announced there was an emergency phone call for an inductee I recognized from my train car. The guy had never used a phone before, so a sergeant took him to the mess hall to show him how to put the call through and how to speak into the handset. I had entered a different world.

In the morning, twenty-five pairs of feet hit the barracks floor at 4:00 a.m., scrambling to a row of toilets and then around the corner to a room of showerheads. I tried following orders the first morning, but I'd never used a toilet without a stall and in front of a bunch of guys except at the YMCA camp where I waited until everyone else had left the latrine. I'd also never participated in the group-shower thing either. The experience was demoralizing and scary. So the following morning, I scrambled to my locker, opened it and wedged myself inside until everyone else was outside in formation for review. I joined my group at the mess hall where breakfast was worse than the truck stop food I'd eaten on the road. My stomach soured, and I belched all morning.

The next day, I was assigned mess hall duty for missing review, but I had a fever and complained I didn't feel well. The sergeant felt so sorry for me; he sent me out to shovel snow for two hours. That's how they are in the army. It doesn't matter what you say; you have to follow orders. I landed in the infirmary for two days with the flu. No one came to look at me, no doctor, no nurse. I lay there until I felt okay enough to eat something. A nurse finally discharged me back to the barracks where my troubles started all over.

My allergies soared and breathing was difficult. I was miserable. I needed a bag to breathe into when I hyperventilated. The wool in the uniforms made my skin crawl and itch. The army told me to wear long underwear under the uniform, which made me sweat, exacerbating the problem. The food in the mess hall must have been cooked in lard because every time I ate there I had an upset stomach, so I ate at the PX instead, living on cheeseburgers and Pepsi, scratching through meals.

Someone sent me to a doctor, Major Drozd. The major looked through my medical record and noted I had already seen a doctor at Fort Meade, Captain Wilkinson, a psychiatrist. I had given the captain a copy of my two hundred allergy test results, and he in return had given me a diagnosis of psychoneurosis, moderately severe. Major Drozd wasn't interested in my allergy tests either. He said, "Show me a rash and I'll show you a discharge. Come see me when you're having an asthma attack and I'll sign your discharge papers."

"I don't get rashes," I said. "I just itch. I've had asthma attacks, but now I just hyperventilate."

What more did the army want? After presenting them with the results of my tests, I expected consideration, but they turned a blind eye. So I refused to do anything—march, clean the barracks, KP.

Uncle Joe told me he had enjoyed his time in the army because he didn't have to make any decisions and had no responsibilities. He just followed orders. I was different. My first response when people tell me what to do is always "No."

Uncle Joe had been in the military police. Once when he was escorting a prisoner to a new location, his route took him through Columbus, so Joe dropped the prisoner off at the local jail and came home for a visit. Joe was the peacemaker in our family but there he was in uniform wearing lace-up boots, an MP brassard around his left arm and a gun at his hip. I asked him what he would do if his prisoner tried to escape.

"Shoot him," he said.

"Aren't you afraid?" I asked. He said no, and I asked why not.

"Because the prisoner knows I would shoot him."

Joe could always reason with people one way or another, but I wasn't like that. Music was my life; I didn't know anything else. If the army put me in a band I might be all right, but there was no indication they were considering it. I had no hope.

Desperate, I tried something even dumber than marrying Jinx. I recalled my cousin telling me you could bring on an asthma attack by ingesting dust or dirt. I went to the latrine, scooped up a lot of dirt from the floor and swallowed it. Shortly, I was choking and couldn't breathe. I barely made my way to the infirmary where someone poured red liquid down me. I passed out—for an entire day.

The next morning, I was sent back to Captain Wilkinson, the army psychiatrist who first saw me. This time, he had me removed from army duty and assigned to the head chaplain of the U.S. Second Army, Roland C. Adams. Tall and slender, the chaplain was a terrific human being. I was so lucky to meet this man. I can't imagine what the next few weeks would have been like without him.

Chaplain Adams had a huge office at Second Army headquarters with double doors he kept open all the time. Many superior officers worked in the building. Before one of our conversations, the chaplain uncharacteristically shut both doors, "The walls have ears," Adams said. "Lots of people don't belong in the military, but they are caught in the system. It costs the government the same amount of money to process someone out as it does to process them in, and the screening system is inadequate." He didn't ask me to explain or defend myself but spoke quietly while enlightening me about the army.

My days improved after my assignment to Chaplain Adams. I reported to him every morning for tasks around his office or in the chapel. I typed up his daily reports and his sermons, a skill I had learned while typing up the weekly menus for Paradise Club, Uncle Joe's popular bar and restaurant. Some days, Chaplain Adams and I would talk; he was a natural shrink. He wasn't judgmental, and he knew the army wasn't a one-size-fits-all. He made music available to me, allowing me to regain a part of who I was. I played the Hammond organ for services on Sundays because his orderly was on leave.

Some emergency called him off the compound one day, but he left me with plenty of typing. An officer with a gold leaf in his lapel opened the door, walked in and stared at me.

I asked politely, "Can I help you?"

"Where's Chaplain Adams?"

"He's out."

He looked at me with baffled contempt and then walked out. Later, Chaplain Adams returned, closed his doors and asked, "Did an officer come in here while I was gone?"

"Yeah," I said. "He was looking for you."

"Did you stand or salute when he came in?"

He knew I hadn't. He'd already heard from the officer. That's the military, stand up when an officer comes in, that's what's important. I'd probably been told to stand in an officer's presence and salute, but obviously, I didn't get it.

The next week, I was sent again to the psychiatrist. Captain Wilkinson was right out of the movies: Coke-bottle glasses, thin and serious. His angular face would have cracked if he'd smiled. He sat behind his desk while I, the patient, sat with my back to the doctor, unable to see him. Prior to my meeting with him, I had a two-hour interview with his assistant, an humongous sergeant whose job it was to pass on my life's story to his boss. The captain wasn't impressed.

"No one likes being in the army," he said, "but as far as your musical career is concerned, you may not see a piano for two years."

"Oh, really?" When people are rough with me, I toughen up. Any shred of hope I may have still had was gone. I must have sounded like a maniac as I continued, "I'm getting out of the army. It may not be at this camp or the next, or wherever else you send me, but I'm getting out. I only need my arms to play the piano, so I'll amputate one of my legs if that's what it takes, because I am getting out."

He didn't say anything. I was angry, cold, almost paralyzed with hatred. I felt contempt for him not unlike what I had felt for my uncle Dave.

Hostility hung in the silence of that odious room until he said, "I'm going to recommend you for a medical discharge and send you back to your ice show."

He said it in a kind way that almost made me cry. I thought it was a different person talking. He asked to see pictures of my wife, asked me about her career. He wanted to know about my family. His demeanor changed completely, as if he had done his job, pushed as hard as he could and then let me win.

Captain Wilkinson officially assigned me to Chaplain Adams to await discharge because nothing happens quickly in the army. Then he asked me one final question. "What will you tell your children?"

"About the army? I'll tell them the truth." I used the chaplain's words. "I'll tell them some people aren't meant for military service. If they'd told me I could be in the band, I might have stayed." I think the captain tried one more push to see if he could make me feel like a coward for wanting out, but it didn't work.

For the next month, I worked for Chaplain Adams and had other duties like KP, which didn't go too well, but I survived.

On the day of my discharge, I dragged my huge duffel bag in and handed the sergeant my uniform. He said, "Don't you want your uniform?"

"No."

"Do you want to take a picture in it?"

"No, I don't."

He shrugged. "Well, I'd love to have all your stuff because I always have guys missing a shirt or underwear."

I gave it all to him and went back to the ice show.

Getting out of the military was like getting out of a bad marriage. Both can be liberating. However, neither divorce nor discharge is necessarily forever, but I didn't know that at the time.

Folks at Holiday on Ice were waiting for me as though I'd been on personal leave. They'd hired a substitute pianist, but the manager, Al Grant, called me once a week asking, "When will you be back?"

"I'm not at a resort, Al, I'm in jail," I told him. "They may call it duty, but it's jail."

Life out of the army was sweet for six months. When I'd just about recovered from my military ordeal, I was recalled. The Korean War waged on until July 1953, so everyone who served fewer than six months was recalled, including me.

This time I reported to a naval hospital outside Memphis, Tennessee. As ordered, I drove directly to the base shrink for re-evaluation. In a brief meeting, he asked me a few questions. I was flabbergasted at the idiocy of the recall.

Then he said, "I'm sending you back to the ice show."

"Thank you," I said.

"Don't thank me. My job is to identify the men who would not be good for the army. You have the type of personality that might lead a group of soldiers off in the opposite direction of your orders. That's not good for the army. You have a problem the military can't solve; you'll have to see someone on the outside."

Then he advised, "If you ever stop traveling, I suggest you seek treatment. When you finally feel the urge to join something—a Rotary Club—something that requires membership, you'll know you're on the road to recovery."

He was right. I didn't want to belong to anything. I felt as though Groucho were talking about me when he said, "I wouldn't belong to a club that would have me for a member." Oddly, I would have to face this issue many years later in Los Angeles with AA ... not exactly a social club, but something that required participation.

I received an honorable medical discharge for "conditions prior to military service." I was free from recall and felt no pangs of conscience for not serving. I guess I did serve for a month and a half—a grim memory—and I learned a few life lessons like not giving up. Chaplain Adams showed me compassion, and he taught me about political games: "If the army gets a major league baseball pitcher, he's going to go to whichever commanding officer has the most pull and needs a good pitcher. Never mind combat. It's politics." The military invented politics.

In retrospect, I probably would have been assigned to a band, but I didn't realize it at the time. Instead, I envisioned pushing a piano ahead of me while playing in a marching band, and regardless of what the psychiatrist Captain Wilkinson thought, I was sane enough to know that was impossible.

NINE

The Second Time Around

Settling back into the ice show was easy; settling back into marriage with Jinx and her mother was not. Louise had her own hotel room now, but she was no stranger to ours, and she continued to rule Jinx's life—making decisions about her clothes, what she ate and whether she was getting enough rest.

Throughout my career, I had played in small groups, mid-sized bands and all-sized orchestras. I accompanied singers and violinists. I played duets and chamber music, but I never liked playing in trios, because musically, it can feel like two against one. That's how I felt with Jinx and Louise. They either ganged up on me or squeezed me out.

I've been told that in the heat of an argument, I sometimes become belligerent and scary. "It's not what you say, it's how you say it," my mother and others would state.

I think my reaction comes from having grown up battling five adults in a family whose pastime was arguing. Maybe I'm too passionate. Sometimes, I feel threatened, so I lash out. It's something I continue to struggle with even today.

One monumental confrontation occurred, just preceding a short upcoming break in the schedule, when Louise waltzed in and said,

"Jinx, honey, you and I are going home to Colorado Springs to check on the house."

I said, "No, Louise. Jinx and I have plans to spend the week together."

Louise began her, "nobody cares about me" routine, claiming she was all alone and missed caring for her daughter.

I snapped back, "You need to get a life of your own. I'll take care of Jinx."

"You couldn't care about anyone but yourself," she blurted in her noxious voice.

"That sounds more like you, Louise. Marriage is for two people, not three," I shot back.

Louise ran crying from the hotel room, and Jinx started after her. I told Jinx to let her go and to stay with me, but she took off. Until then, I thought I understood her mother's protective nature, but this was beyond anything I'd seen. Married two years and in our early twenties, neither of us was prepared to stand against her mother's relentless emotional onslaught. It reminded me of my mother's attacks on Gloria and Midge. Louise was a force of the unnatural.

After Jinx ran out the door, I felt defeated. I wanted the marriage. I loved this girl, but with her meddling mother in the middle, it was hopeless. I was losing my wife to her mother. I looked out the window and before I knew it, I had stepped out onto the ledge. My knees were shaking, and I was sobbing. I looked down and actually thought of jumping, but I saw Louise standing at the front of the hotel. Was I going to let a mother-in-law destroy me? I had talent, a career I loved and promise for a great life. Cautiously, I reached for the window frame and inched my way inside. Hell no!

Jinx chose Louise. After telling me she couldn't deal with my anger towards her mother, she left for Colorado. Still, I plunged back in, determined to make my marriage work. Louise was only forty. Surely, some lonely man would come along and take the woman out of our lives.

Not so. Louise continued to pull every mother-in-law trick. If we had a schedule break, she would try to convince Jinx to go home with her. If Jinx decided to stay with me, Louise would call after a day and say she was going to kill herself.

"Oh Mommy, Mommy, please, Mommy," Jinx would cry frantically into the phone. She was the type who couldn't stop crying once she started. No matter how I tried, I could not do or say anything to comfort her. It upset me to see her in such a state. She'd hang up the phone and say, "I've got to go to her; my mom is going to kill herself."

"She's not going to kill herself," I'd assure her.

"I've got to go."

Resigned, I'd call the show manager and say, "Your star is leaving again, and I don't know when she'll be back." Then I'd borrow money from the company and buy her a ticket to Colorado. Someone would call Jinx's understudy out of the chorus to headline the show for the new booking until Jinx returned.

One time when Louise threatened suicide, Jinx threw herself on the floor screaming, "Don't, please don't!"

I grabbed the phone and said, "You know, Louise, if I beat your daughter, it wouldn't hurt her as much as you do. Do you understand what you are doing to her? She's hysterical."

"Well, it's all your fault, you son-of-a-bitch," she said in a tone that reeked of loathing. I knew then it was all an act she was putting on for her daughter. I felt like I was in a movie and Louise was determined to win the academy award.

I said, "Why don't you go kill yourself, Louise, and don't bother calling us." Boy, she really took off on me.

I wished Jinx could have heard her so she'd know it was all an act—a way to control her—but a little doubt crept in and I began to wonder if maybe they were in cahoots. What could they possibly want—

the money I earned? Of course, Louise didn't kill herself. I think she died of meanness years later.

Meanwhile, these unpleasant episodes dotted our life on the road. Jinx was like a little girl around her mother and called her Mommy, but when Louise was gone, my gorgeous twenty-five-year-old wife showed up out of a dream. We'd go out for dinner with friends, go sightseeing or shopping in towns where the show was playing, and we'd enjoy each other as if we were on a honeymoon.

When the show took time off around Easter, I took Jinx home to meet my family. Our visit coincided with Passover, when all the family gathered for a ceremonial meal honoring the liberation of the Israelites from Egyptian slavery. Jinx sat next to Joe and asked questions about the traditions of the Seder. All my uncles were taken with her. She engaged everyone in conversations and was interested in their stories. Charming and gracious, she complimented the ladies on the food they prepared for the celebration. I watched my mother take in the whole scene. She was impressed, partly because Jinx was the star of the ice show, but I think Mother wanted to like her. Though the religion thing loomed large as always, I was encouraged because the visit concluded without incident. I thought we might even be invited back. My family behaved, and Louise was in Colorado.

Jinx and I enjoyed each other's company and wanted a family, not in the usual way, but a pet. Because we drove from venue to venue, the "no animals" rule didn't apply to us. We shopped for a dog and bought a smart, fawn-colored boxer with a black mask and white markings named Poncho. A playful dog, he made us laugh, and he sopped up our love like a sponge. He was a perfect distraction during confrontations with Louise. He was also my buddy when Jinx ran off with her mommy.

Poncho's ears perked up whenever I put on a particular old shirt. It was a signal we were going to the park in Sioux City, Iowa, where I wrestled with him daily during weeks of rehearsals. He'd growl and tear away at the shirt, but he never left a mark on me except slobber from licking me into submission.

One rough spot in the marriage that I couldn't blame on my mother-in-law occurred in Asbury Park, New Jersey, where the company was rehearsing a new show. Muriel Bentley, a talented dancer, later known for her significant Broadway roles and her association with choreographer Jerome Robbins, was assistant to Holiday's choreographer Donn Arden. Donn assigned Muriel to start rehearsals and work on routines before he arrived. Since I had a car, I picked her up on my way to the hockey rink. One day when I honked, Muriel didn't come out, so I knocked on her front door.

"Come in a minute; I'm not ready yet," she yelled. I opened the door and stepped in. There she stood, naked, in an open bathrobe that she let drop to the floor.

"I'll wait in the car," I said, turning and shutting the door behind me.

Nervously tapping out rhythms on the steering wheel, I wanted to drive off and leave her. A few minutes later when Muriel got in the car, I couldn't look at her. We drove in silence to the rink.

Jinx was frosty the next couple of days. I kept asking her what was wrong.

She finally told me Muriel had said something weird to her like, "Your husband must need more sex than you're giving him."

"What the ****," I exploded. "Let me tell you what happened." I relayed the whole scene while Jinx paced back and forth in the room. I told her I didn't have anything to do with Muriel, that I had walked out on her. "Jinx, honey, I'm sure my indifference made Muriel angry, you know, the *woman scorned* thing. She was probably afraid I'd tell you, because as the star of this show, you could ruin her career."

After an hour of tension and talk, Jinx believed me. She knew me well enough to know I'm a terrible liar and was telling the truth. I was grateful her mother was gone for a couple of weeks so she couldn't meddle or make things difficult for me. When Louise wasn't around, Jinx and I understood each other. I never picked up Muriel again.

One night, I decided to buy dinner at an upscale restaurant for some of our friends in the show and for the owner, Mr. Chalfen. Jinx was always an outgoing, congenial hostess and had a good sense of humor. We had a great meal and a fine evening of conversation, laughing and telling stories about the show. Before I knew it, though, Mr. Chalfen beat me to the punch and paid the tab. I had a serious talk with him to say he had to let some of us reciprocate. He accepted my complaint and thanked me for setting up the dinner, but he wouldn't let me pay.

Jinx consoled me, explaining it would have set an uncomfortable precedent for other cast members, and Chalfen couldn't have that. As she said, *"Pianist pays boss' tab* doesn't play well on the marquee." Then she kissed me. These were the good times without Louise, but they didn't last. As Jinx's skating career blossomed, she began to treat her mother like a confidante, shutting me out of half her life. Problems always followed when Louise returned, and she was a bear if I made plans that didn't include her.

Jinx pulled away from me more and more as Louise stayed on through the fall of '53. Sometimes I saw my wife only during the show. At night, she'd pop into bed after I was asleep. When I complained about the change, she told me she detested the tension between her mother and me. "It's the way you argue with her—the way you say things and put her down," she blamed.

I'd heard these complaints before, but now, she said I was immovable, and that she didn't always agree with me. This was a big surprise. I thought we had solved the Louise problem, but apparently, I was wrong. Either the mother-daughter relationship was too strong, or Jinx had discovered I was not the person she wanted to spend her life with.

My schedule left little time for anything but meals because I was still rehearsing both principals and chorus. Yet Jinx started eating night lunch more often with her mother, or other skaters, instead of with me. I considered she might be involved with someone else. She was partnering with a new line skater, a HAP (half-assed principal) in skaters' lingo, and claimed she had to rehearse a lot. We made it through the holidays, but Jinx went back to Colorado with her mother for most of the time off.

When she returned, I could see a big change in her. She was pleasant, but the love was gone, and I could tell she was unhappy and wanted to end the marriage. Louise came to me with papers.

"I want the marriage annulled," Louise said.

"On what grounds? Jinx and I have been married over two years, and in spite of you, we've managed to consummate the marriage."

"We can get it done in Colorado," she continued. "I have connections there."

She thrust a fistful of papers at me to sign, the gist of which accused me of psychological abuse.

"This is baloney," I said. "I'm the one who's abused here."

"Just sign," she ordered.

I obeyed. Numb, I felt exactly as I did when the sergeant had yelled, "You're in the army." I just marched down the hall and gave Louise what she wanted. It's strange when I think of it now because I wouldn't take that from a boss. My sense of justice made me stand up against the musicians' union several times. An orchestra contractor who broke the rules didn't have a chance against me, but I always gave up against the women in my life. This time, I was tired of fighting with Louise. It wasn't worth the effort if Jinx didn't love me.

Jinx's top billing in the show meant she and Louise continued to have a presence in my life even though I kept my distance. All I wanted was to keep Poncho close to me. Wherever I went, he went. One day at a drugstore where I shopped, I took Poncho inside on his leash. He stopped abruptly in an aisle, splayed his legs and refused to move. He was staring up at a rack of stuffed bears. A lady in the same aisle said, "Oh look. Your dog wants one of those toys. You should buy it for him."

It seemed ridiculous. Poncho had never had a stuffed toy before, but he kept staring. So I took one down and handed it to him. He let it drop and kept looking up.

The lady said, "I think he's looking at the red one. Give him that one."

I did and he carried that red bear all through the store while I shopped and then to the cash register where I checked out before leaving. He carried it to the hotel with his head high in the air as if he were clenching a trophy, and when we were back in the room, he attacked the bear, threw it up in the air, chomped on it and tore it to bits. He was such a happy dog. At that moment, I was happy, too.

Then one day Jinx came to me and said, "I'd really like to have Poncho."

Reminiscent of Henny Youngman, I thought, "Take my wife, please," not my dog, but I heard myself say, "Okay." Was I that beaten down? The next thing she wanted was our new Cadillac, a green four-door sedan, because she couldn't take Poncho on the company train. I didn't want to part with the car either, but again, I said, "Okay."

She took off with the dog and the Cadillac. Later, I saw Alfredo Mendoza, her new HAP skating partner, driving the car, so I knew I'd been right about him. I was angry and told her so. It didn't do me any good.

During a week's break, Jinx and Alfredo drove the car and Poncho to her mother's place in Colorado Springs and gave the dog to a family with acreage because she thought it would be a great place for him to run. She sold the car to get a down payment on a beauty shop for her mother. All I got was an awful heartache over Poncho.

Years later, I was still haunted at how the relationship had ended. With coaxing from a friend of mine, I phoned Jinx, and after several conversations, flew her to Los Angeles where I was living alone in a rented house after my fifth divorce. I recall picking her up from the airport in a limo. When I saw her, I didn't recognize her. She had changed from that charming ice skater I had married into a hard, been-around-the-block woman. After going over the sour end to our marriage, she admitted the other guy she'd been seeing hadn't worked out, and she apologized for her mother and for taking my dog. Our meeting ended that chapter in my life. We had nothing more to discuss. I flew her back to Colorado because we both understood Thomas Wolfe who wrote *You Can't Go Home Again*.

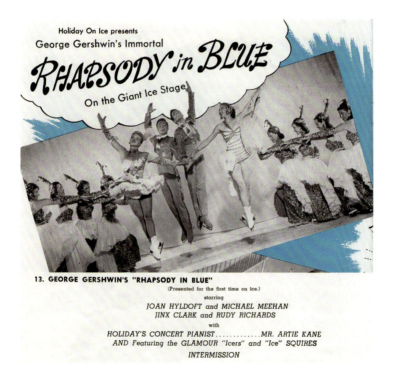

After the annulment from Jinx, my personal life was in shambles, but my professional life was in high gear. Dolores Pallet, musical director of Holiday, and my boss, knew about my Gershwin performance with the Columbus Symphony, so she and the Tysons, our producers, created a new show featuring me on piano for a special *Rhapsody in Blue* segment. Gershwin and I have had a long, ongoing relationship.

For the performance, I dressed in light blue tails with powder-blue golf shoes and accessories. Assisted by a line skater, I walked across the ice in the dark and climbed a ten-foot-high platform to a baby-blue, Gulbransen grand piano. I played an edited arrangement of the *Rhapsody* with the Holiday on Ice orchestra while the entire company, all wearing costumes of various shades of blue, skated.

The show's conductor and crack trumpet player, Ben Stabler, and the orchestra were also on a ten-foot-high platform, but they were fifty feet from me. Many conductors ignore soloists, but Stabler made it easy for me to perform, nodding at me when to begin and end my solos and

PIANIST RETURNS WITH ICE SHOW—Aaron Cohen, youthful Columbus pianist who played a number of radio and concert engagements here a few years ago, has returned with "Holiday on Ice of 1954." Now using the name of Artie Kane, he is soloist in the "Rhapsody in Blue" number which highlights the skating revue at the fairgrounds Coliseum all this week. Above, he is shown playing the Clavioline, a piano attachment that can simulate the tone of 30 different instruments, which he uses during the show. Looking on are two of the "glamour icers."

when to come in with the orchestra. Audiences loved the performance, clapping and whistling long into intermission.

Halfway through the tour, we played my hometown, Columbus, Ohio. My mother asked for fifteen tickets for the Saturday show, the busiest night, when it's nearly impossible to reserve company seats. The show sold out, but somehow I got her the tickets.

After the show, I met the whole family as they walked out of the Coliseum. Everybody was raving about the show and congratulating me, except my mother, who was silent.

"Well … did you like the show?" I asked.

She frowned, and in her best Anglo-Russian accent asked, "Tell me this, do all those people have to skate while you're playing?"

I always took the bait. "What do you mean? It's an ice show, for God's sake."

Uncle Joe smoothed things over as always and told me how proud she was of me, though I never saw it that way.

I think the family was sad Jinx and I were no longer together. She was one of my wives they met and actually liked. They even forgave her gentile roots, but my mother was always impressed with stars.

However, with me, I never measured up. I kept trying, though. One year I sent flowers to Mother for her birthday.

"Don't you know lilies are for dead people?" she asked.

I bought her an expensive black leather purse from Italy for another birthday. She loved soft leather. "I thought I told you to save your money," she scolded. Never a thank you, just a rebuke. Joe, the peacemaker, would come to me later to say how much she liked what I gave her. I appreciated his effort but wished my mother would tell me herself. At least I found affirmation in my music.

Rhapsody with everything in blue

TEN

SHORT PEOPLE

JEAN CHEADLE

EVERY ASPECT OF MY POST-JINX ROMP WAS SHORT: the woman, the courtship, the marriage and the divorce. Laura Jean Cheadle came from Montana where her father was a state supreme court judge when he was sober. I'm not sure what prompted Jean's interest in me. One of my friends said she was trying to get even with Marshall for leaving her.

Marshall Beard, the superb, former skating partner of Sonja Henie, had a long career with Holiday on Ice, Ice Follies, Stars on Ice and many other shows. He and Jean were recently divorced. Marshall and I were friends and remained so until his death at age ninety-three. Over the years, he rarely missed an opportunity to rib me about marrying his ex.

Jean started paying a lot of attention to me during rehearsals, asking questions about her routines or requesting another run-through. She would hang around after her rehearsal until I had a break, then we'd talk or go to lunch. I'm a sucker if someone's nice to me or shows an interest, and even today, I never consider the possibility of a hidden motive. It was a huge relief not to have a mother hanging around us, and I'm sure that contributed to how much I enjoyed Jean's companionship.

A principal skater, she partnered with the athletic Bob Saccente. Jean was very small and easy to lift. I referred to her as the midget. She and Bob specialized in spectacular routines.

Most of the troupe traveled by company train, but I bought Marshall's car, after Jinx took the Cadillac, and after the last show in Sioux City, Iowa, I took off in it with his ex-wife and two other skaters for the next venue, Little Rock, Arkansas. Since I loved driving, I told my three passengers, "Just get me on the right road and then you can all go to sleep."

Two hundred miles later, someone in the backseat woke up and asked, "How come there's snow on the ground?" They had me on the right road, but I was going north instead of south. Eight hours after our departure, we were back in Sioux City in time for breakfast at our hotel where the rest of the company was boarding a bus to the train station.

Marshall Beard

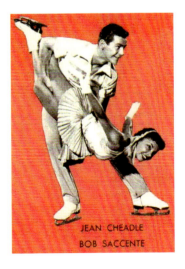

JEAN CHEADLE
BOB SACCENTE

I've never had a problem finding my way through a piano part or any musical score, but I admit that I'm geographically challenged. My passengers had a good laugh, and I drove eight hours more than planned. Still, we beat the train to Little Rock.

Although Jean and I had occasional disagreements, which often ended with her hanging up the phone on me, we continued dating. After ninety days, we leapt into marriage. Maybe I was getting even with Jinx, maybe Jean was getting even with Marshall, but for sure, we were both on the rebound.

Serious arguments began when she wanted to be married in a church.

"What for?" I asked, when I should have been asking myself what I was doing even thinking of marriage.

Jean wasn't religious or even involved with a church, but she stuck to her demand. My only affiliation with anything other than a synagogue stemmed from my years with the Columbus Boychoir at the Broad Street Presbyterian Church where I had played organ for Sunday services. One of the ministers, a phenomenal speaker, had been a philosopher who made bible stories relevant to everyday life, a welcome change from my childhood memories of ranting rabbis. I searched out a Presbyterian church in Corpus Christi, Texas, one of the stops on our ice show tour of the southern states. Jean and I met with the minister. She told him she'd been baptized into some Christian religion in Montana.

"You've been married before?" he asked me.

"Yes," I answered.

"Was the divorce your fault? Because if it was, I can't marry you."

"Oh, no. It wasn't my fault."

"Okay then, but you'll have to be baptized."

"Fine," I said. After the baptism, I was a member of the Woodlawn Presbyterian Church, which made me a Presbyterian Jew. I also carried a St. Christopher's medal given to me by the woman who had run the refreshment stand at the Ice Palace in Brussels. We often had talked during breaks. She said the Pope had blessed the medal and that it would protect me. Ecumenically, I was well covered.

After Jean and I married, we celebrated at a dinner with friends that night. Jean picked on me throughout the evening. She didn't like my clothes or the way I talked, and she was tired of my friends. I think everyone was uncomfortable; it was a bad way to start our marriage.

Later I told her the things she'd said puzzled me, and I asked, "Was I Cary Grant when you met me, and have I morphed into Lon Chaney now that we're married?"

"No, I just don't think you're funny anymore."

I was stunned. It was a mean, hurtful thing to say, and I couldn't figure out what had changed after the ceremony. Our relationship started down an unending path of arguments.

She wanted me to go to Billings, Montana, to meet her family.

"It's premature," I warned. "I don't get along with families, and yours will be no exception. It's a bad move at this time. Let's give it a while. We can go during the Christmas break."

She was having none of that. After touring a few more southern cities, the ice show returned to Sioux City, Iowa, for more rehearsals. We combined that trip with the Montana visit.

Jean wanted to stay with her family. I lobbied for a nearby motel, one point I won. The visit was awful. We never had a real conversation with her parents. Unlike Jinx, Jean didn't have a mother problem. She had a family problem: alcohol. Her parents drank nonstop through dinner and every time we visited their home.

The Martin Hotel, Sioux City, Iowa

We drove back to Sioux City and carried our marital tension, along with our baggage, into the Martin Hotel. By now, all kinds of things bothered me about Jean. She was so short her heels kicked my knees when we slept spoon fashion, and I was tired of hearing about Marshall. Clearly, she wasn't over him, and I could feel her resentment of me.

Some elements of rehearsing a new show brought a measure of stability to my life. For six weeks, I didn't travel, and life took on a routine. The hotel had a coffee shop in the corner of the lobby, across from the elevators, and every morning I came down just in time to make it to rehearsals at the hockey rink. Like clockwork, the waitress at the coffee shop handed me a fried egg sandwich and coffee as I passed by her station.

The arena was a short walk across the tracks from the hotel. Back on my schedule, I was playing rehearsals for both chorus and principals ten to twelve hours a day. I dashed from one rehearsal to another like a robot, but I was happy about the long hours because they meant less time with Jean. It was the wrong way to have a relationship and to start a marriage when my only enjoyment came from the music and the work.

One night another argument ensued. I can't recall what it was about, but I remember that my lack of interest in the subject, along with my firm desire to get some sleep, amplified Jean's fury. She jumped out of bed, grabbed a pillow and blanket and curled up on the sofa in our room.

"What are you doing?" I asked.

"I'm going to sleep on the couch."

"Don't do that."

"Why not?"

"Because I'm not bothering you. I'm not going to attack you. This is your bed. You should sleep in it. If you sleep alone on the couch tonight, you're going to sleep alone every night."

Her action was like hanging up the phone on me. Insulting. I hadn't touched her or demanded anything from her. Nothing warranted her move to the couch, but she slept there all night.

The next day during lunch break, I went to the hotel, packed my steamer trunk and moved into another hotel closer to the hockey arena. She soon found my new hotel and burst in sobbing.

"Let's just forget last night," she pleaded.

But I'd had enough, and I felt stupid for getting involved with her. She didn't like me. I was only a substitute for Marshall. I had mistaken attention for love that didn't exist. If I'm honest, I didn't love her either. We were both victims of a loneliness brought on by life on the road. This would not be my only role as a substitute in a marriage.

Jean and I were married ninety days, the same length of time as the courtship. It took another ninety days to get the divorce.

ELEVEN

Brother, Can You Spare a Dime?

In October of 1955, before the divorce papers with Jean came through, I steered my mind away from women and bought a new '56 Thunderbird in Philadelphia. I wasn't earning the kind of money that puts you in a high-income bracket like today's performers, but I was doing well enough to afford a new car. I was crazy about that car.

Tommy Collins and Jinx Clark, skating partners in Holiday on Ice

When I was between marriages and on the road, I roomed with Tommy Collins, a lead skater who partnered with several of Holiday's stars. Later in his career, Tommy owned and produced twenty-five years of Champions on Ice, taking Olympic medalists on show tours through forty-some cities in the United States. Morris Chalfen was his mentor, and Tommy was a good student.

On tour, before Tommy married a pretty skater named Janie (the Georgia Peach), he and I always booked two accommodations: a room to store our steamer trunks and a suite with a separate bedroom and a living room for our nightly card games. Those were carefree days with good friends and fun times. Tommy and I continue to see each other at least once a year and reminisce about the road, the Muehleback Hotel in Kansas City, the skating stars and the characters we knew.

Tom Collins, owner & executive producer: Champions on Ice

Tommy roasts Artie, 2006

The company had its own train and provided everyone with a berth whenever the show traveled, but about twenty-five of us opted to drive instead. One day, an attractive blonde skater, Sherry Wells, approached at the close of a show and asked if she could ride with me. She said she didn't like traveling on the train. I agreed to let her ride with me if she agreed not to bother me. I told her I didn't like to stop often. She said that was fine with her. It seemed okay, and I didn't have to water her or walk her at rest stops like I had done for Poncho and Lady. Sherry didn't ask for much, just a ride.

After hours on the road, I wanted some conversation, so I asked her where she was from.

"Louisville, Kentucky."

I told her I was an only child and asked her if she had brothers and sisters. She said she had three brothers, but she didn't elaborate. As I recall, she had little to say about any subject I brought up.

Sherry Wells, Glamour-Icers, Holiday on Ice

I asked her where she learned to skate. She said she took lessons at a rink and that she had always wanted to be in an ice show. Mile after mile, that was pretty much all the information I got from her. I didn't know if she was uninterested or uninteresting.

The Thunderbird had a bench seat; Sherry would lie down halfway across it and sleep for most of the trips. We travelled together all winter for the full lineup of shows, and we consistently beat the train to the next stop. No personal connection grew between us, and none would have except for a calamity that occurred when we returned from a stint of shows in Mexico City starring Sonja Henie.

Back in 1953 the most famous skater in the world had formed a partnership with Morris Chalfen to skate in his European Holiday on Ice tour. Three years later, Sonja was in the States rehearsing at the Toledo hockey rink for Holiday's Mexico City run, and I was to be her rehearsal pianist.

I studied her music in advance so that I would be prepared when she arrived. On her first day, our crew set the piano on a platform and pushed it out onto the ice. I began playing Sonja's opening number and soon noticed she was off her routine, so I stopped. She skated right up to me, digging in her edges and spraying ice over the piano and me.

"Why'd you stop playing?" she demanded.

"Because you're off the routine."

She bristled, giving me a "don't you know I'm a star" look.

"I thought I was here to rehearse you on the routine," I said. "If you don't want me to point out musically where you are wrong, get another piano player."

Icicles shot out of her eyes, but she calmed down and learned to trust me. I think we had mutual respect, which makes for a good working relationship. She knew I was on her side and had her best interest at heart.

After rehearsals finished up in Toledo, it was time to head to Mexico City. As much as I loved the Thunderbird, I decided it was impractical. It was such a hot car that the police would pull me over for speeding even when I wasn't. I also worried it might be stolen along the way or in Mexico, so I traded it for a Mercury Montclair.

On our drive south, I told Sherry what it was like to rehearse a star like Sonja. I asked Sherry if she was

Sonja Henie and Morris Chalfen, partners in Holiday on Ice

The incomparable Sonja Henie

interested in working up to a chorus skater and maybe a principal skater one day. She said she liked being one of the Glamour Icers and having her name in the program but was afraid to try solo skating. Apart from that, she had little to say. Somewhere on the long road, between Sherry's naps in the front seat of the Mercury, I learned that her father was a civil engineer and that her mother didn't know how to drive. That was nearly the sum of our conversations.

With Sonja as the star, all shows in Mexico sold out. One day, she asked my opinion about getting a piano in her hotel suite so we could rehearse there. She interrupted herself, and before I could answer, she said, "Of course I can have a piano if I want one. I'm Sonja Henie."

She was good-hearted and friendly, and she often amused me with her odd behavior. When I picked her up in a cab for the first band rehearsal, she handed me a large, leather pouch, and said, "Take care of these. It's all my jewelry, and everything's real. Take them up on the bandstand with you."

"What if I decide to leave town with them?" I asked.

"Won't matter. They're insured."

We got on well because of her sense of humor. After the show one night, we went out for dinner. Seated at the table, she pulled out an elaborate gold box with a gold swizzle stick and handed it to me to read the engraving. It said, "To Sonja Henie from her most ardent admirer, Sonja Henie."

I admired Sonja for her professionalism and work ethic. Audiences admired her for her sensational performances.

During the run of shows, I rarely saw Sherry except at final rehearsals and performances, but at the end of the engagement, we made plans for the trip back to Toledo. On the long drive, Sherry was so quiet that I grew tired of her silence and began to wish she were more of a companion. She was definitely in the right skating group, and I did notice that she was the prettiest of all the Glamour girls, a strikingly tall blonde. I just couldn't find a topic she had an opinion about or wanted to discuss. With my questions and her short answers, all I found out was that she had two older brothers and one younger.

By the time we reached Arkansas, I was exhausted from driving and squinting through drizzle on narrow country roads. I asked Sherry if she had any experience driving on a two-lane highway in the rain.

"Sure, I can drive if you need me to."

"Great." I found a safe place to pull off the road. She took over driving.

I fell asleep in the passenger's seat until I was jolted awake by her screaming. I felt the car slide downhill and roll onto its side, landing on the passenger door. I pulled myself upright and felt water creeping up my legs. Drowning would be a bad ending for a mid-western Presbyterian Jew wearing a St. Christopher's medal. Sherry was on top of me screaming. Through the front window, I could see a man careening down the embankment, hurrying toward us.

He yelled, "Roll down the window." The motor was still running, so I reached for the power window switch. The window opened. Sherry kept screaming as I sank deeper into the creek.

A conscientious truck driver had seen the accident and stopped to help. He grabbed Sherry's arms, and I pushed her up and out the window. Then he pulled me out. We had bruises and cuts, but that was all, except for Sherry's incessant sobbing.

The man took us to the nearest farmhouse. I'd never seen such poverty. The screen door on the ramshackle house was busted. All floors were laid in linoleum, clean but torn up in places. Except for the kitchen table and odd chairs, there was little furniture. Unshaded light bulbs gave the place a harsh look. But these people were generous and kind. They fed us and then drove us in their rusted pickup truck to a nearby motel.

At the motel, Sherry explained the accident, how some man in an old pickup had pulled out of a driveway without looking. Coming down a hill, she had slammed on the brakes to avoid him. The car swerved, and because the back roads in Arkansas don't have shoulders, the right rear wheel slid off the pavement. The car flipped. The fellow in the pickup never saw what happened, but the oncoming truck driver had, or we might not have made it out.

Sherry was inconsolable. I sat her on the bed and wrapped my arms around her, tried to comfort her, but couldn't get her to stop crying. Accidents and tragedies bring people closer. I felt responsible for her. I should never have put her in that situation. I kissed her tears, stroked her beautiful hair and apologized for asking her to drive. She stopped shaking, and her tears dried up as I reassured her it was not her fault. I cradled her face in my hands, looked in her sad eyes and kissed her. She returned the kiss. I held her until we fell asleep in each other's arms. That night, we became lovers, of course.

The next day, I hired a tow truck to rescue the car. Two guys ran lines down the embankment and attached them to the Mercury. The truck operator started the winch and the tow truck's front end bolted upward. After repeated efforts, they finally dragged the car out. The insurance company tried to have it fixed, but the car was unsafe, and eventually it was hauled to the junk yard.

At the Missouri Pacific Railroad Station in Arkadelphia, Sherry and I kissed and held each other a long time. Then Sherry took a train to her parents' home in Louisville, Kentucky. I took a train to Columbus to see my mother and Uncle Joe before heading to New York to look for interim work before beginning preparations for a Sonja Henie production in New York. I called Sherry every night.

NBC executive producer Max Liebman had hired Sonja for the first color television spectacular, scheduled for broadcast December 22, 1956. It was titled *Sonja Henie's Holiday on Ice.*

The NBC staff orchestra and a giant cast of ice skaters would accompany her during that hour and a half extravaganza, which would appear in people's living rooms across the country. Producer Perry Cross directed a lineup of talent such as host Art Linkletter and guests Jaye P. Morgan, Ernie Kovacs and Julius La Rosa.

Rehearsals for the show were to begin at an NBC facility in Brooklyn in early fall. The details of the television special had been set months earlier. Sonja offered me a cut-rate deal to do the whole package.

"I belong to the American Federation of Musicians and have to be paid union scale," I told her, "and I should be paid over scale for a show with this kind of responsibility." Sonja was silent, but her look let me know I was on thin ice. So I added, "I also want travel expenses."

She trotted off to Mr. Chalfen and asked him to negotiate a lower fee. He told her he wouldn't negotiate with me because I was good at what I did and that I was reasonable about money.

She thought about it, came back to me and said, "Okay, we'll pay it. You're a son-of-a bitch, but you're worth it."

In New York, I couldn't get Sherry out of my mind. My continued emotional turmoil over her emotional turmoil about the accident swept me into that abyss between love and thralldom. Yet, I knew I wanted a loving and stable relationship with a future—a caring partner to share my life. At the time, I probably didn't know what I was doing. Was there a basis for a relationship here, or were my ongoing feelings of guilt shining a false halo around Sherry? Time would have answered those questions, but in my eagerness to settle my personal life, I called Sherry and arranged for her to travel to New York. I convinced myself that this was the right thing to do and thought she was the right person to marry. She wasn't a star, so no temperament; she didn't travel with her mother, she hadn't been married before and her father didn't have a shotgun. Also, I had been thinking about her day and night since the accident. When she arrived, we couldn't keep our hands off each other.

I didn't look for work for a week. She admitted she'd always wanted to be with me. That was why she'd asked to ride in my car.

We got married at the Riverside Church in Manhattan in a private ceremony. We were alone—no friends or relatives. The church provided the witness. That was the beginning of the strangeness. Sherry never mentioned wanting her parents at the wedding. I'd never met her folks, and we had no plans to meet them. When I think about my other unions, I recall Joy's mother went to the courthouse with us, and her father gave us a new car. Jinx's mother was definitely present and snarling as I married her daughter. Though her family wasn't there, Jeanne insisted we take a trip so I could meet them soon after our wedding. With Sherry, it never occurred to me to invite her family or mine. Maybe I was unsure of my decisions and didn't want anyone's opinion.

I rented an apartment on Long Island, the first stop out of Manhattan on the subway. The first night of our marriage, I remember deciding I was going to be normal now. "I'm not going to wear protection; I'm going to be a normal husband and we'll get on with our lives." It seemed like Sherry woke up the next day with morning sickness.

For the first few weeks in New York, I played for Broadway rehearsals and a couple of nightclub shows. I didn't make much money and had some lousy auditions, the kind where I was so hostile about auditioning that I ruined any employment chances. Sherry was sick, pregnant and stuck in the apartment while I looked for work. She didn't complain, but I felt sorry for her. I'd never thought about what she would do in New York.

In August, Sonja arrived, and rehearsals began for the television show, which helped financially. Sherry's pregnancy kept her from working in the show. It was torture for her to sit through rehearsals and not skate with the company, though I didn't realize her pain at the time.

Sonja lived in a five-story apartment in Manhattan with her new husband, Niels Onstad, a Norwegian ship-owner and art collector.

He executed her deals and enforced her contracts. One day, Sonja didn't show up for rehearsals at NBC and the executive producer called to see why. Niels explained that the three large color televisions in Sonja's contract hadn't been delivered. He said Sonja would return to rehearsals when the TVs arrived.

On occasion, I went to her apartment to play proposed musical numbers for her approval. She had Steinway grand pianos on three different floors and each was painted to match the décor of the room. It was a ghastly thing to do. I'm sure the pianos were embarrassed because they sounded uncharacteristically timid and reserved when I played them.

Wayne Thompson, emcee for Holiday on Ice, lived in New York with his wife, Pat. Sherry became friends with her, which was a relief because it gave Sherry someone to spend time with while I worked. Pat was an overweight intellectual. I thought she would be a good influence on Sherry who, I discovered, didn't say much because she didn't have anything to talk about. She had never held a job except for the ice show, and she didn't want one. I began to understand her silence during our long car trips. So I would go off to rehearse, and Sherry would wave bye and either stay in the apartment all day watching television or run off somewhere with Pat.

Piano rehearsals for the TV special began in Brooklyn at a hockey rink. As the show took shape, the NBC orchestra moved into the rink. This was a great opportunity for me to meet some of New York's finest musicians such as the great drummer Bobby Rosengarden, probably best remembered as the bandleader of *The Dick Cavett Show*. Legendary pianist Dick Hyman was in the orchestra, too. He was one of the nicest people I met, and we still talk occasionally.

Through these contacts, I hoped to meet Marion Evans, whose outstanding arrangements for various acts and shows were magnificent. I'd played some of them in jazz clubs and they were inspirational. He had a few students, and if you were lucky enough to get an invitation to "fall by" his studio, you could learn volumes about the business and about how to write the best vocal accompaniments and band charts.

Sonja was impatient and didn't like Harry Sosnik, the music director and conductor. He was unfamiliar with ice-skating and couldn't get the tempos right. As Sonja's pianist, I cringed each time she threw a fit and said, "No, no, no; NO" to Mr. Sosnik. No one was a bigger star than Sonja was at the time, and she expected star treatment. She was in business with Chalfen, owned half of Holiday on Ice, and her husband was rich. She would glare at the conductor, point at me and say, "Artie, play that section for him."

That was not a good way for me to establish relationships for my future, which was my long-range goal: to play with the big boys in New York. However, I played what she'd ask, and she'd smile and say, "That's how I want it, Mr. Sosnik."

Except for those few rough spots, the whole New York experience with the show went smoothly. The show was a huge hit, and I found it exciting to be part of that historical moment that inspired people all over the country to buy color TV sets.

Sherry and I spent Christmas together in New York and then returned to Asbury Park, New Jersey, so I could rehearse a new show. Sherry was uncomfortable in a hotel and unhappy she couldn't work. She stayed with me until the last month of her pregnancy when she returned to her parents' home in Kentucky to have our baby.

It was terrible timing because I was on my last twelve-city tour with Holiday and couldn't be with her for David's birth. A year before, I'd given notice to Mr. Chalfen and Dolores, my musical boss and mentor, that I would leave the show and try to make it in New York. This was my final tour. They both tried to change my mind.

"Artie, you could stay with the show, keep making money and have employment the rest of your life," Mr. Chalfen offered.

"That's what I'm afraid of," I told him. I've got to find out if I'm just a big fish in a small pond, or if I'm as good as people say I am."

The ice show was no longer a challenge to me. It had been an outstanding employment opportunity for eight years. I learned an enormous amount about commercial music, business and getting along with people—not wives, but colleagues and bosses. Cast members of Holiday on Ice were mostly supportive of my decision to leave the company.

My close friend Tony DeVito was a terrific saxophone player and key musician in the band with whom I remained good friends for fifty years. He was worried. "Kid, I don't think you know what you're doing. New York is a really tough place, and you haven't saved much money." Tony knew I always spent everything on new cars, the best hotels, great clothes. Putting money away was not my style. Finally, he said, "Look, I've saved $25,000. You're covered for half of that if you need it."

Tony DeVito —
best friend in the world

I'll never understand why Tony made such a generous offer to me. I was grateful but cavalier about it. I'd never had to struggle. Things always dropped in my lap. My reputation was my ticket to employment. People had offered me the old, "If you come to New York, I can open doors for you." Such phrases, I've learned, rarely produce a job, but I was confident I'd find work.

When the tour ended, I told Sherry I would find an apartment in New York and be ready for her and David's arrival. He was a beautiful boy, and I was scared to death.

I refused to live in a tenement with our baby. So Dolores, my former boss, switched roles and became my surrogate mother. She helped me find an apartment in Queens on the top floor of a four-story building that was only about three years old. It cost $150 a month, expensive for 1957, but it had two bedrooms, a bath, kitchen and a living room. With key in hand, and the rest of my savings from the tour, we went on a shopping spree for a crib and every piece of equipment needed for a newborn. When Sherry arrived, she liked it, and I was hopeful and happy because I didn't feel guilty when I looked at my son.

Sherry couldn't work other than skating in a show or teaching ice-skating because that was all she'd ever done. She was a stay-at-the-apartment mom, but she missed skating and performing with the show. She was depressed after David's birth, always tired even though she slept soundly through the night and David's crying. I would get up, change him, walk him, warm the milk and feed him. He had colic, and there was nothing to do for him except hold him and rock him and try to comfort him. I thought there must be a way to cure him, but the doctor said it would pass. Luckily, it only lasted about three months, and then he grew out of it. I had mixed feelings about Sherry during that time because she barely had energy to care for David. She was irritable and often complained of fatigue. She also griped about wanting to go back to the show and lamented that we didn't have a babysitter.

"My mother could take care of David if we didn't have to live in New York, and I could go back to the show," she said.

It never occurred to me she could have had a serious disorder like postpartum depression syndrome. I don't think the medical profession had such a diagnosis back then, but if she had it and I knew it, I would never have judged her so harshly.

Reality struck when the few hundred dollars I'd saved flew out of my pocket and no jobs with my name on them surfaced. One of my problems finding work hinged on the union. Although I was a member of the American Federation of Musicians and the Columbus Local,

I was not a member of New York's Local 802. I joined, but there was a six-month residency requirement to get a union card, which keeps itinerant musicians from taking work away from those already living in the area. While waiting, I spent my days rummaging for work in the city, which meant taking the subway in to play rehearsal piano jobs for singers and dancers auditioning for Broadway shows. If they paid me at all, it was way less than scale, maybe five dollars for the rehearsal and audition. It wasn't unfair; everyone was broke and living on hope. I spent a lot of time riding that subway. At least it was a cheap way to get around.

I got the most work from Jose Duvall, who played the Juan Valdez character for Columbian Coffee. He was a singer and recorded an album, *Songs of Juan Valdez*. I met him through the ballet company. He still owes me fifty dollars, but he died in 1993, so I gave up trying to collect.

I also got a job at the Viennese Lantern, a high-end dinner restaurant that catered to clients with money. Three strolling violinists provided the atmosphere, but when they took a break, the pianist filled in—that was me. Unfortunately, no one told me there would be requests, something I loathed. Drunks would come up, drop money on the piano and order a shot of "Melancholy Baby." I always played the requests if I knew the tune. For the most part, I used the time to practice my piano stylings and improvisations during those twenty-minute periods. No one was listening; I was providing background music. The job was uncomfortable and produced almost no money.

One night, I subbed at the Blue Angel Cabaret in Manhattan. A fellow came up to the piano and, like a gangster, pulled out a wad of money. He flipped through it carefully until he found a one-dollar bill, peeled it off, dropped it on the keys and requested something. I played whatever it was, but he and his friends were drinking and talking. When he walked out, he said, "I know you didn't play what I requested."

"Yes, I did," I hollered, but he didn't hear that either. I felt like a jukebox, not a musician.

The night jobs were hard on Sherry's and my relationship, and I worried more and more about David. If I could have found good paying work, we could have afforded a baby-sitter. A few dinners out and an occasional show might have taken the pressure off our marriage and family.

Sherry wasn't much of a partner. She didn't seem to care that I was having a hard time, that I couldn't find steady work, and that I was as depressed as she was. I knew she was unhappy, but I couldn't think of what to do for her. When we were together, all we seemed to share was a lot of silence and resentment. I suppose I didn't consider what it was like for her to give up her career. In those days, it was the man's role to have the profession and be the breadwinner. Some sympathy from me might have saved our marriage. I came to understand this better a few years later in another marriage.

Around this time, Mr. Chalfen was in New York. He called to see how I was and wanted to come over. I had no job, just a wife, a baby, and an expensive, nice apartment. I told him I'd be honored to see him.

The first thing he said was, "You know you are crazy, Artie. Do you know that?"

"Yeah."

"You could have your job back and continue with the show for as long as you like."

"Mr. Chalfen, I told you, that's what I'm afraid of. I have to get into the competition."

He was very nice. He always extended himself and treated me well. He told me to call him anytime.

I continued to accompany a variety of singers and dancers for their auditions. I also got a call to play for a backers' audition for a possible Broadway show. Two choreographers were preparing the show *Packaged in Paris.* One was Luigi Faccuito, an Ohio boy who later had an illustrious career working with Gene Kelly, Fred Astaire, and Cyd Charisse. Luigi told me a friend of his, a busy Hollywood composer, had written a ballet on spec for the show.

During the backers' audition, composer Dominic Frontiere walked over to the piano, handed me a score, and asked me to sight-read the ballet he'd written. It was black with notes and very difficult, something for which Dominic was known, I later discovered. I did a pretty good job, I thought, and so did he. He was extremely complimentary, told me he was from Los Angeles, and said if I ever came to the West Coast I should call him. Right, I said. He insisted he was serious and gave me his card. This tactic hadn't worked in New York, and I had little faith it would do me good elsewhere, but I kept the card. Turned out to be my best move ever, though it took time before I would benefit from someone who meant what he said and had the heart to help a struggling musician.

After many low-paying gigs, and no indication that things would improve, panic plagued me. I'd never been where nobody knew me, where I had to prove myself each time, and where life seemed like a perpetual audition. Every time I looked at my son, I felt like a failure. I called my mother and said, "This is a serious phone call. I'm in trouble, and I need a thousand dollars right now."

"What have you done with all the money you earned? Haven't I told you to save for a rainy day?"

She must have derived satisfaction from being right. I suppose I could have planned better; I could have saved money; I could have listened to the warnings. None of those realizations helped, and she didn't help either.

At the last second, I called Tony DeVito and told him what I had told my mother.

Tony said, "The banks are closed now. Can it wait till morning?"

He sent $1,000 the next morning and eight times after that. It took me six years to pay it off. He refused interest. His only condition was that I would never mention it. I took out term insurance with him as the beneficiary in case something happened to me. I could never repay that kind of goodness, but I kept in touch.

When I became successful in Hollywood, I tried to convince Tony to move there. He would have done well in the studios, and I would have sponsored him, but he was content to work the garbage truck detail in Oak Park, Illinois, and play gigs on the weekend at clubs and events. His family was there. He and his wife, Dottie, didn't want to move to Los Angeles. Decades later, my wife JoAnn and I brought him and Dottie out to Whidbey Island for a couple of visits. Tony loved our video room chairs, so we sent a set to them.

Meanwhile, life with Sherry deteriorated. She complained nonstop when I was home. She didn't know anybody except Pat. We couldn't afford to go out or to hire a baby sitter. We argued, David cried more. I would take him out and he'd cry because he wanted his mother. One particular argument ended with a brilliant line from her: "You're nothing but a second-rate talent with a first-rate temperament."

The line was so good, I couldn't be angry. I stopped ranting just to admire it. Then I wondered where she got it because she wasn't smart enough to think it up. Turned out it came from Pat, her fat friend who had plenty of lousy things to say about me. Maybe I deserved it because I hadn't considered how a marriage and a baby would work out living in New York without a job.

Another argument ensued over a *Playboy* magazine. It was a new publication then and contained mostly articles with a few photos. I'd buy it, look through and throw it out. I wasn't hiding it. When I came home one night, Sherry was pouting on the couch.

"What's the matter?"

"Oh nothing."

"Come on, what's the matter?"

"Nothing."

I don't understand the game. It drives me crazy. What am I supposed to do to find out what's going on? I yelled, "Something is the matter, tell me what."

"Well obviously, I'm not enough woman for you."

"What does that mean?" I asked.

"I found this *Playboy* magazine." She held up the latest issue I'd brought home.

Since I'd made no effort to hide it, I wasn't surprised. "So what do you mean that you're not enough woman for me? It's a bunch of articles and pictures. It's just a guy thing. It doesn't mean anything."

We were both trapped in a relationship fraught with money problems. Except for Tony's regular contributions, we were drowning, but I wanted David to have a happy first Christmas. There was a tree lot on the way home from the subway. I always wanted a Christmas tree because I couldn't have one at home, so I bought a six-footer. Sherry and I decorated it with lights, globes and a lot of tinsel. We put our

Christmas in N.Y. 1957

squabbles away for a few days, bought a stuffed dog and some other toys for David, and had a nice time as a family. David was a beautiful child. At least we did that right.

Our discontent culminated one day while I practiced on the spinet piano in the apartment. Sherry sat down next to the piano and in a sympathetic tone told me that she understood the music business was really hard. She suggested we leave New York and move back to Louisville with her family where her father had found a job opening for me at the local hardware store. Sherry had it all figured out. Her mother could take care of David while Sherry went back to the ice show, and I could play clubs on the weekend.

Good God! How could she not know who I am? How could she think I could work a day job as a clerk and be a musician on the weekend? I recall Leonard Rosengarten, my analyst later in life, explaining that a man needs a partner who knows what a relationship with that person entails. A doctor's wife can't be angry if an emergency call comes in at two in the morning. I'm a musician. I realized Sherry had no clue who I was or what that meant. At least I knew she was an ice skater and that was all she was.

I bought her an airline ticket back to Louisville.

"I wasn't really serious," she pleaded.

"I am. I don't bluff or say things I don't mean. I know you're unhappy."

Sherry and David at her folk's home in Louisville

David at 3½, November 1960 in Atlanta, GA

Sherry stayed in Louisville long enough to park David with her parents, and then she rejoined the ice show. I missed David but not Sherry.

I moved out of that expensive apartment and found a place on Fifty-eighth Street right in the heart of Manhattan. It had a tiny living room, an even tinier bedroom with enough room for a mattress that took up the whole floor, a bath, and a Pullman kitchen. It was fifty dollars a month, partly because it was in the middle of an area famous for gays and hookers—neither of whom ever approached me. The good news was I was able to send a hundred dollars to Sherry every month for David.

Still broke and out of work, I received a call to audition for the position of assistant conductor and pianist at the Roxy. I followed directions to the stage door and was guided to a band room with a grand piano. There, I met two managers, who were friendly, and their leader, Bob Boucher.

Bob explained, "Here's the thing, Mr. Rothafel owns this place and he wants to feature music for the dancers in the opening production number. The song is *Autumn Leaves*. He's crazy about Roger Williams' recording of it. The number will feature piano, and we need to know if you can play that run at the beginning of it."

The managers interviewing me didn't appear to know middle C from their middle ear, but Bob seemed all right. For once, I was thinking I shouldn't be a smart ass. Even though the run was not musical rocket science, and any good pianist could probably play the thing, I was still respectful and asked, "Which direction did you want the run?"

"What do you mean by that?" Bob asked.

I sat at the piano and played the beginning melody with the run cascading down in thirds just like Roger Williams had recorded it. I said, "The run can go both ways." So on the second phrase of the song, I played it going up the keyboard.

The managers stared at me openmouthed, and then Bob said, "You got the job, man."

It's the only audition that resulted in employment for me. I became the pianist and assistant conductor at the Roxy. The salary was okay, but the hours were long. I played four shows a day, seven days a week. I'd lost my family, but I'd made it to New York and survived for nearly two years, honing my musical skills and finagling an invitation to study arranging with the incomparable Marion Evans. New York provided invaluable lessons in music but also in humility. I found that success in one field doesn't guarantee triumph in another. I gained respect for the process and curbed my impetuous tendencies, at least in my career.

TWELVE

New York, New York

The first time I entered the Roxy was for my audition when I was shepherded through a stage door to the basement. The next time, I entered through the main doors on West Fiftieth Street to my new place of employment and was stunned by the grandiose architecture, multi-tiered balconies, and lavish interior. The Cathedral, as the Roxy was dubbed, seated nearly six thousand ticketholders. With its Cinemascope screen and multiple shifting stages, the Roxy combined motion pictures with vaudeville for entertainment. Beneath the palatial main floor, five additional floors included support facilities such as dressing and rehearsal rooms, dry cleaners, barbers and hairdressers, an infirmary, a gymnasium, a dining room and cafeteria, a library, and even a menagerie for show animals. If I'd had a dog, I would have boarded it there.

From 1:00 p.m. until eleven at night, seven days a week, the entire cast performed between movie showings. I played piano or conducted our twenty-piece band for four shows a day. Many of the show segments featured the band and the Roxyettes, a precision dance company now known as the Rockettes.

At first, the work was grueling. I rarely saw my apartment, except to sleep, because I spent breaks learning music for each act. The small underground city served entertainers and theater staff, which made it easy for me to stay there sixteen hours a day.

The Roxy stage door provided the easiest access for musicians. Stairs led down to a huge room that served as a refuge for the band members between shows. Amenities such as lockers for our instruments, changing rooms, offices, bathrooms, plus two poker tables offered musicians a habitat away from home. At each end of the room, payphone booths linked us to the outside. Many friendships as well as a few battles were forged over card games. No blood was shed.

Occasionally, I'd sneak in a poker game with band members during the day and a hand of gin rummy with my boss at night. I got to know the musicians and their stories. The shrink in the army who chided me about never belonging to a club must have made an impression on me, because I worked on being a member of the band instead of the leader.

More seriously, I recalled the European ice show and wished I'd taken the opportunity to become a better conductor then, both musically and as a leader. Instead, I'd been arrogant and demanding. I thought I knew everything. I wanted to learn from that experience. If I had the opportunity to conduct shows again, I wanted to do it right, to be prepared and to have the right attitude.

The opportunity came when Bob Boucher, the man who hired me, took an interest in me. Highly regarded by the musicians, he was an accomplished show conductor. He had a clear conducting style and knew every act's music cold. From Bob I learned to think ahead and prepare for every change, every skipped beat, forgotten lyrics, and

Bob Boucher

all types of calamities such as falling scenery and escaping animals. A consummate musician, he was a wonderful mentor.

Bob made sure I learned more than the music for the shows. He taught me the importance of timing. I learned the jokes and how to bring the orchestra in without stepping on punch lines. The length of a pause was crucial to a comedian, and the audience's reaction could make or break a performance. I practiced tempos religiously and often used a metronome so there would be no difference between Bob's conducting and mine. Just as it is with skaters, a dancer's tempos—the speed the music is played—shouldn't vary much or else the choreography won't work.

Bob had a good relationship with all the entertainers. He was easy going and avoided confrontation. Performers knew he was there to support them and serve their needs musically. I struggled to learn that lesson, especially with Count Carlo and Constance de Mattiazzi.

They had an act known as The Dancing Dolls. In the act, Constance wore men's shoes on her feet and women's shoes on her hands. She bent over at the waist so that her shoed hands touched the ground, which made her arms resemble a woman's legs. Upper torsos of two life-sized mannequins were mounted on Constance's back in a position that looked as if a man and woman were dancing together. Carlo waved a stick, my cue to start the music, and then, as if he were the dolls' master, he directed Constance to dance. When she moved, it looked as if two dancers were twirling, lifting and prancing to the music. Audiences were delighted and astonished at how brilliantly Constance performed the feat.

Count Mattiazzi was a sour fellow, probably because Mrs. Count got the applause, bruising his ego. He was especially unhappy with me and complained that my tempos were different from Bob's tempos. After his reproach, I carefully worked on the dances and asked Bob if I was doing something wrong.

"No," he said, "I wouldn't worry about it."

The next day, Mattiazzi hunted me down after the performance and accused me of ruining the act because I was either too fast or too slow with the music. His wife was standing off stage, so I asked her to tell me where the tempos were wrong.

"Your tempos are fine for me," she said in broken English.

"They're not fine for me," claimed the count.

"Well," I said, "your wife is doing all the dancing. You're only waving a stick."

On his way out, the count spit in my face. I reported him to the stage manager who handed me a towel and agreed to keep Carlo off the stage unless he was performing.

Artie at the piano with the Roxy orchestra

I realized that I attracted confrontation, whereas Bob Boucher avoided it. He was always respectful and deferential but pleasantly firm. He listened politely and had a knack for leaving another's ego intact. I admired this quality in Bob along with his overall temperament. He was a good example for me, and I made an effort to follow his lead with not always perfect but increasing success.

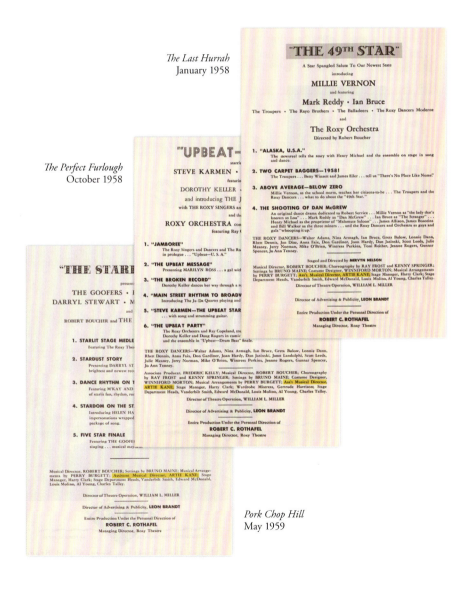

The Last Hurrah
January 1958

The Perfect Furlough
October 1958

Pork Chop Hill
May 1959

THIRTEEN

The Party's Over

Although my life revolved around an unrelenting routine of rehearsals and shows, I found time to study arranging and to date Helen Wood, an extraordinarily multitalented Broadway singer, ballerina and violinist. My life was full but good. My salary from the Roxy allowed me to make payments to Tony and send money to Sherry, who called me from various cities on the ice show tour to pass on her parents' report on David. Her calls always depressed me and ramped up emotions of guilt over my son. Then one day during a Roxy band rehearsal, Sherry phoned me, sobbing hysterically, exactly the way she had after the car wreck in Arkansas.

More than a year had passed since we had formally separated and she'd called me the "worst son-of-a-bitch who ever lived." Her father wrote me a six-page letter confirming that.

"Sherry, I'm in the middle of a rehearsal. What's the matter?" I couldn't get a coherent sentence out of her. I was worried. "Has something happened to David?"

"No," she managed to blurt out.

Relieved, I told her I'd call later when I could talk. After rehearsal, I ran back to my apartment and dialed her number. I could hardly believe it when she told me she was pregnant and needed my help.

"Why don't you call your father?"

"I can't," she said. "He'd kill me."

A smart man would have hung up on her, but Sherry knew—SOB that I was—that I couldn't walk away when she needed rescuing. Besides, she was the mother of my son. A shrink later told me that, like Sir Galahad, "You're one of those guys whose white steed is parked in the garage ready to save a damsel tied to the tracks."

"Whose is it?" I asked Sherry.

"A new guy in the company. He's a principal skater, with a wife and a new baby."

I was angry. This prude, the mother of my son, who got upset because I had bought *Playboy* magazine, was on the road screwing a married guy who had a newborn. I told Sherry since the guy was working, the least he could do was take care of the financial part of her dilemma.

"No, he can't," she sobbed. "He doesn't even know. I need to get rid of it. I want an abortion."

There was no talking her out of it.

I'd heard about the horrors women suffered trying to end unwanted pregnancies, and I knew that several died each year from botched procedures. I had connections. I knew dancers who knew doctors who knew how to go about this safely. No back alley guys. It had to be done soon, in the very early stages, before the end of the first trimester. For the first time in my life, I had a savings account of a thousand dollars, and that was the exact cost of the abortion and Sherry's expenses.

I called my old friend, one of the managers of the ice show, and said, "Kenny, don't ask any questions. Release Sherry Wells from the show. I'm doing you a favor. I'm sending you a prepaid airline ticket for her."

Four days later, Sherry arrived in New York. The doctor had helped several dancers in the show who vouched for him. He warned me the procedure would require a three-week recovery period before Sherry could travel again. After the abortion, I brought her back to recuperate in my apartment, the shoebox with the Pullman kitchen and a bedroom the size of the double mattress on the floor. I slept on the pullout couch in the living room. I was up and out of my cramped quarters early in the morning. I used the band room at the Roxy as my office to study and practice. I had no idea what Sherry did all day. We never had a meal together or talked. After three weeks, I told her to make other arrangements or go back to the show.

At five feet nine inches tall, she got right in my face and backed me against a wall. "I'm not going anywhere," she said. "I want a chance at our marriage, and I'm not going to be persecuted for making a mistake."

As she screamed in my face, I had an out-of-body experience where my hands closed around her throat. I knew if I stayed in that apartment, I would actually do it. I would throttle her. I pushed past her and called my lawyer, Robert Garlock, who had helped me arrange support payments for David. He told me to leave the apartment immediately and to stay out until he had her removed. I don't recall how he handled that, but she was gone, and my divorce came through three months later on January 29, 1959. Garlock sent me a bill for the personal service of a restraining order, plus a plane ticket for Sherry back to the show, and her cab fare to the airport.

I learned later from my mother that Sherry returned to New York with our son that September. She took photos of David playing in a fountain in Central Park and

David at the Freidsam Memorial Carousel in Central Park

riding the Freidsam Memorial Carousel. She never contacted me, but sent a small album of pictures to Columbus. I expected her reports about David would continue, or that I might get a thank you for my help with her pregnancy problem. A call never came, but she kept in touch with my mother. On my side, I didn't call her either. Tony let me know she was still skating with the show. I worried she and her father would load David with negative information about me, and plenty of it was probably true. After I moved to California and had a house, she refused to send him to me for visits. However, every summer, she packed him off to Columbus for a few weeks to visit with Uncle Joe and my mother. They made sure he had new clothes for school and anything else he wanted. Mother would call me and say, "David's coming. Why don't you come see him?"

But I was hurt. "I'm not playing those games with Sherry," I said. "If she doesn't want David to know me, so be it. One day he'll look me up if he's interested."

I know now this was a mistake. Treating David poorly and trying to justify it because of the angst between his mother and me was irrational and dumb. Too angry and self-absorbed to understand the effect my behavior could have on my son's life, I let him down, quashing any relationship that might have developed between us.

In contrast, my mother loved David probably more than she loved me. She and Joe offered substantial money to Sherry if she'd

David in Columbus with Grandmother Sally

allow them, instead of her parents, to raise him in Columbus instead of Atlanta where they lived. I don't know how they broached the subject or what they offered, but I know they couldn't do enough for him and treated him royally during summer visits. Apparently, Sherry didn't accept the offer.

Joe taught David to play golf. One day, after alluding to his role in my becoming a pianist, Joe jokingly asked my mother, "What shall I make this time?"

I had visitation rights. I could have hired an attorney and gone through the courts to set up a schedule for visits, but I copped out using the excuse that I didn't believe in forcing a tug of war on a kid. The final blow came when Sherry married again and changed David's last name to Russell. I told myself I didn't care if I ever saw him again.

As it happened, Sherry's new husband, George Russell, gambled away their money and family home, forcing David to go back to his grandparents in Atlanta. I missed this opportunity and one other where I could have made a difference in my son's life, but I rationalized my way out of it all by using anger and hurt as justification for my failure as his father.

FOURTEEN

California Here I Come

Shortly after my final episode with Sherry, John Berkman, my replacement at Holiday on Ice, followed me to New York. John was searching for work on Broadway, same as I had done when I left the ice show. I asked him if he had a place to stay.

"Not yet," he answered. He was looking for a small apartment, centrally located like mine. I told him he could share my place until he found one. I gave him the couch.

John's father, Samuel Berkman, was cofounder and trustee of the performing arts conservatory Hartt School of Music in Hartford, Connecticut, and John's mother was on the teaching staff. John had a well-rounded musical education in piano, violin and woodwinds. He played piccolo in the Marine Corp orchestra and marching band. He's a first-rate studio musician.

After John moved in, I hardly recognized my apartment. I'd come home late at night from the Roxy and find my apartment buried under his clothes. Every item he took off resided in the very spot where he stood when he removed it. Mounds of manuscript paper harbored piles of beer cans. He never finished a project. Everything lay in waiting. When I questioned his progress on apartment hunting, John admitted he couldn't find a place he liked as well as mine.

John was one of those guys who defied reasonable behavior. I couldn't get rid of him like I couldn't get rid of Sherry. The difference was I didn't want to throttle him.

I liked working at the Roxy, but its heyday was over. Closure seemed imminent, and with that, my steady paychecks would vanish. LuAnn Simms, a featured vocalist in the Roxy shows, had recommended me to Jaye P. Morgan as a pianist. When my apartment phone rang, Miss Morgan's personal manager, Bullets Durgom, offered me a job as Jaye P.'s on-the-road conductor/pianist. I looked over at John, his piles of clothes, heaps of beer cans and stacks of paper, and asked Bullets, "When do we leave?"

A popular jazz singer with two hit records, "Life Is Just a Bowl of Cherries" and "That's All I Want from You," Jaye P. Morgan was a solid entertainer with lucrative bookings across the states. My insecurities about employment in New York vanished when I signed an open-ended contract with her manager.

John kept the apartment, and I sold him the bed, convertible couch, and my piano, all for $200. For years, he bragged about negotiating such a good deal.

During my last weeks at the Roxy, I studied Jaye P.'s arrangements and learned where she stretched a phrase, where she took liberties with the melody, where she needed extra support from the band for an effect in a song. I knew when she needed a jazzy piano fill to spice up a lyric. I'd learned these and other tricks from Bob Boucher.

I hit the road with Jaye P. and her drummer, Jerry Tomlinson, for Chez Paree in Chicago, a big-deal nightclub where singer Bobby Darin and comedian Mort Saul were the main acts at the time. I felt prepared and excited about a new chapter in my career.

Blonde, wholesome and big-eyed, Jaye P. had a magnetism that captivated an audience. She could personalize a song. Some parts of her performance were sassy, some were desperate. Her fans and patrons couldn't take their eyes off her.

When you work with great singers—such as Barbra Streisand; the incomparable Sinatra; cool, intense performer Bobby Darin—or gutsy personalities—such as Sonja Henie—magic happens. Jaye P. was one of the magic makers. When her show cooked, it was thrilling. We knew it, and the audience knew it.

Along with the magic comes the pressure of making it happen show after show. You have to produce; you're not allowed an off night. We played two shows every evening and went out afterward for night lunch. One a.m. was our time to relax, our time to come down from onstage tension. Back in Jaye P.'s suite, we'd sit around and talk. We'd discuss the show—what worked and what to change the next night. She'd have a few drinks, after which Jerry and I would put her to bed. She blamed her drinking on her second marriage.

"If I could get this divorce over, I could stop drinking," she said.

"Well do it then," I said.

"Go with me," she begged. "I can't do it alone. I need you to hold my hand."

That sort of vulnerability has always led me to trouble. After a few months of bookings, we had a schedule break, so I flew with Jaye P. to Juarez, Mexico, and helped her with the paperwork. She came back divorced.

Soon after, we started *getting together*. Our onstage connection generated excitement that spread to our relationship and led to marriage in July 1960.

Between road gigs, we lived in Jaye P.'s posh apartment on the Upper East Side. Life was exciting, and we were making money. Did she stop drinking? No, but her excuse evolved. She needed to drink because she wanted a baby and couldn't conceive.

Jaye P. was funny, clever and a natural jazz singer who refused in-depth music rehearsals. Her background was country music. In the fifties she'd had her own variety show where she sang with her brothers, who were all vocalists and musicians, but Jaye P. couldn't read music. Not only did I teach her new material, I also rehearsed her for shows. Our musical connection drove our personal relationship and excited our performances.

One afternoon while I was hammering out a melody line for her to learn, she continued to sing the wrong notes, so I stopped. "Listen, it goes like this," I said, and played it again.

"I don't have to sing what's written," she barked.

"You have to learn the correct melody in order to improvise on it," I snapped back. "Otherwise, you won't know what fits with the chord structure, and the band parts won't work in the arrangement. Do you want it to sound wrong on stage?"

She stomped off but learned the correct melody.

Jaye P.'s unpredictable nature was one of the reasons her performances were fresh and sensational. She didn't script me into the act, but one night she sang Cole Porter's "All of You" as she slowly vamped toward me at the piano. "I love the look of you, the lure of you ..." She lingered on each word. The spotlight followed her while she sang to me in her sultry voice. I moved as far over on the piano bench as possible to avoid the light. I was embarrassed that she would bring our relationship onstage, and I was angry; I thought she was taking a chance with the show. The audience got involved and egged her on. I didn't know how to ad-lib. Out of my element and uncomfortable, I waved her off.

A heckler yelled, "Hey, why don't you slap her?"

I freaked and motioned the band to play the closer, ending the set. I was on my way into the audience to beat up the guy who ruined the act when the drummer, Jerry, stopped me. "Leave it," he said. "The guy was drunk. Don't make a problem." He was right; I had overreacted.

Tension raced through our performances onstage and off. Our competitive careers added pressure to our relationship. Applause and successful performances eased the tension. So did sex. Both produced an adrenaline rush that was addictive.

With an addiction, you're never satisfied, and as a performer, that's a good thing because you strive for something greater. Always looking for the next break, Jaye P. wanted out of New York and suggested we try California. I, too, was intrigued by the music business on the West Coast. We talked about it, and in the summer of 1960 we decided to move to Los Angeles.

Artie and Jaye P.

The day we were to leave New York for Los Angeles, I was driving. As we entered the Holland Tunnel, I started to sweat and became short of breath. A feeling of panic set in as I gripped the steering wheel, a kind of foreboding I'd never experienced before. It was different from the nerves of a new show or audition or competition. I pressed on, but by the time we reached the Pennsylvania Turnpike, I couldn't continue. Jaye P. told me to turn around and head back to New York. As soon as we got through the tunnel, I calmed down. Jaye P. called her doctor, a nice woman who came to the apartment and checked me out. She determined that I'd had a panic attack and prescribed a low dose of a designer tranquilizer called Miltown. It worked well, took the raw edge off my nerves, and within a couple of weeks, I was able to drive us across the country. First though, after a performance in Connecticut, we married, on July 31, 1960, in Greenwich.

We still had bookings in and around Las Vegas, and a two-week run at the Riviera, which helped ease our decision to move west. One good-sized casino with an elegant nightclub had a marquee outside that read, "This Week Jaye P. Morgan," with an opening act listed in small letters.

Everyone treated us like family, welcoming and friendly. I liked watching the blackjack tables, so one day a manager asked if I'd like to see the office. Inside were huge stacks of money piled up. "This is amazing," I said. "Aren't you worried?"

"About what?"

"Being robbed."

He laughed. "You want to try it?"

I'd been oblivious until he pointed out all the security: No uniforms, but every other person was a watcher, and they had all smiled or said hello to me.

"Haven't you noticed all the people here who know your name and that you have the run of the club? All the employees are obligated to learn who the performers and band members are and what they look like, and when your name comes down, they learn the personnel in the next act and your time is over."

Within a week, I got what he meant. After our closing night and before I packed up the music, I stepped outside to smoke a cigarette. Jaye P.'s name was already off the marquee, and a guy on a ladder was spelling out the name of next week's big shot. Later, I would learn the same lesson in the studios. In the entertainment industry, it's always queen for a day.

While we finished our Vegas commitments, Bullets was negotiating Hollywood television appearances that promised stability and greater fame for Jaye P. He arranged for her to guest star on Tennessee Ernie

Ford's *The Ford Show* and on the *Pat Boone Chevy Showroom*. Because these shows had their own conductors and bands, Jaye P. didn't need me, so I figured there might be an opportunity for me to pursue work in the film and recording studios.

We settled into Los Angeles, bought a house in Studio City, met a few people and established ourselves with doctors. Milton Uhley, a Beverly Hills internist, continued my prescription for Miltown, which calmed my turmoil over moving and trying to gain entry into a new arm of the music industry.

Jaye P. was having medical issues, so a friend referred her to Dr. Maury Lazarus, a prominent OBGYN in Beverly Hills. Jaye P. wanted me to meet her doctor because she wanted a child and needed my participation. I liked Maury immediately. A swarthy, Sephardic Jew, he had a successful practice but also spent one day a week at a free clinic in Venice treating poor, uninsured women. A friend who contributed generously to the clinic told me Maury sometimes treated some free-clinic patients at his own office. One Friday, Maury's receptionist ushered in a wealthy Beverly Hills dowager. In a stern tone, she questioned Maury about the black woman in the waiting room. "You don't treat colored women, do you, Dr. Lazarus?"

Dr. Maury Lazarus

"Oh, you mean Ruthanne? She's not my patient; she's my sister. She came by for lunch." The dowager shrieked, grabbed her purse and rushed out of the office.

During his internship, Maury house-sat for a medical professor who lived on the perimeter of a private golf course in the affluent Toluca Lake neighborhood, a restricted golf club that discriminated against Jews. Maury studied all summer on the backyard patio overlooking the course.

One member of a foursome hit a ball over the fence, which landed near Maury. The golfer walked over to the fence and asked Maury to throw the ball back so he could continue playing. Maury picked up his books and walked toward the house, turned and said, "Sorry, I can't; I'm Jewish."

THE MYSTIQUE OF MAKING IT IN THE L.A. MUSIC BUSINESS hinged on studio work. Record and jingle companies, television stations, and motion picture studios offered musicians the best employment opportunities in the world. The most talented players, arrangers and composers flocked to Hollywood.

When I had been struggling in New York, Dominic Frontiere had said, "Call me if you come to California." With no expectations, I thought, what the hell, and called. True to his word, he opened countless doors for me. He muscled me into Local 47, bypassing the waiting period, and used me as his pianist for the TV series *The New Breed*. He hired me throughout the sixties as he composed music for producer Leslie Stevens' weekly television shows, including *Outer Limits* and Quinn Martin Productions' *The Fugitive*. Through Dominic, I met producers, orchestra and studio contractors, and scores of talented musicians.

Meanwhile, Jaye P. was cast as Adelaide in a summer stock production of *Guys and Dolls* starring Tony Martin and Alan King. She wanted me to travel with her to Framingham, Massachusetts, and Oakdale Musical Theater in Wallingford, Connecticut, so she could bounce ideas off me about her character, but I didn't know anything about musical theater or acting. I could advise her about the music and tell her if she was singing the right notes, but acting wasn't my bailiwick. She persuaded me that our marriage wouldn't survive unless we shared every moment of OUR lives. I went with her, but there was nothing for me to do except praise her performances and boost her ego, which is what she really wanted. I dreaded each empty day and took extra Miltown to get through them. After many rehearsals and three weeks of performances, I was sure the marriage wouldn't survive with me sharing every moment of HER life.

In an in-depth interview with the *Bridgeport (CT) Post* about the show, Jaye P. said, "There's no point in being married unless you can be together. It's rough for Artie to stand around while I'm working, but when we married, we decided we could be together and our careers wouldn't interfere."

That philosophy may have been fine when I conducted her shows and recordings, or played piano for her performances, but it wasn't okay for me to sit around for hours of rehearsals or sit in the audience and watch six performances of her show every week. Marriage has to have equality.

During afternoons, we played cards or watched daytime television, which Jaye P. loved. We were together, but it was a forced togetherness. One day, we shopped for a puppy to take back to L.A. For once, we made a mature decision and decided to wait. Mostly, we talked about how people juggle two careers and concluded it's a difficult task in the entertainment field.

In the spring of 1962, Jaye P. had an important week-long booking in Palm Beach, Florida, for which she wanted me to conduct and play. Not only was I happy to go and work with her for a special engagement, I suggested we go to Columbus afterward so I could introduce her to my family. It was Passover, time for the tribe to get together. That year, family and friends were also planning a surprise sixtieth birthday for my mother. Several people wanted to honor my mother for her generosity, including a grateful couple who wanted to thank her for playing matchmaker. The family gave Mother a specially designed bracelet. I arranged for Jaye P. and me to arrive at the end of the celebration. Our presence seemed to delight my mother. Again, the family was on its best behavior and accepted Jaye P., who entertained them like the star she was, during our just-long-enough stay.

When we returned to L.A., Jaye P. asked me to shape my work schedule around hers so Bullets could book more plum jobs for us in Vegas and Miami Beach. What she didn't understand was that I had to be available to take studio calls in Los Angeles. If I was out of town repeatedly, contractors would go on to the next name on their list. After much discussion, we agreed that a one-sided deal wouldn't work and that I should pursue the studio work I wanted. Still, Bullets booked her in some nightclubs and shows and called to give me the dates, expecting me to go with her.

"I can't be out on the road with her, Bullets. I'm trying to break into studio work in L.A."

"Oh my God," Bullets yelled to his partner, Ray Katz. "We've got a problem."

"No you don't," I said. "Jaye P.'s music is in perfect shape for any conductor and orchestra to play. I made sure of that."

Jaye P. didn't want to go on the road without me. Even though she knew I was trying to make a studio career for myself, she resented it and blamed me for not supporting her. Bullets cut out the club bookings and arranged appearances and acting roles for her in a variety of television series. She worked a lot and made good money. I thought she would be happy, but I think she missed the thrill of a live performance every night. Meanwhile, I accepted all work offered, studied composition and arranging, and practiced many hours a day.

The prolific Italian composer Mario Castelnuovo-Tedesco was a faculty member of the Los Angeles Conservatory of Music. He taught composition to several Hollywood film composers including John Williams, Jerry Goldsmith, and Henry Mancini. Awed by his reputation and tremendous output of music, I had the privilege of studying under him when he was in his seventies.

Castelnuovo-Tedesco inspired me, but I was also scared of him. I'd come in with my lesson—something like assigning instruments to the lines of a Beethoven piano sonata—and he would ask, "How low does a violin play?"

"Down to the G below middle C," I answered.

"Then why do you write F?"

He would catch my every mistake, and I'd feel stupid, but I learned. I was determined to master orchestration. He knew I had the creativity to compose, and I knew I had the film sense. If I ever got the chance to score a piece of film, I was going to be ready.

Working with phenomenal musicians in a rarified business never ceased to amaze me. Part of me worried the phone wouldn't ring. When it did, I worried I wouldn't be up to the task. Would I be able to sight-read the music and serve the composer?

Not only did the composers and orchestra contractors audition me at every session, the orchestra musicians judged me as well. These were not formal auditions; I had the job for the day. The question was whether they would call me back for another studio session in the future. When I walked across the stage to the piano, no one said hello—not the musicians nor the studio personnel. They must have known how cold that felt to someone new entering through the stage door that could as easily swing the other way. It takes toughness to get past that audition. I surmised the musicians didn't want to be friendly until they knew I'd made it into the fold.

Tension ran high for me on studio sessions. No matter how early I got up to practice before the call, my cold hands trembled as I sat at the piano waiting for the composer's downbeat. My stomach was in knots. Often, I'd take an extra Miltown to calm my nerves. When I asked my doctor about it, he said I was on a very low dose of the drug, and it was fine to double it when I felt anxious. Fear of not doing well on the job created my anxiety, along with the lack of camaraderie and the standoffish attitude of the other musicians. The only people who spoke to me when I was breaking into the studio business were Red Mitchell, the greatest jazz bass player I ever knew, and Frankie Carlson, the jazz drummer and percussionist who played for big name stars from Doris Day to Elvis Presley.

André Previn, in his book *No Minor Chords,* said the reason he is so fond of jazz musicians is that they only care how you play. "Their friendships … tend to be governed by one simple rule: If they like the way you play, and if they believe you to be a nice fellow, then fine. If one of those two elements is badly missing, forget it."

That defined Red and Frankie, and Red played a lot of jazz with André. After we became good friends, I told Red, "You saved my life in my early studio days because it felt really unfriendly in L.A."

The *studio system* in which each company—MGM, Paramount and Warner Brothers—had its own orchestra on staff, was discontinued in the fifties and replaced with a freelance structure. Getting your name onto a contractor's call list took considerable maneuvering. Orchestra contractors had favorites, or key players, but they filled out the orchestra with available players. I had the chops to do the job, but I was a social misfit, unfriendly, couldn't make small talk, and probably came off as arrogant. I should have practiced smiling when the Langfords brought it up at the Roxy, but I was shy and didn't think anyone would take me seriously if I smiled. Besides, I was self-conscious about looking insincere. Moreover, when people smiled, I thought they were phony. Too many times in business, someone would be all smiles until someone left the room, and then the smiley guy would say, "What an ass."

Somehow, I managed to stay on the good side of the contractors. Fortunately, the more I worked, the more calls I got.

A musician had to stay in good with Local 47 as well. I kept track of all my work, paid my membership and work dues, and stayed squeaky clean, avoiding any cash calls that teetered on nonunion, that is, on *dark dates*. The union had a strong position on the West Coast, providing health care and pension benefits, making studios the top place to work. Busy players were big earners, and if sessions were canceled with fewer than ninety-six hours' notice, you still got paid.

Known as the Hollywood Pianist, studio musician Ray Turner was in high demand. At MGM he was first call, and wherever he played, he received top dollar, over scale. Then television shows blossomed. TV producers didn't have the budgets to pay more than scale. Actors had an audience following and were irreplaceable, but anonymous musicians didn't appear on screen and didn't command loyalty. Ray was pricing himself out of television work.

In came my champion, Dominic Frontiere, a fine musician and composer and a savvy businessman. He built relationships like Hitchcock built suspense. Dominic hired MGM's music contractor, Mickey Whelan, to contract a television show and touted me as the new pianist in town. Mickey was impressed with my ability to sight-read Dominic's complex compositions and, as a result, called me for several MGM television shows that didn't have the budget to pay Ray's above-scale rates.

The relationship-building continued. Dominic and Mickey knew Paramount's music contractor who hired me as part of the orchestra for a series of western television shows. I remember that day at the scoring stage vividly. I didn't know anyone, and no one spoke to me. Terrible at small talk, I sat at the piano, adjusted the bench a couple times and opened the music folder. The first piece, or music cue, had TACET stamped on the piano part. It meant there was nothing to play. I sat up straight, tried to look interested and was quiet when the red recording light lit. The conductor announced the next cue. I turned the page and found another tacet sheet. Paging through the entire book, I discovered every cue was marked TACET. I had no idea what to do, so I sat at the piano three hours. Someone might have suggested I sit in the orchestra room and wait to be called, but no one said a word. I wished I had a book to read. I noticed several other musicians reading or working crossword puzzles when they weren't playing.

One person finally said hello and invited me to lunch in the cafeteria. He observed that I didn't have much to play on the session. I agreed. Back on the recording stage, I sat through three more hours with no music to play. After the orchestra was dismissed, the contractor told me to stay. I watched as stagehands shoved an old upright piano called a *Golden Oak* onto the stage. The piano looked a hundred years old, like it belonged in a bar in the Old West. It had tacks inserted in the hammers to make the music sound metallic and loud. Rarely tuned, tack pianos have a twangy, tinny, strident sound.

A music librarian brought me a stack of lead sheets. "We need source music for our western series," he said, "so we're going to record tunes for the library."

Source music refers to music from a radio, or an instrument on screen, like a piano in a bar. The audience thinks the music comes from the visual source, but the music editor actually dubs it in after filming the scene. Actors don't have to pretend they are playing because the film won't show their hands.

Lead sheets are melody lines with chord symbols. Much is left to the pianist's imagination. Finally, I knew why I was there. For the next two hours, I coaxed my imagination into an old time bar setting and played like a performer at Tin Pan Alley. I held the sustaining pedal down and banged away playing waltzes, polkas and old ballads from the turn of the century. After each one, someone in the booth yelled out, "Okay, that's a print. Next." At the end, the scoring mixer hollered, "Thanks." I went home not knowing if I'd done a good job or if I'd ever work again. That evening, I couldn't eat dinner. I had a panic attack, took an extra pill that didn't help, and paced most of the night.

Next day, Dominic phoned. "What did you do at Paramount yesterday?"

When I explained, he said, "My God, they're in ecstasy. They want to know where we found you."

Once again, my background of nightclubs, variety acts, theater and ice shows had paid off, this time on a Hollywood job. Every job I took, no matter how obscure, added to my experience and led me to another job.

It wasn't long before I got a call for motion picture work, the big carrot job. Frank DeVol composed the music for *Boys' Night Out,* an MGM picture with Kim Novak and James Garner. In the fifties, Jaye P. had sung with the Frank DeVol Orchestra. Frank had been a close friend of Jaye P.'s since the beginning of her career and had written arrangements for her. Once I had proven myself, he used me often on his sessions, and we, too, developed a close friendship. Because of that connection, Frank asked Mickey to book me, instead of Ray Turner, for his film scoring sessions.

On the first day, I noticed a large instrument covered by a tarpaulin. Five pedals stuck out from the bottom. On the break, I asked Mickey, "What's that?"

"It's a concert harpsichord. You're playing it this afternoon."

"Mickey, I've never seen a harpsichord."

Unfazed, he said, "You better stay here during lunch and figure it out."

I looked under the tarp at an unfamiliar keyboard with the white and black keys reversed. They were shorter and narrower than a piano keyboard. I didn't want to let Frank down now that he'd taken a chance on me. I was certain the Hollywood Pianist, Ray Turner, knew how to play the instrument.

Ray and I had met at an earlier session when Mickey needed two pianists and had hired us both. When I reached to shake Ray's hand, he spread my third and fourth fingers apart, pretending to break them. "This is what we do to new pianists in Hollywood," he joked.

He let me know I was making a dent in his income. Naive, I didn't consider myself a replacement for Ray. I got the chance because his reputation demanded more money. As the new guy, I played for scale, and if the session called for it, I'd play the harpsichord.

During lunch I learned the pedals were couplers that activated strings an octave higher and lower. I familiarized myself with other levers and practiced music cues marked harpsichord. My nerves were as tight as the strings on the instrument, and I didn't have my pills with me, but I got through the afternoon session and didn't embarrass myself.

A studio guitar player, Barney Kessel, said recording work was 99% boredom and 1% fear. The problem being, you never knew when the 1% would strike. That was the case with the harpsichord.

While work continued to fill my calendar, Jaye P. made several appearances on the *Johnny Carson Tonight Show* and the Steve Allen Show between her television roles. She seemed happy with her career, especially her appearances on the talk shows.

In the summer of 1963 recording artist Peter Nero was hired to compose music for MGM's movie *Sunday in New York,* starring Jane Fonda, Rod Taylor, and Cliff Robertson. Music contractor Mickey Whelan engaged me to be there as orchestra pianist, but when I arrived for the sessions, I looked through the piano book and discovered every cue had Peter's name on it, leaving nothing for me to play. I brought this up to Mickey who said, "You're our studio pianist so you have to be here in case Peter needs you to stand in for him. You'll be paid time and a half whether or not you play."

Peter had featured the piano throughout the score and had meticulously written out every note to sound like he was improvising while playing with the orchestra. The copyists had taped his long piano parts accordion style so they would stack up on one side and stretch across the Steinway's music rack with only four pages visible at a time. They were unwieldy and prone to cascading to the floor during page turns. I talked to Peter who was relieved at my offer to turn pages for him.

Sessions were booked the entire week, and everyday I'd show up and take my position at the side of the piano ready for crisis management. Of course, the musicians gave me nothing but trouble, making snide remarks, teasing and making fun of me as the highest-paid page turner in the business. Peter was aware of the ribbing I was taking.

The music was difficult; Peter played brilliantly and was extremely appreciative that I kept his music organized and silently turned every page at the exact moment required. It was a great experience, and I was glad to get to know him over the five days.

The following week I received a thank-you package from Peter's manager containing every piano album Peter had recorded. The same week, I was booked at MGM on recording sessions for the television series *Dr. Kildare*. I sat ready at the piano. When the show's composer, Harry Sukman, called up his first cue, a wave of laughter rolled through the orchestra as Peter Nero walked across the stage and stood next to me to turn my pages.

JAYE P. KNEW HOW DIFFICULT IT WAS TO BREAK INTO THE STUDIOS, and I thought she was rooting for me; however, as I got busier, she descended into depression. I would come home and find her drinking. She'd say it was because she wanted a baby.

"If you want a baby, don't get all uptight about it; let's adopt one."

There we were in L.A.—she in her third marriage and me in my fifth—deciding to adopt a baby. We could have done it privately through a lawyer, where they didn't ask so many questions if you paid big bucks, but I wanted it to be legit. We went through the county where the average time was three months. The examiner assigned to our case took nine months to complete the process.

"We don't care about you," the examiner said. "We care about the baby. You two are a bad risk—individually and together. It's likely there'll be another divorce."

I used every negotiating path to convince her we'd make great parents. I believed we had an enduring relationship and the means to give a child a wonderful home. Every time we left a meeting, Jaye P. would say, "I have a splitting headache. We're never going to convince this woman to give us a baby."

I'd say, "She's got a headache, too. I'll keep working on her. Persistence is the key." I was certain a baby would make Jaye P. happy because she'd stopped drinking already.

Born August 30, 1963, Paul Steven Kane arrived in our lives. We adopted him right out of the oven. We met his birth mother briefly but knew little about her except she was Dutch. She called him Brett, but we named him Paul. Jaye P. was happy. She quit working for several months to be home with him. We lived in a comfortable house with a swimming pool in Studio City in the San Fernando Valley. Jaye P. and I had a stable relationship. Everything came together for the first time, and I loved being a dad. This was much different from life with Sherry and David. We could afford whatever Paul needed. Jaye P. was happy

Happy Mom and baby

Paul breaks out of his playpen

Counting on food

Paul — fun at my piano

being a mom, singing to him, rocking him. When I came home from a recording, I played with him, carried him around. We fed him together, and he smiled all the time. He grew into a cute toddler.

We were happy at home and in the neighborhood. Judy Garland had brought jazz pianist and conductor Jack Elliott from New York to Los Angeles in the early sixties as musical director for her Sunday night shows. Jack and his wife, Bobbi, bought the house next door to Jaye P. and me. We quickly became great friends. Jack later went on to conduct *The Andy Williams Show.* In his authoritative, deep voice, Jack hollered across the yard one day, "Hey Ace, here's the deal. Sid Caesar's in town, and he's starring on Andy's show."

Artie, Alan Elliott and Paul at the park

Jack Elliott

"Yeah, so what?" I asked.

"His pianist, Earl Wild, has the flu and can't fly in from New York for a comedy sketch he created for Sid."

Jack was up to something; I could tell. Earl Wild was a remarkable pianist who'd performed with major symphonies around the world and premiered the *Shostakovich Piano Trio* and other major compositions.

Jack continued, "The routine is based on Grieg's Piano Concerto. Earl plays the piece off stage while Sid pantomimes the performance onstage at an imaginary piano. Sid's in a panic, but I told him I knew someone who could do it."

"No, you don't, Jack," I hollered back. Earl had to follow Sid's hands, and for someone unfamiliar with the routine, it would be like driving a car with a blackened windshield. *Live television* meant the show was taped in front of a live audience—no time for do-overs. Besides, I'd have to learn Grieg.

"I know it sounds like a lot of work, but I got you $500."

"I'm sorry, Jack, but I can't do it."

"Don't worry, Ace. I'll send you the kinescope tonight so you can study the act."

I don't know how NO became YES, but by show time, I could play the opening of the concerto and the comedy routine in my sleep.

Sid was a larger-than-life person. Fans of his popular, ninety-minute variety show, *Your Show of Shows,* sometimes hounded him and costar Imogene Coca. He carried two guns, for protection, he said, in case his followers included a few nuts. Sid traveled with a personal staff of two or three people. Insanely serious about comedy, he rehearsed endlessly.

On the verge of a nervous breakdown at the thought of working with him, I popped an additional tranquilizer and traipsed into NBC.

Jack introduced us, and Sid began explaining the act. "Now look, I come out, sit down, but there's no piano. I adjust my cuffs and roll the bench up and down, and then my hands come down as if I'm starting the piece. DON'T PLAY! You see, the lid is down on the keyboard—the imaginary keyboard."

"Yeah, I know. I watched the kinescope," I said. "Could we rehearse it?"

"Oh, of course." Sid raised his eyebrows. And so we rehearsed.

Comforted by warnings that Sid was a rehearsing fool who didn't stop till the scene was perfect, I sat at the stage piano, watched his every move and followed his pantomime perfectly through the entire routine. Sid came over and said, "Great. Thank you. See you tomorrow."

"Wait a minute. They told me you like to rehearse all night. Where are you going?"

"I wouldn't touch what just happened. You were perfect," he said and left.

That boosted my confidence, then smashed it. Maybe one perfect rehearsal was just dumb luck.

The next day at dress rehearsal, complications ensued. The crew set my piano in a location that blocked my view of Sid onstage. I explained to the director that I had to see Sid in order to play when he played. We took a short break while the crew rearranged the furniture.

This time the crew set up a monitor and aimed a camera on Sid's face. "Jack," I yelled, "I've got to see his hands, too." They pulled the camera back so I could see all of Sid.

The performance was solid; the audience howled. As far as Sid was concerned, it was a big hit.

When Jack announced break time, Sid made his way through the orchestra and presented me with a dozen roses. The band teased me unmercifully, but these are the memories that make me smile. Later that night, Jaye P. and Bobbi joined Jack, Sid, his entourage and me for dinner at the Tail of the Cock, a popular restaurant and hangout for personalities.

It was an honor and high spot in my career; however, when Sid and Jack praised me for my timing and playing, Jaye P., irritated, played with her napkin, looked the other way, and started talking to Bobbi. I wanted to share a terrific evening with her and celebrate a small career triumph. Instead, I had a rude awakening about the strife Hollywood couples suffer when one achieves success and the other is jealous. Jaye P. ordered too many drinks, and, in an unsuccessful attempt to grab the spotlight, boasted about her TV shows and bookings. Clearly, she was feeling insecure and looking for praise. I was embarrassed for her.

EARLY IN 1964 television opportunities surfaced for Jaye P. in *The Joey Bishop Show* and *The Merv Griffin Show*. Bullets had worked hard to reinvent her career and booked roles for her in the series *The Eleventh Hour* and *Make Room for Daddy*. When she worked, she was happy. I took care of Paul. At first, I always kept him beside me. When I ate, I fed him at the same time. He seemed to like music, so I often put Paul in his playpen in my studio while I practiced. Sometimes I held him at the piano so he could play on the keys. His bedroom was next to my studio, so even when he slept, he was exposed to music. Jaye P. was taking work she wanted, and I was busy in the studios. Our lives were on an even keel.

Mother and Joe visited us at the house on Mary Ellen. They couldn't get used to the security system or the time change. When Joe got up at four thirty to walk in the neighborhood, he left the front door open and the alarm beeping. My mother, still on east coast time, rummaged around the kitchen long before we got up. Hearing sounds, I imagined looters packing up our pots and pans.

Fame was a serious draw for my mother. Impressed by names in lights, she always used Jaye P.'s full name when speaking about her. "This is my daughter-in-law, Jaye P. Morgan." It was reminiscent of my second marriage when my mother would say, "I'd like to introduce you to my daughter-in-law, Jinx Clark, star of Holiday on Ice."

Jack and Bobbi were entertained by Mother and teased me—not in a mean way—about her mannerisms and Yiddish accent. She delighted them with her honesty and worldview. Of course, everyone loved Joe.

I took Mother and Joe to the Fox scoring stage where I was again playing piano in the orchestra for Frank DeVol during the recording of his score for *Hush, Hush Sweet Charlotte*. I had prerecorded Bette Davis singing that title song a few weeks prior. She was delightful and nice to work with. I thought Mother and Joe would enjoy the orchestra session and be impressed that I'd played for Ms. Davis.

On the first union break, I asked them what they thought. Scrunching her nose, Mother said, "Is this what you do?"

Of course, I couldn't let it go. "What do you mean? I'm recording with the best musicians in an industry that pays me a small fortune and is respected throughout the world. I thought you'd be proud and happy for me."

Uncle Joe piped up, "We are proud. Your mother thought you'd be playing solo concerts. We've never heard of this kind of work."

Joe was right. How would they know about the film recording industry? When I had called home, I hadn't explained my job; I had simply told them I was employed as a pianist and making a lot of money.

Regardless of my mother's thoughts on the subject, I knew I was doing well, yet, despite my success in the studios, feelings of panic plagued me, and I was living on Miltown. One afternoon while I played on the Fox scoring stage, I thought the piano was moving, but realized I was swaying instead. Feeling unsteady, I put in a call to Dr. Uhley on the first orchestra break. He agreed to stay late and see me after the session.

After I described the motion I was experiencing, he referred me to a neurologist, Dr. Frumanski, who ran a series of tests and determined I had a temporal lobe disorder. The diagnosis freaked me out, but the two doctors assured me that with a low dose combination of two drugs, Dilantin for the brain seizure and Valium as a tranquilizer, I'd be able to function just fine and continue with my career. Over the next few weeks, I seemed to be better. The pianos stayed put, and I stopped swaying.

My circle of work expanded when Warner Brothers' studio contractor called me to play for *Looney Tunes* sessions. I didn't even try to explain this to my mother and Joe. Composer Bill Lava was well known for writing fast-moving, difficult cartoon music with many intricate passages between xylophone and piano. I didn't know this when I took the call, but when I opened the piano book, it was a sea of black dots, fast tempos and full of runs. I felt like I was at a competition of Czerny piano exercises. They were tough piano parts, but I enjoyed the session and must have done a good job because, one afternoon while Joe and Mother were still in town, Bill Lava stopped by my house with a check for fifty dollars, a bonus, which he said he'd pay me each time I played his sessions. I told him that was completely unnecessary, and I would gladly take his calls if I wasn't already booked. He seemed relieved when I said I enjoyed the challenge of playing his music. I learned that other pianists avoided his calls. He lived up the street from me, and we had a cordial, professional relationship while my chops improved playing Road Runner cartoons. Uncle Joe never got over my turning down the bonus.

Jaye P.'s and my life revolved around Paul and work, and our home didn't lend itself to entertaining guests, so after a day or two, I booked rooms for my mother and uncle at the Sportsmen's Lodge close to our house. A hangout for old Hollywood, it had a decent restaurant and grounds for early morning walking. It also gave them something to do during the day when I was working and Jaye P. was filming.

Joe sometimes played with Paul at the house, but Mother was barely tolerant of him. "He doesn't look like any of us," she said. "The family doesn't recognize adoptions."

"He's part of my family whether you recognize him or not," I snapped.

The next year when Mother and Joe came to visit, my cousin Aaron Berman had just finished his residency and had opened an Ear, Nose and Throat practice in Encino, an upscale suburb in the San Fernando Valley. Mother was so proud of Aaron—a doctor, no less. She bawled me out for calling him by his childhood nickname, Bunky. "He's a doctor now and deserves your respect," she admonished.

"Okay," I said, "I'll call him Doctor Bunky."

Cousin Aaron, a wonderfully good natured and talented doc, offered to take Joe and Mother to Disneyland, which relieved me of two days of entertaining. Mother spent the second day recovering from her ride on the Matterhorn. I'm not sure she ever forgave Aaron.

Between her visits, Mother must have done some homework and decided my film music career was a worthwhile and noteworthy pursuit. During her next visit, I arranged for a chauffeur to drive her and Joe to Universal Studios where I was recording. I was at the piano when the contractor's flustered secretary rushed over and said, "Artie, your mother is at the gate berating the guard because he doesn't know who you are or where to find you."

During Mother and Joe's stay, Jack Elliott hosted a wrap party after recording his score for *Where's Poppa?*, a film I had also worked on. Carl Reiner was the producer. Carl hung around the piano at the sessions, and we exchanged childhood stories about our mothers. So when Jack extended the invitation, I thought it would be okay to bring my visiting relatives.

Jack Elliott & Carl Reiner at *Where's Poppa?* party

At the party, Carl came over to meet Mother who was truly in awe of the man. She certainly knew who he was and was all aflutter. Well over six feet, Carl bent down to talk to her.

"Mrs. Kane, you must be so proud of your son. He's the finest pianist in the studios and has a wonderful career."

Mother, in nearly a back-bend position, looked up and said, "That's what we're hoping."

Carl never got over that. Years later, my eighth wife, JoAnn was working on a recording session at Fox where Carl was the producer. She introduced herself to Carl as Artie Kane's wife, and as he shook her hand he asked, "Did you ever know Artie's mother? I've never met such a marvelous example of a Jewish mother."

In the fall of 1963, I played in the Peter Matz orchestra on a few Edie Adams television shows. I was at the piano when Edie's guest André Previn introduced himself to me. He explained that the director wanted him on a platform above the orchestra at the start of the show. "I'm supposed to play a few bars of music," he said, "but they can't get a microphone up there. I'd like to show you what I intend to play so you can play it. You'll be heard, but I'll be on camera. Is that okay?"

I stood up and said, "Excuse me. I've got to call my mother."

André frowned and said, "What?"

I explained, "I was born eight days after you, and all my professional life my mother has continued to admonish me, 'Artie, look how well André is doing and look what you are doing.'"

"Good God, you must hate me," he said covering a laugh.

"No, on the contrary, you've become my holy grail."

I really did call my family during an orchestra break and told them to tune into *Here's Edie* on the show's scheduled airdate. I reminded them, "When they introduce André, don't forget, I'm the one playing the piano."

Later at lunch, André and I discussed our familiar circumstances growing up in a persistent family. His father was like my mother: relentless.

LIFE WAS GOOD, and then I came home after a day of recording and found Jaye P. in the den unconscious. Frantic, I checked to see if she was breathing and smelled alcohol. She was drunk. I looked in Paul's room; he was down for a nap. When Jaye P. sobered up, I tried to find out why she would do that, but she couldn't give me a reason. She was simply unhappy. I didn't know what to do. I was afraid for Paul. Fortunately, Jaye P. and I were making enough money that we had a housekeeper. I asked her to work extra hours every day and watch Paul until I got home.

When possible, I took Paul everywhere except to work. On weekends, if I went shopping, he went shopping. If I went for a drive, he went for a drive. As soon as he could walk, we walked everywhere. I went to a department store and let him try out the escalator. Once when he was running beside me to keep up with my longer stride, a woman asked, "Why don't you pick him up?"

"Look at him!" I said. "He's having a good time. He's excited, he's learning. He's a happy kid." I had him by the hand, so it would take longer to get places, but we were both having fun. Helping Paul experience life felt like normal parent behavior, and he was safe with me.

Meanwhile, Jaye P. was sliding downhill and so was her career. I worried about her ability to care for Paul every time I left for work. We needed a full-time nanny. When I learned Jaye P.'s mother needed a place to live, I moved her into the housekeeper's rooms and hoped she would have enough influence over Jaye P. to curb her drinking. At last, there was a mother who wasn't a negative influence. A strong country woman, she knew what she wanted in life. She'd never touched a drop of liquor.

She had five boys and two girls. Most of them drank like their father. They'd started down that path early in life.

One time Jaye P. said, "No man is ever going to treat me like Daddy treated you." Her mother stood right up in Jaye P.'s face and said, "Don't you talk about your father like that. I loved him and he loved me; and when he came home from work, the house was clean, you kids were clean and dinner was on the table; and if he wanted me, I was ready."

I thought to myself, what a woman. The man was a drunk. His last act was to pull all his teeth out with pliers while in a drunken stupor. However, she wouldn't allow her daughter to berate him. As soon as Mom, her name was Josephine, moved in, I felt relief about Paul's well-being.

I TRULY ENJOYED STUDIO WORK and played keyboards for sixteen years before I started my composing career. Movies, television film, jingles, records and television variety shows—it didn't matter—I made it a point to be available when I got a call, and I accepted the first booking. Some players waited before accepting a call in case a higher paying or better job came along. My insecurity and sense of fairness forced me to take the first offer.

Sometimes those first offers were exciting, such as the time Michel Legrand hired me for a Barbra Streisand recording session, and I nearly blew it. I approached the podium and noticed a Styrofoam cup filled with steaming hot tea sitting on the piano next to the music rack.

"Whose tea is this?" I blurted.

"It's mine," answered Barbra.

"Well, get it off the piano."

"Michel …" she called out to the podium.

Michel raised his arms and said, "I'm not getting between you two."

Barbra gave me an exasperated look and removed her tea.

I may have been out of line. I admit I was thrilled to be on Barbra's sessions listening to that beautifully clear and true voice in my headphones and enjoying her artistry, but hot tea on the piano? No.

She forgave me and later asked me where she could buy a good piano. I recommended Comsky's Pianos. I met Barbra and her entourage there, introduced her to Bernie, the owner, and argued with him to give her a discount, which would be good for his business. While there, I played a seven-foot Grotrian-Steinweg grand that had just arrived from Germany. I loved the piano, dreamt about the piano, but I couldn't afford to buy it.

Each time I went to the bookstore or drugstore near my home in Studio City, I passed the Bank of America branch where I banked. I'd go in to make a deposit and loiter, trying to get up enough nerve to talk to someone about securing a $5,000 loan so I could buy the piano. After a couple weeks, I advanced on the assistant manager, Joe Perches, fittingly pronounced *purchase*.

"What can I do for you, Mr. Kane?" He could see I was surprised he knew my name, so he elaborated, "I know you're a customer of the bank and a musician."

Introductions aside, I told him I needed a $5,000 loan.

"What do you want the money for?"

"Well, I want to buy a new piano," I stammered.

"That's good because if you wanted to buy a tractor, I wouldn't consider it."

I laughed. He continued, "You see, I know you earn a living as a musician, so your request is reasonable. If I approve the loan, I have one condition. When the piano arrives, I'd like to come to your house and play it."

I said, "Yes, of course, that would be fine."

I got my piano. After it had acclimated to the house and been tuned,

I called Joe, who came over and turned out to be a pretty decent amateur pianist.

The only social life Jaye P. and I had revolved around Jack and Bobbi. A few dinners at their house and an occasional restaurant meal barely fit our busy schedules. Jack was in demand as a music director; I accepted every studio call and Jaye P. bounced around several television series, including *Vacation Playhouse, Hennessey, General Electric Theater* and the *Joey Bishop Show*. Her numerous appearances on the *Tonight Show* kept her name in front of the public. She seemed to have a special relationship with Johnny Carson. They had chemistry on screen; it sparked reactions and banter alongside Carson's many characters. She often flew to New York to do his show between her Los Angeles TV series.

When she was gone, I'd hang with Jack and composer/jazz pianist Dave Grusin.

During one of Jaye P.'s out-of-towners, the king of bossa nova, Antonio Carlos Jobim, visited Los Angeles. Jack and Bobbi invited me to their Sunday dinner party thrown for Jobim and his entourage from the Brazilian embassy. I wanted to meet him. Grusin was also a huge fan along with Ronnie Kaufman, wife of the general manager of Zody's, a chain of discount stores. I offered to pick up Ronnie on my Yamaha 125 motorcycle and take the shortcut through the canyon. I told her to sit straight and not lean when we went around curves, but she leaned and we went down, sliding up against the mountain with my foot caught in the wheel. Ronnie was unhurt.

Two young guys in a pickup stopped, loaded my bike in their truck and took us to Jack's house. I was in pain, so Jack called an orthopod who was in his office for a weekend emergency. Jack and Dave drove me over and waited while the doctor took an X-ray of my foot. Nothing was broken, but I was shocked to see my big toe upside down with the toenail on the floor.

"Dislocated," the doctor declared as he filled a big needle and injected Novocain between my toes. He waited a few minutes, then grabbed and turned the toe to its correct position. I didn't have time to wince.

Back at the party, I mixed pain medication from the doctor with alcohol and lost track of time. Jobim and his groupies arrived late and more thirsty than hungry. Jack told me he was running out of booze and needed more, so we moved the party to my house.

I don't know what I was thinking except I felt like a big shot—a host with a nice house, a grand piano, and the bar was stocked with liquor. Everyone was drunk and smoking pot. Jobim was on the floor disrobing an actress, and Grusin, who can't resist playing any piano within a hundred feet, noodled jazz riffs on my new Grotrian-Steinweg grand, with his drink sweating circles on the piano's glossy finish and his burning cigarette hanging off the edge of the keyboard.

The alcohol and pain pills wore off quickly when I realized what was going on. I couldn't imagine people behaving so poorly. I hadn't even met Jobim. He was too busy with women, but I threw him and everyone out. Sex, drinking and drugs were inappropriate in my house, especially with my mother-in-law and Paul in the back bedrooms.

IN EARLY 1966 WHEN MY CAREER WAS COOKING, Maury Lazarus called and said, "Let's have lunch. I'll meet you at Nate 'n Al's." It was an odd call out of the blue, so I met him at the deli with my stomach in knots. I ordered cottage cheese and peaches that arrived just as Maury said, "Jaye P. needs a hysterectomy." At the time, many doctors performed hysterectomies, needed or not, but Maury said the surgery wasn't optional for Jaye P., that she'd die without it. She might die with it, too, because, Maury explained, a hysterectomy usually causes depression, something Jaye P. couldn't handle.

I remember dropping my face into the cottage cheese. I was devastated and in tears.

Maury told me my wife could die without the surgery, but that she might kill herself because of the depression. He knew the condition of our marriage, about Jaye P.'s drinking. And I think she must have told him the same thing she told me about her second husband, that she could stop drinking if she could just get a divorce, this time from me.

Leonard Rosengarten

Maury walked me outside to a phone booth, called Leonard Rosengarten, a psychoanalyst, and sent me to see him. I was defeated, unable to tell this shrink why another of my relationships was failing. I should have been the one seeking a divorce. I hated her drinking and could not understand what was so wrong with our marriage that she had to drink. I loved her. We had this sweet child we loved. Why tear our lives apart? Give me a reason. Was I a wife beater? Did I see other women? NO! This appointment was the start of a long relationship that saw me through the demise of this marriage plus two more.

Leonard was the youngest member of a team of wartime psychiatrists sent to Nuremberg Prison in Germany after World War II. It was his assignment to determine if the Nazi prisoners were sane enough to stand trial. Now he'd have to determine if I was sane enough to go through another divorce and still hold on to my career. On our second meeting, he tantalized me with a few accounts of the trials and asked if I was interested in hearing more. I told him I was very interested, but I didn't want to pay for the privilege. We got on well after that.

Not long afterward, I came home from a late session to find my house all lit up; Jack and Bobbi were there. We were often in each other's houses, but not at 11:00 p.m.

They told me Jaye P. had overdosed on pills. They took her to have her stomach pumped. Thank goodness her mother was home with Paul. Life with Jaye P. became impossible. I never knew what I might come home to. In an interview years later with an L.A. jazz critic, Jaye P. said, "I had three wonderful husbands, but I guess I just don't enjoy being married. I have a son, Paul Steven Kane, by my ex-husband Artie Kane." She was always grateful to me for going through the adoption hurdles, but that wasn't enough to keep our marriage together.

I moved out of the house during the divorce proceedings and had to fight for everything, including my piano, and especially for time with Paul. In the sixties, the courts made it impossible for a father to gain custody of a child unless the woman was a real train wreck. I would have had to engage in serious character assassination, which I wouldn't do. I found some comfort knowing Jaye P.'s mother was there to protect Paul.

With her mother's help and the threat of losing Paul, Jaye P. eventually straightened up and stopped drinking for good, I think. She was a good mother to Paul, although she gave him too many things. We had joint custody, which slowed down my feeling of loss for my son. Jaye P. spoiled him so much that whenever he came to my place for the weekend, he wanted to go home almost immediately. "Dad, I'm used to having my own TV in my room."

I'd take him to an amusement park, but he only wanted to go home and play with his toys. There's something sad about all those single fathers clasping their kids' hands, trying to build a relationship on a merry-go-round. My apartment couldn't compete with the house Paul enjoyed with his mother and grandmother.

When I'd take him home, Jaye P. would stand in the driveway with her hands on her hips, looking at her watch if we were two minutes late. I kept on though. I missed him.

FIFTEEN

CHARADE

At least I had my career. In 1966 I met Dimitri Tiomkin, a Russian pianist and composer. He'd immigrated to the United States in 1925 and had become a film composer. Tiomkin had scored pictures for Frank Capra and Alfred Hitchcock, for a spate of westerns during the fifties, for J. Lee Thompson's *Guns of Navarone* in 1961, and went on to score numerous other films.

Tiomkin often composed by writing the music for two pianos and then recording the pianists playing, with the film, to see how the music fit. This gave him a chance to audition the music and make changes before orchestrating it, and it gave the producer a chance to hear and approve the score before hiring a full orchestra to marry it to the picture. The process saved money in case the producer didn't like it.

In his thick Russian accent, Tiomkin called me Professor Art, and I addressed him as Maestro. He corrected me: "Maestro is a shmuck; my friends call me Dimi." I had tremendous respect for him and found it thrilling to work with such a prolific composer whether it was on a motion picture or for television themes, such as, *Rawhide* or *Wild, Wild West*.

Dimi asked me to meet him and a singer at CBS Television City to audition a theme song he'd written. At the meeting, the director of music, Lud Gluskin, presided over a room of humorless studio executives, all dressed in the same style suit. I accompanied the singer, after which the suits left without a word. Except for tapping a pencil on his desk, Gluskin remained silent. California has a warm, sunny climate, but Hollywood is cold.

Dimi thanked the singer and ushered him out the door.

Gluskin nodded toward me and asked, "How much do I pay your piano player?"

"Piano player? You think I find this boy in gutter outside studio? This boy is fine artist."

Gluskin's phone rang and we had to step outside. Dimi whispered to me, "Keep eyes and ears open, mouth closed. I give you beezness lesson." We were called back in.

Gluskin said, "Okay, I'll pay your boy $150."

Dimi said, "Fine, I pay him rest myself."

"I can't let you do that. How about $500?"

Walking out of the building Tiomkin said, "We may not get main title, but we fock company leetle bit."

Tiomkin's sense of humor peppered his scoring sessions, and musicians clamored to take his calls. During an orchestra recording session on *36 Hours,* a James Garner, Eva Marie Saint picture, he stopped the orchestra when the trombone entered, and complained, "Too loud vas."

The player said, "Okay, I'll come in softer."

We began again and just after the trombone entered, Dimi objected, "Too loud vas!"

The trombone player said, "Sorry, I'll make it even softer, Dimi."

We started again and at the same spot Dimi dropped his arms and yelled, "TOO LOUD VAS!"

The trombone player called out, "Dimi, I didn't play at all that time."

Dimi raised his head, closed his eyes and said, "If you had played, vould have been too loud."

One of my first sessions at Warner Brothers was with Ray Heindorf, an American songwriter, composer and conductor who held the reins forty years at Warner's Music Department. A gruff and impatient fellow, he had a short fuse when stressed. The orchestra was slow to return after lunch one day, and the din of their voices and instruments tuning grated on Ray's nerves until he roared from the podium, "Shut up!"

A pall settled on the room. Ray knew he'd stepped in it, so he forced a laugh to lighten the mood. "Well, you never have to worry about me having a heart attack because there's nothing in here," he said, pointing to his chest.

A violinist in the first row stood up and said, "You never have to worry about a brain tumor either."

Laughter erupted in the room. Ray doubled over and steadied himself against the podium, shaking his head and grinning.

IN THE THROES OF ANOTHER MESSY DIVORCE, and with no place to live, I took over the lease of a Malibu Beach house from my friend Dave Grusin, who used the house on rare occasions as a get-away with his wife, Sara Jane.

My neighbor Jack Elliott had introduced us three years earlier when Dave came to L.A. and took over the *Andy Williams Show*. We got to know each other hanging out in Jack's studio. In January of '64 Dave had several projects going and couldn't leave town, so he asked if I would play and conduct Andy's show at the new Kahala Hilton in Hawaii where NBC had booked its annual affiliates meeting. Andy was NBC's star entertainer.

A gifted pianist and arranger, Dave had written orchestra charts for the show that captured the essence of the songs and supported Andy's smooth style and phrasing. Though the orchestra parts had been kept up-to-date with changes and cuts, Dave hadn't marked anything in his own music because he had the show memorized. During rehearsal, Andy would stop singing and say, "Hey Artie, Dave played a clever piano fill in that section. Can you play it?"

"I could, Andy, but Dave didn't write it down," I'd say. Then I'd have to cover and sketch in some appropriate piano riff. When I complained to Dave, he responded with his inimitable smirk, which meant, "I know, but you'll fix it."

Dave's beach house hadn't been kept up-to-date either. It was funky, right out of the movies—a one-bedroom pad with shag carpet, thrift-store furniture, and a half-assed stereo system with a collection of Sinatra records. Even so, I liked it because it had a front-and-center view of the ocean. The sound of the surf crashing and waves bubbling up under the stilted porch gave me a sense that the earth was solid on its axis.

I left this ideal spot every other weekend to pick up Paul and take him to Beverly Park where all the Sunday fathers gathered with their kids. It wasn't the relationship I wanted with him, but it was good for us to share time twice a month.

Meanwhile, I had no career complaints; my studio calendar showed bookings six weeks in advance. When I wasn't recording, I went back to composition, revisiting my work from New York with Marion Evans and continuing my studies in Los Angeles with Professor Tedesco, who took students only on recommendation. Dominic Frontiere had gotten me in when I'd been married to Jaye P. Each week I'd go to Tedesco's small, Spanish stucco house on the outskirts of Beverly Hills. He was old school—like working with Beethoven.

Dominic had warned me, "If he gets too close to you, he's not trying to kiss you; he just can't see, even with his thick glasses. He's affectionate, and he'll call you 'dear,' but don't think anything of it. He's Italian."

I could tell that my professor shaved before each lesson because he'd forget to wipe off a dab of shaving cream in front of his left ear. Leaning toward me, he'd peer through Coke-bottle glasses and say, "Hello, dear," then start correcting my homework, which had taken me hours to write. He'd begin erasing parts and whispering in a soft voice, "no, no, no."

I'd think, hell, I'll never learn this, but then he'd encourage me with "yes, yes, good, dear," and we'd go on.

His system was to take a piano part and say, "Okay, you will put this in orchestra now. How will you divide it?" I'd wait, afraid to give the wrong answer, so he'd continue. "Piano plays this line. What instrument do you want to play this one?"

"Violins?" I'd guess. He'd mark it and go on to the woodwinds, brass, and the rest of the orchestra, explaining the reasons for each decision. Then he'd tell me to go home and write it all out on score pages. Even with all his markings, it was a lot to remember. Eventually, I graduated to the next step where he wouldn't let me mark down what he'd said. We'd talk about it at length, and then he'd send me home with the work. I complained to Dominic that by the time I got home I couldn't remember Tedesco's instructions.

Dominic said, "Do what we all do. Drive around the corner, park and write everything down while it's fresh."

If I came back the next week with things wrong, the professor would examine my work, his nose inches from the music, and start erasing again. The process was tedious, but when I got it right, I felt like I'd found the missing piece to a puzzle. I was thrilled to learn from this great musician. Composition didn't come as easily as learning the piano, but I worked diligently.

I also practiced regularly on my Grotrian-Steinweg piano, the only item I'd managed to wrestle away from Jaye P. after the breakup of our marriage. Music is totally personal for me, and I turned to it as a companion and savior. It had saved me through my childhood, and now it was my refuge in adulthood.

During this intense period, when I was immersed in music and trying to save my relationship with Paul, contractor and trombonist Tommy Shepherd called me to play the Hammond organ at Frank Sinatra's upcoming recordings. Nelson Riddle was writing the arrangements—for a swingin' band plus organ. Months earlier, I'd played piano and organ for Nelson's sessions on the score he'd written for Howard Hawks' film *Red Line 7000*. Nelson liked the sound and decided to add the Hammond to his Sinatra band.

I've always admired Sinatra and was flattered to be called for his *Strangers in the Night* album and the subsequent television special, *Frank Sinatra: A Man and his Music, Part II*. As the recording dates approached, I had misgivings and tried to cancel out of the sessions because I didn't consider myself a jazz organist. Fellow musicians, however, urged me to show up. So I did.

Frank invited around fifty people to the session. He thought performing before an audience added an element of excitement to the recording, and he sang better to an audience than into a microphone. On edge and uncomfortable in a sport coat, I put on dark glasses and swallowed an extra Valium, which didn't help after I saw the organ. It sounded all right, but it looked like a piece of crap, beat all to hell from hard use. The instrument was on a platform in Frank's line of sight, and no one had told me I'd be featured on a couple of songs.

Sinatra had a reputation for excellence and no nonsense, so the musicians were on good behavior. The first tune was a wailing, up-tempo version of "The Most Beautiful Girl in the World." We ran it down twice, and the band nailed it!

"Okay, guys," Frank said, "let's do it." He sensed the right moment to record a high-energy performance, and we all knew the band cooked.

After the take, producer Sonny Burke announced over the speaker, "That was wonderful, Frank, but I think we can do a better one in here," meaning they wanted to try another setup of mics and equipment.

Sinatra said, "You should have thought of that before. Next song." That's how it went down with The Man in charge, recording his album in May of 1966 and taping his television special a month later in June. Occasions like this stand out as a career high—something that becomes apparent when you work with the best.

Peter J. Levinson singled out another song on the album in his biography of Nelson Riddle, *September in the Rain:* "'All or Nothing at All' began at a hearty medium temp—much different from the original Sinatra/Harry James version—but after Artie Kane's organ solo the band began to roar with Sinatra on top wailing to the finish."

Frank Sinatra: A Man and His Music Part II
Artie on Hammond Organ, "You're Nobody Till Somebody Loves You"

Artie and the orchestra accompany Frank Sinatra on "That's Life"

Evaluation of the work was confirmed, even fifty years later. I received a call from Marc Myers who writes on music for the *Wall Street Journal*. He had become enamored of the *Strangers in the Night* album and wanted to interview me as the organist. In his article he said, "The organ brilliantly mirrors Sinatra's middle-age sass without feeling out of character." Again, I was overwhelmed with gratitude for the abundant opportunities I've had in my career.

That same year, during a session at RCA studios, I met Dave Grusin's sister-in-law, back-up singer Susan Tallman. A pretty girl with long, reddish hair, a captivating smile and beautiful eyes, she had been a busy studio singer in Detroit before coming to L.A. to live with Sara Jane and Dave. Both Susan and Sara Jane found work with West Coast record companies, television variety shows and film studios. They were versatile singers who could sight-read and blend their voices, singing choral parts or echoing phrases behind pop stars.

Susan Tallman

Sisters Sara Jane and Susan

Before long, Susan was spending time at the beach house with me. She'd drive her old, green Chevy from her apartment near Universal Studios all the way to Malibu and stay a few days. Not only did she cook and do my laundry, but we also had a great time between the sheets. We were just hanging out together, sharing experiences we'd had with characters in the music industry—the politics and union troubles. While I practiced, Susan painted; she worked in oils.

I should have known it was too good to last. The wrecking of a perfectly neat relationship with Susan began when her sister, Sara Jane, phoned me one night to say Dave was divorcing her. On the way out of the house, I told Susan I was going to check on Sara Jane because she sounded suicidal. When I arrived, I found her sobbing, but within ten minutes she came on to me, and I struggled to get away from her advances. Much later, I returned exhausted and red-eyed from the intervention. I sensed Susan was disappointed that I'd raced off to console her sister. Even so, she kept coming to the beach house, and I kept answering Sara Jane's calls.

I remembered meeting Sara Jane at Jack and Bobbi's when she came over with Dave for dinners or parties. She looked like a country girl with rosy cheeks and long straight hair that she sometimes wore in a messy up-do. Unlike her sister, she was buxom and had that come-into-the-bedroom look. Her cherubic cheeks had a warm glow as if she were hot and bothered; I imagined her removing pins from her hair and letting it fall to her shoulders. Although she was devoted to David, she seemed detached and kind of bossy, probably because she'd become a vocal contractor in the studios and controlled the hiring of other singers. She wore her position like a mantle.

At those get-togethers, I felt like an outsider when I would hang out with Dave and Jack. They were both engaged in extracurricular relationships and had plenty in common. They were tight friends and could drink me under the table. The first time they convinced me to smoke pot, I was in the back seat of Jack's car. We'd gone to the store for something Bobbi needed and the two of them wouldn't let up on me. "Come on, Artie, try some. Just take a drag off this." When I did, I started to laugh and couldn't stop. I laughed till I cried. We had to park down the street till I came out of it so our wives wouldn't know. Jack said my eyes were a dead giveaway. Not only was I kind of square, I didn't like the feeling of being out of control smoking weed. I got along better with their wives because they liked deep conversations—my specialty.

I don't know why two years later I was drawn to meddle in Sara Jane's life. Maybe she was always in the back of my mind. Maybe I felt noble, or had a need to soothe her. Maybe it was the bruising I took over Jaye P.'s rejection of me. Maybe it was because Susan's and my relationship was just for fun and Sara's desire was exciting and provocative. I knew it was only a matter of time before I let it go further.

The house off Laurel Canyon where Sara Jane had lived with Dave was like a cottage in a hamlet. I called it the Snow White house. I was uncomfortable going there, as if I were intruding on her former life. Since the forty-minute drive from Malibu was inconvenient, I let the lease lapse and rented a furnished guesthouse for a month next to Sara while I looked for a new place to live. I mentioned to my shrink, Dr. Rosengarten, that I was considering dating Sara, taking her to dinner and working out a normal relationship. He said, "Are you nuts? Don't do that to Dave."

"Why not? I'll call and ask him if he minds."

"I don't care what his answer is," Dr. Rosengarten said. "When a man gets rid of a woman, he doesn't want anybody to have her, particularly a good friend. You'll ruin your relationship with Mr. Grusin. It's not logical, but that's how it is. And what about Susan? I thought you liked her."

"I do, but our relationship isn't serious; she's a friend. Susan's a free spirit. She doesn't have an agenda, and she's not interested in settling down. She's just a nice person."

Ignoring my shrink and his advice, I asked Dave if he minded if I dated Sara. He blurted, "I don't care what you do. I'm involved with someone else for chrissake." I don't think I paid attention to his feelings or the dismissive tone of his answer.

Dave and Sara Jane had a child, Michael. It also didn't dawn on me that he would be a complication. How could I be so oblivious that I didn't think their cute, smart, little boy would affect our relationship?

While Dave and Sara Jane sorted out the parameters of their divorce and custody situation, I moved out of Malibu into my new apartment over a garage on Sunset Plaza Drive, walking distance from the Hamburger Hamlet, where I subsequently took Sara on our first real date. Climbing the stairs to my place after dinner, she removed her blouse.

"What are you doing?" I asked.

Shrugging, she said, "I assume we're going to go to bed, and I don't think it will happen with our clothes on."

My thoughts turned to Betty Moon, my old nightclub flame. My disdain for her rush to sex flashed through my mind, but it didn't stop me from following Sara into my bedroom. If I'd had any common sense, I would have stopped everything right then. Sara Jane solved everything with her genitals, including her anger and agony of losing Dave. I wasn't exactly innocent in that area either.

As it turned out, we both lost him. I counseled Sara about her divorce and romped around in her bed while their son, Michael, slept down the hall. It felt devious, like I was cheating on a friend. In spite of it, Dave continued to hire me for his recording sessions. The irony of working for him on his first film project, *Divorce American Style,* escaped me, though he was scoring the film while divorcing Sara and courting jazz singer Ruth Price. Oddly enough, he was civil to me during sessions and answered any musical questions I had, but he never said hello or goodbye or spoke to me otherwise.

Divorce American Style was the second film I'd worked on for producers Bud Yorkin and Norman Lear. Bud hung out onstage, so I got to know him a little—enough for small talk. During an orchestra break, I walked outside and down the loading ramp where Bud sat on the railing. I took a pack of Pall Malls from my shirt pocket and tapped out a cigarette.

"Why don't you throw those away, Artie?" Bud said, more a suggestion than a question.

I laughed. "Don't you smoke?"

"Not anymore." He explained that the insurer of his and Norman's company, Tandem Productions, required that they get regular health checkups. "Occasionally, things show up that need attention," Bud said.

"Are you all right?" I asked, concerned.

"I'm fine, but Norman got a warning and was told to stop smoking if we wanted insurance for the company. So why don't you do yourself a favor and throw those away?"

"Okay, Bud." I took his advice, threw the pack away and quit that day. Unfortunately, I didn't have as much sense about Sara Jane as I had about cigarettes. Whenever Dave came to the house to see his son, he'd wait in the car until Sara brought Michael out. That stung. Now, I realize Dave was hurting too. Perhaps I wasn't a good enough friend to ask him how he felt or what had happened between him and Sara Jane. He was stoic, but I did understand his heartbreak over leaving Michael. During this time, I had three appointments a week with Dr. Rosengarten, who reminded me at each meeting how I hadn't heeded his warnings.

One night while Dave waited for Michael, I went out to his Porsche, opened the door and sat in the passenger seat. Dave stared straight ahead with his hands on the wheel.

"I can't stand this silence," I said. "Hit me. I won't fight back. Just get it out of your system because I'm willing to apologize for whatever I'm guilty of."

He was a stone. Even worse, when I made the life-altering mistake of marrying Sara Jane, I thought he would be ecstatic because I was saving him a ton of alimony, but the friendship was gone.

It was April of '67, just before the release of Franco Zeffirelli's *Taming of the Shrew* starring Richard Burton and Elizabeth Taylor, when I married Sara Jane, the woman who could have taught a PhD course on *controlling behavior*. We began the marriage without a honeymoon because my work calendar was booked weeks in advance. I wanted to make it up to her, so I blocked out time for us to spend at a cabin we had purchased in Idyllwild above Palm Springs where we could ride horses on mountain trails. Unfortunately, I had a panic attack on our first trip, either from the change in altitude or from unfamiliar surroundings, but Sara was unsympathetic and dismissive of my distress. It set the tenor of our early relationship. I remember the sales person had asked me what name I'd like on the sign at our cabin since we'd bought it under both our names. I suggested "Kane Mutiny." When the man next door came over to welcome us, he called me Mr. Mutiny.

Artie in the pool with Michael Grusin

Shortly after Sara and I returned home to the odd little house she and Dave had shared, we had a disagreement because I had scolded Michael for not responding when his mother called him. He was the sweetest kid, brilliant like his father, and Sara didn't want me to interfere. She stood with her hands on her hips and said, "The last guy who lived here didn't learn the rules, so I'm going to tell them to you right now."

From then on, I could do nothing right where Michael was concerned. Sara knew best how to raise the child and her judgment trumped mine.

"This is how the house operates," she said. "I'll discipline Michael. He's special and you don't know anything about how to raise him."

Instead of talking or reasoning with Michael like I wanted to do, she'd send him to his room as a punishment. That bothered him a lot but he didn't sulk. On the contrary, he'd build things—like rockets—and stay there for hours. Later, Michael became an aerospace engineer, building systems for real rockets. He was in the gang of geniuses NASA calls on to solve rocket science problems.

Sara could switch modes in a second, especially after she'd won a battle. It seemed as if a fight turned her on. Wild and uninhibited, she was ready for sex. Still reeling from her insults, I wasn't so interested in making up in the sack. Sara would say, "I don't see what one thing has to do with the other." I had a nagging feeling she didn't like me because of her constant criticisms, but she'd stop just short of name-calling. If I'd had any sense, I would have beaten a path out the door and never looked back.

Instead, my panic attacks increased, so I looked for diversions. I enjoyed riding horses at Griffith Park with drummer Johnny Guerin and bassist Joe Mondragon. These musicians were experienced riders who trusted and could handle their horses on narrow paths and ledges. When I rode these paths, I could see great views of the Griffith Observatory and the rugged landscape, but I couldn't enjoy them for fear my horse would misstep and plunge down the steep terrain. Once, my rental horse hit the trail galloping at what seemed a hundred miles an hour. It was all I could do to hold on. I discovered that all the rental horses knew their way home and ran like hell to get there. At the last minute, I ducked just in time to avoid getting my head knocked off as the horse charged into the stable. That ride convinced me to get my own horse, one that was not too feisty or too slow.

I bought two horses, one for me and one for Sara Jane, plus a house with acreage zoned for horses, in Studio City. The property had a small barn that I had remodeled into a pair of stalls with an automatic watering system for the horses. I put in a saddling paddock and a small ring. My builders, Nohles and Walker, were tough, sage characters who never let up teasing me about life-lessons, tools and everyday problems a sissy piano player couldn't grasp, such as manure. These two salty fellows built a ramp so I could run the wheelbarrow up a platform to a small dumpster that I had hauled in for waste management. The first time I cleaned the paddock and barn, I wheeled the stuff across two hundred feet of grass, wrangled it over to the ramp, took a running start up the platform, forgot to let go and followed the horse manure into the dumpster.

A rancher I wasn't, but I have great memories of riding lessons with Cathy Walters, a horse handler, who had a terrific sense of humor. I spent many pleasant hours in a saddle on Gamie, a huge, muscular eighteen-year-old Morgan gelding Cathy had found for me that was gentle as a fawn. When she rode Gamie, who was parade trained, he pranced, galloped, parade rested and swished from side to side, all without much coaxing. When I got on him, he wouldn't budge.

"It's not the horse, it's you. You're not clear what you want from him," she said.

She didn't know how true that was. I didn't know what I wanted from any of my relationships.

One day, during a lesson on saddling tips, I felt a painful pressure on my right foot. "Jesus," I hollered, wriggling my foot free. Gamie was standing on the toe of my boot.

"What's the matter?" Cathy said.

"He stepped on me. That's what's the matter."

She laughed and said, "It's your fault, Artie. I told you, when you lead a horse, lead him away from you. You led him toward you and onto your foot instead of pushing him an arm's length away."

Sara Jane's interest in her horse lasted less time than her interest in me. I sold it back to Cathy shortly after Sara surprised me with the news she was pregnant. Cathy's goal was to teach me how to enjoy and handle my horse. Eventually she succeeded. Griffith Park brings great memories with my crazy recording colleagues. The well-maintained trails ran across meadows where I could practice gaits and work on form and handling while surrounded by acres of wilderness in the middle of a metropolis.

Plenty of men play golf and schedule weekly games, allowing them four hours away from home without an explanation. But I was a poor golfer, and the game was too slow. Riding got me out of the house and gave me pleasure, but it didn't reduce the tension between Sara Jane and me.

NINE MONTHS AND TWO WEEKS AFTER OUR WEDDING and hours away from delivering our son, Adam, Sara Jane woke me about two in the morning and announced her water had broken. "I need to go to the hospital now, Artie," she said calmly. A nervous wreck, I jumped into the car and drove like Parnelli Jones down Riverside Drive, hoping to attract a cop for an escort.

"Artie, are you taking me to the hospital?"

"Of course I am," I bellowed.

"Well, you just passed it."

Sara Jane and Artie holding Adam at home

Having a baby was wonderful but frightening, especially with the rocky relationship between Sara and me. However, all that trouble disappeared with Adam's birth. These are the times I recall sharing loving and happy times with Sara as well as scary, but close times.

Shortly after bringing Adam home, a crust formed over parts of his tiny body. It must have been painful because the little guy cried constantly. His scabs seeped and scared the hell out of Sara and me. I called Maury Lazarus, my friend and OBGYN doc. I was off the wall, in a panic, and could hardly get the words out. He told me to bring Adam to Cedars, the giant L.A. hospital where he was now the head of the department. Maury called in an elderly, retired specialist who diagnosed Adam's problem as Leiner's Disease, a rare systemic skin disorder found on newborns that spreads rapidly if untreated. Our sweet infant remained in isolation at the hospital for a few days while he was continually bathed in pHisoHex and treated with an ointment.

When we brought him home, we carried on the treatment and fed him a special formula that I couldn't find anywhere. I called every drug store and market that sold baby formula, but even the pharmacists treated me as if I was speaking Mandarin. Like a nagging wife, I called Maury again, yelling over the phone that no one knew what the hell I was talking about, and none of them carried a special formula for a crusty newborn.

"Will you just shut up a minute, Artie, and listen to me? I'll take care of it. I'll get it from the hospital."

I cried. I still break down when someone is nice to me.

"Drive your car back to the entrance where you picked up Adam," Maury instructed. Give them your name and a nurse will bring you a supply of the formula. Don't say anything except thank you and don't try to give her money."

What a wonderful friend. Maury had commandeered a supply of this scarce food from the hospital for our baby. Over a couple of months, Adam's crust disappeared; he got stronger and became the cutest kid on the West Coast, at least to Sara and me. When I see photos of Adam and Michael playing in the pool or sandbox, I have good memories of times with both boys and their mother. Adam was the bond between Sara and me—the focus of the love we shared at the beginning when she was vulnerable and needy. When we had rough patches, Adam's laugh, his needs and his sweet nature surpassed our urge to quarrel.

She was a good mother in many ways, forever protective and thorough in her care of the boys, but in certain situations, she was bananas. One day she admonished me: "Mothers' instincts are perfect, so don't argue with me." That was her response any time I opened my mouth about the kids or had ideas about their care. It didn't matter that I'd had two other children. I don't recall ever having trouble with kids, only their mothers.

One early morning, I fixed my breakfast and set it on the dining room table. Michael got up early, too. I dressed him, fixed his breakfast and sat him next to me. He was about four and a half years old and very smart. I was reading the paper and eating. Michael was whimpering, a habit of his when he wanted attention or when Sara was with Adam. "What's the matter, Michael?" He continued whimpering. "Michael, don't do that. You are ruining my breakfast."

He continued to whimper, "Mommy, Mommy, I want Mommy …"

"Mommy is busy with Adam right now. Why do you want Mommy?"

"I want my mommy," he said, slamming his spoon on the table.

"Michael, if you won't stop that you'll have to eat in the kitchen."

Sara Jane appeared in the doorway and Michael got louder until he was yelling. I stood up and told him to take his dish and go to the kitchen. He stopped whining, and gave me that "I'll show you" look as he slid off his chair and whisked away his dish of cereal.

Sara Jane marched in, grabbed his dish from him and said, "I'll take your food, darling. Come with Mommy." At that, Michael yelled and stamped into the kitchen where Sara lifted him into his toddler seat, his screams growing louder and louder.

I followed them and said, "Michael, go to your room."

"He doesn't have to go to his room," Sara Jane said, blocking the kitchen exit. "I'll deal with him."

It was the only time I ever touched a woman when I was angry, and it still bothers me when I remember it. I should have walked away, but instead, I shoved her from the doorway.

Michael stopped yelling in mid-breath, escaped off his seat, and said with eyes wide, "I'm going, I'm going."

He was smart enough to stop his bad behavior. Sara and I weren't.

Over time, she became more critical of me and took total charge of the children as if I were retarded or incompetent in handling them. But whenever she had studio sessions at night, I was the one who took care of the boys, gave Adam his night bottle, bathed them, and put them

Adam steals my heart

to bed. I think Michael knew that I liked him, liked to talk to him. I would ask him lots of questions to get him to talk. He was an amazing kid who needed attention and nurturing. Adam was an adorable, easy child who needed my protection from his older brother who liked to pick on him.

None of my success with the boys altered Sara Jane's attitude. She would give me detailed instructions about their care, as if I were an alien who dropped in for the day.

"Be sure you dry them completely after their baths, and watch Adam so he doesn't slip out of his tub seat. Maybe you should buckle him in, in case you're not paying attention.

"Michael's toy is on the side of the tub. He's probably going to cry when I leave, so give him the toy. It will distract him."

"Got it. Go Sara. You're going to be late."

"Adam will never go to sleep unless you give him some more of his bottle, so be sure to warm it—not too much—and test it before you give it to him."

"Sara, I know all this. I did the same thing last week. Just go to your session. We'll be fine."

"Okay, but you'll be sorry if you don't follow my instructions."

The evening went like this: Michael whimpered a bit, and I informed him his mother would be gone all evening. "It's just the three of us. Now we can have it nice or not nice. Which do you want?"

"Nice," he said with a slight pout.

We had a fine time playing in the tub. Adam didn't slip out of his seat. I helped Michael with his pajamas, creamed and powdered Adam and put on his diaper; and before I could warm the bottle for the "few sips he had to have, or else," he was sound asleep in my arms. I read to Michael before I put him to bed.

Battles over ridiculous things were sport for Sara. The house had a fine swimming pool, but it didn't have a heater. I wanted to put in a heater so the kids could swim year-round. Sara said, "Absolutely not. I swam in Lake Michigan when I was a kid, and besides, we can't afford it. If the water's too cold, the kids don't need to swim." Money for the heater was not the issue; control was.

The only time my opinion mattered was when I had my son, Paul, over to play with Michael and Adam. Sara hardly said a word while he was around, but then neither did he.

We had a big yard, a pool and a horse with a riding ring. Paul was moody, so different from the happy little boy I used to take everywhere. I took him to the Pony Park on Beverly Drive one day to get him interested in a small version of our horse, but again, he wanted to go home. Raised as an only child, he didn't interact well with our boys. He seemed glum until we were in the car going back to his house. I think Jaye P. was so upset when it was my turn to take Paul that he felt disloyal to her and too guilty to have fun.

I continued to see him, but I felt more and more helpless as I observed his unhappiness when he was with me. He was even more withdrawn with Sara. My failure to sustain the relationship upset me, and with each visit, I seemed to lose ground, so I quit forcing the issue. I was sad, but both women seemed happier.

Otherwise, life with Sara was a constant duel—a test of wills. I know some of the blame was mine. I couldn't control my need to win a point and neither could she.

Adam was two and a half when I knew it was the end. Sara grabbed a suitcase, left me with the boys, and went to Las Vegas to get away from me. When she came back, I packed a small bag, and as I was leaving, she said, in front of the boys, "I've never loved you. I've always loved David and I always will. You were just a poor substitute."

As I listened to her, a flood of memories washed through my mind. Joy had sliced up all my clothes with a razor blade; Jinx had run off with her mother and some new skater in the show; Jean told me I was only a stand-in for Marshall; Sherry had loathed me for the hard times in New York; Jaye P. didn't want to be married to me anymore and nearly drank herself to death; and finally, Sara Jane said she had never loved me and I was only a poor substitute for her previous husband. Obviously, six women couldn't shoulder all the blame. I owned plenty of it.

My judgement was so impaired that each time I made bad choices I blamed my wives for my mistake. But no one forced me to marry these women I slept with (except for Joy), especially when the hazard signs were staring at me.

Years later, during my twelve-step program when I finally apologized to Susan for running off with her sister, she frowned and said, "What are you talking about? We had a great relationship, a little peculiar but fun and no strings. I loved it. I was just shocked when I got back from my job in Vegas and a friend told me you and Sara were getting married."

"Are you serious?" I asked. "Sara told me the two of you had talked and that you were really excited and happy about our plans to marry."

"Not so, Artie. Sara never called me until a few weeks after you were married. She was crying and complaining that she should never have done it, that after David left she was scared and was looking for financial security. She said she didn't love you at all. I was so angry with her that I didn't speak to her for months."

I felt sad and stupid.

Susan said, "What I don't understand, though, is how my crazy sister managed to marry two wonderful guys like you and David."

Rosengarten was right. I was a poor judge of character, and it was my habit to pick women who were incompatible with me. I felt a deep despair about my personal life and relationships, especially over the consequences to my three boys, David, Paul and Adam. I resigned myself to having an affair with my piano and my music.

Meanwhile, I was in another custody battle for weekend visitations with Adam. Of course, I couldn't see Michael, even though I wanted to take both boys so they could play together at Beverly Amusement Park. You think you have no rights as the father of your own son? Well you have fewer rights with your son's half-brother, even if you spent three years raising him. It was a painful time with lawyers, alimony, child support, plus edicts and hassles over seeing Adam. A year later, Sara Jane took me back to court for more child support. She was quite the actress in front of the judge. Scrubbed of all make up, and with her breasts bound like a pair of Japanese feet, she played the waif card so well that the judge turned his chair to face her, waved off my lawyer, and announced that he would question the witness himself. I hadn't balked at paying more for Adam; Sara never asked. She just took me to court.

One thing I knew for sure, I didn't want to abandon another child. I had the closest relationship with Paul because I'd taken care of him the longest. Maybe I felt sorry for him because he'd already been abandoned by his birth parents. I had continued seeing Paul until he was about five and a half, including bringing him over to play with Adam and Michael. Adam was only three and a half when I gave up fighting Sara Jane for my scheduled visits. Ultimately, I left Paul, Adam, and my oldest son, David, with women I didn't respect and who didn't like me. I know I gave up the kids too easily when I should have waged a court battle to maintain my visiting rights and preserve some kind of father-son relationship. I was a failure as a father. I made an appointment for a vasectomy.

SIXTEEN

Love in Bloom

Two weeks after the vasectomy, I returned to the doctor's office to provide a specimen. While I was waiting for the results, a nurse stuck her head in the door and announced, "Mr. Kane, you are free to roam."

Great, I thought, driving home to yet another rental house on Sepulveda Boulevard where I had no wife, no girlfriend and no appetite for sex, proven by the headache coming on after the ordeal of jerking off to a *Playboy* centerfold. I had begged the doctor to lend me one of his nurses for inspiration. "Sorry," he'd said, "not at these prices."

With no place to keep my horse and no funds to pay exorbitant boarding fees at Riverside Park, I gave Gamie and my horse trailer to Cathy Walters and plunged headlong into my career. I took refuge in the one constant in my life, music. As soon as my hands touched the piano, life was good. I took every recording call I was offered: jingles, record dates, TV shows, movies. If they needed a pianist, I was their guy. I would often work three calls a day, the first at 20th Century Fox where Lionel Newman started sessions at 8:00 a.m. so he could make it to the Hollywood Park racetrack by three.

My relationships with the music department heads at Fox, MGM and Universal were solid. These studios were my mainstay of employment. I also recorded commercials for Bob Bain, a well-known guitarist who wrote jingles for the ad company, Klein & Barzman. Bob Bain called me into a meeting with Bob Klein who wanted to start a new record company called Alpenstock. They asked me about recording a piano album that they wanted to sponsor and produce. I was flattered and excited about the prospect. I didn't know I was their third choice.

Bain and I put together lists of personnel for two orchestras, plus the names of ten hot arrangers in Los Angeles to write charts for piano and orchestra. As we got further along with the project, Bob Klein demanded control over personnel and the content of the album. Since he and his partner Alan Barzman were bankrolling the sessions, he watched the budget; I wanted my guys and never considered the costs. I hired my friend and former neighbor Jack Elliott, an experienced music director worth triple union scale, to conduct several numbers and to be the producer. I hired the powerful L.A. contractor Bobby Helfer to contract the musicians. Like a steamroller, I just did what I thought was right without asking or showing deference to the backers. These guys wanted a spectacular first album for their label, and I told them I knew the best people to accomplish that. But when they wanted to pick the songs for me to play, meetings became contentious. I rarely stayed for them. It was obvious to me they had no idea about the type of music that could be arranged into great piano solo pieces. I'd argue for a while and then walk out. Bob Bain tried to calm me down, but I was determined that I knew how to produce an album better than they did. I acquiesced to a couple of lame songs that I thought I could replace when they heard how good the rest of it was.

By the time the first session began, Bob Klein was fed up with me and had lost interest in the project, but he couldn't pull the plug on the recordings because they were booked through the union and had a long cancellation clause, so we recorded. Bob Bain told me I was blowing the whole thing because I was blatantly hostile toward Bob Klein, but

I wouldn't listen and had an argument with Bob Bain, too. I was confident that after they heard the product, they'd all love the results.

Michel Legrand, composer on *The Thomas Crowne Affair* and *The Happy Ending*, both of which I had worked on, wrote a special arrangement of "Windmills of Your Mind" for me and had Dick Hazard create a gorgeous string arrangement featuring piano for "What Are You Doing the?" My old friend Dave Grusin was speaking to me again because he knew I'd been miserable living with his ex-wife, and now that I was divorcing her, he realized how much alimony I'd saved him by marrying her in the first place. I'm sure he wanted to rub in the fact that I'd soon be knee-deep in payments to her.

Dave wrote two dynamite charts, one on "Everybody's Talkin' at Me" from *Midnight Cowboy* and another, "When Summer Turns to Snow," a song he wrote for a Sergio Mendez album. The piano part on "Everybody's Talkin'" was tricky because he'd written it like a banjo part, and working out the fingering was an essential element to making it come off. When we got a good take on it, the band hooted their approval. The producers insisted it be the opening number on the album—one thing we agreed on. Quincy Jones created a funky chart on a tune, "Lonely Bottles," that he'd written and that I'd played on for the film *In Cold Blood*. For that piece, I played the clavinet, a strange-sounding, popular keyboard instrument of the late sixties. Johnny (John) Williams wrote a chart on "Make Me Rainbows," the love theme he wrote for a Dick Van Dyke film called *Fitzwilly*.

I was humbled by the musicians who created material for me and grateful for friends like Jack Elliott who conducted and helped me pick the best *takes* each day. Nerve-wracking describes my feelings during the recordings. I think it takes a certain outgoing kind of personality to be a solo recording artist. Soloists are under pressure to perform; pressure always created problems for me, but I had come a long way in my career and thought I could do it even though I preferred being in the background. I invited other friends to sit in the booth, like my builder friends, Nohles and Walker, the guys who teased me about all the practical things I didn't know. They added humor to the mix.

Artie and Ray Brown

Quincy Jones

Artie and Chuck Domanico

Ray Brown

Shelly Manne and Larry Bunker

Artie at the piano

Artie, Quincy and Dave Grusin

When it was over, I had twelve tracks on an LP that I was proud of, but Bob Klein was so angry with me, he decided to take a financial loss and refused to fund the record company. In a panic, I got a test pressing of the album to peddle to Herb Alpert at A&M. I remember climbing the steps to Herb's office on Sunset and LaBrea, the old Chaplain Studios, and the courage it took to knock. Herb opened the door while chewing on an apple. I stepped back to allow a thick fog of marijuana to escape before I handed him the album and told him what we'd made. Herb squinted to read the hand-written label and said, "We've already got Pete Jolly on our roster."

"Pete's a jazz pianist, Herb. What you don't have in your stable is a commercial pianist like Peter Nero or Roger Williams. I could be that guy; my album could fill that spot."

Herb looked right through me, took another bite of his apple, shoved the LP in my hand, and slowly closed the door. I backed out and stared, mouth open, as if I'd been shot.

Without an agent, or a connection to a recording label, there was nowhere to go. I was angry—angry with myself and with Bob Klein. I couldn't admit that I was wrong, that I'd handled meetings and relationships with the backers poorly. I worried that my music career would become another failure for me like my marriages. I couldn't see that my uncompromising attitude and resistance to negotiation on this project were the same issues that plagued my relationships with women. The reality hit me that all the work of the talented arrangers and musicians would be lost, not because I didn't make a good album, but because I couldn't get out of my own way. My impatience and inability to work out logistics and details with the entrepreneurs, or even to leave a negotiation with a compromise so both parties felt good, had ruined a wonderful opportunity for me.

The sting of rejection didn't fade quickly. It felt like my New York failures, only in a better climate. I think I wanted the album because more than anything else, it would have been a validation of my work—proof that I was a recording artist. My mother and Joe would have something to show for all those piano lessons they paid for. My studio work meant nothing to my mother because she couldn't point to any accomplishment. When I was with the ice show, she had programs she could haul out and point to with my picture and name in them. Studio work isn't glamorous, nor was it something she could talk about to her friends or the family. When she attended a recording date during an L.A. visit and asked, "Is this what you do," I was crushed because she didn't understand my work. But here was a whole record album—something that would have made her proud.

It would also have steered me on a different musical course, making appearances and touring. That kind of life and career may have been out of my comfort zone. I'll never know if I deliberately created the negative atmosphere around the album, but I went back to my studio and film work and decided never to record a piano album again. On breaks during sessions, musicians would ask me when the album was coming out. It was like a knife in my gut. I'd say, "I don't know. We haven't signed with a label yet." Word got around and, eventually, no one bothered to ask.

In spite of my depression over the album, my work with the studios remained abundant. One day, Kurt Wolf, contractor at Warner Music Department, called and said, "Artie, you've made a big problem for me."

You never want to hear those words from a contractor who controls a significant amount of your work calls. "What did I do, Kurt?" I asked apologetically.

"Michel Legrand is composing the music for *Summer of '42*. It's a big summer release with lots of promotion scheduled. He's driving me crazy because you turned down his calls for the recordings. He insists he's writing a piano score for you, won't take no for an answer and refuses my substitutes."

"Kurt, I already accepted a three-day call with Billy Goldenberg. I can't cancel Billy's TV movie to do Michel's film. It would be like canceling a dinner date with a brunette because a better-looking blonde came along."

I suggested my protégé, Ralph Grierson. He was a beautiful pianist and could certainly perform brilliantly for Michel. Kurt seemed to understand and booked Ralph.

A few days later, Michel called, irate, and speaking so loud and fast through his French accent that I could barely understand him. "What are you doing to me, Artie? I want you on my film, not some Ralph."

"Michel, I can't. I'm working for Billy; I've had the call for a month. Besides, Ralph Grierson is a wonderful pianist. He plays all the literature and works with Michael Tilson Thomas. He's better than I am."

"If he's better than you are, send him to the other date, and you come to my date."

Richard Roth produced *Summer of '42* for Warner Brothers Pictures in 1971. I wanted to play on that film because of my friendship with Michel, because of his marvelous music, because it featured piano, and because the film was sure to be a big hit, since Herman Raucher's novel was a runaway best seller. Michel's soundtrack sold a lot of records, but what I said about Ralph was true. Recommendations are tricky. Some people suggest less capable replacements to protect their employment or territory. Ralph was up to the task, and Michel eventually forgave me.

Despite my resolution to avoid another attempt as a recording artist, Henry Mancini called me using his best East Coast accent.

"Hey Audie, it's Hank," which is all it took to make me sit up straight and listen. "Remember that little source piece you did on the organ for the Pacino film last year? Well I like it. Would you be interested in making an album or two with Ray and Shelly?"

Drummer Shelly Manne, bassist Ray Brown—both music giants—and I had played on a 1969 film Hank scored called *Me Natalie*. Hank was smitten with the trio work we'd recorded.

"I'm not a jazz organist," I said. That was my first no. I felt the same when I played for Sinatra, although that worked out well.

"I don't want a jazz player; I just want what you did on the film. This isn't going to be a hot album."

What he meant was he wanted a commercial record, not unstructured variations on a theme where the players get together and jam. Jazz artists don't care what sells; they just play from the heart. Hank wanted a "vanilla" album that would make some money. He had an idea the Hammond organ was making a comeback, and the fact that Hank called me was already a compliment.

"Sorry, Hank, I don't want to be in the record business. I made a piano album last year and trying to get it sold almost killed me. I don't want another door slammed in my face. I finally gave up, and I never want to go through that again." That was my second no.

"You don't have to go through anything," Hank said. "I'm sponsoring you with RCA Victor. It's under my contract. You don't even have to say hello to anybody."

Hank was a friend who would rescue me at parties or awards dinners when he'd see me bristling with discomfort. He'd whisper something rank in my ear and I'd crack up, so it wasn't easy to turn him down. I agreed; we recorded.

The toughest part about the project was taking pictures for the album cover. Hank was worried about his bald spot, and I wouldn't smile. The photographer found a cute girl with Betty Grable legs wearing a short skirt. He set up a ladder near the piano and asked her to sit on the top rung and flirt with us. Then he shot two rolls of film. Hank had no trouble keeping his chin up, thereby reducing the light reflection off his head, and I looked pleasantly stoned.

Good photographer!

Recording the organ albums with Hank

Unfortunately, Hank was wrong about the market. The organ sound was not coming back; neither recording sold well.

COORDINATING VISITATION DAYS for Paul and Adam was a nightmare. Both mothers had issues with whatever dates I arranged. It seemed they were in cahoots though I knew they didn't speak to each other. Distance added another obstacle when I rented a swell house in Beverly Hills, ten miles across the Hollywood Hills from where they lived. The house was convenient to Fox and MGM, and it was on a quiet street where I could practice without disturbing the neighbors. Since the rental had hardwood floors, and I had only a few pieces of furniture, a natural reverb embraced the piano like a concert hall stage. I rationalized the high rent because my session calls were consistent. I was meeting my expenses and making my child support. Being alone was a good thing, not answering to anyone about my whereabouts, eating whatever I liked from whatever restaurant would prepare a take-out dinner for me. Esther was my housekeeper, a kind, thin woman recommended by a friend in my same divorced and unattached circumstance. Esther washed my one set of sheets each week, kept my barely-used kitchen clean, and organized and dusted my piano; but she refused to have lunch with me until we had a frank exchange of views. One day while she was there, I worked a morning session and stopped for sandwiches on the way home. She unwrapped both and set mine on the counter, then took hers into the laundry room. I found her sitting on a stepstool using the washing machine as a table.

"Esther, unless you are prejudiced against Jews, I wish you'd join me for lunch." She smiled shyly and explained that black people are usually expected to eat in a separate area. When she joined me, I told her I enjoyed her company. It was the start of many good conversations about people, bigotry and Beverly Hills.

A week after that conversation in the laundry room, two jolts knocked me out of bed at 6:00 a.m., February 9, 1971. I grabbed my revolver and ran halfway down the stairs to see if there'd been an explosion or if someone was breaking into my house. Instead, I saw my piano dancing across the living room floor. An earthquake. Running out the front door in my jockey shorts and T-shirt, I met my neighbors for the first time. The epicenter of the 6.6 quake had been in the San Fernando Valley, so after confirming that my kids were okay, I was glad I'd moved to Beverly Hills. The damage and mayhem from that event disrupted many lives. Music sessions were cancelled, and several colleagues who lived in the San Fernando Valley had to relocate due to tremendous damage to their homes. Because of the upheaval in their lives, they were unable to work for weeks.

By the time the earthquake dust settled, it had been a year since my sixth marriage had flatlined. My contact with the opposite sex had been minimal, relegated to lunches at a studio with fellow musicians and sometimes with pianist Pearl Kaufman. Pearl told me about a "dear friend" she wanted me to meet, saying we would make a wonderful couple. I said I was doing fine without a woman in my life for once, but Pearl was a born matchmaker. She brought Jack Benny's daughter, Joan Blumofe, to the next recording session and introduced us as kindred spirits.

Joan Benny and Artie

She was night and day different from women I'd been with. She looked like she'd stepped out of a glamour magazine: blonde hair perfectly coiffed, smart, designer clothes, size six. I wouldn't usually notice, but even her purse matched her shoes. Wary of stars or people with a pedigree, I was surprised to find Joan a comfortable, easy-to-talk-to person. We agreed to a meal at the Aware Inn in Sherman Oaks, famous as one of the first organic restaurants on the West Coast.

In an unhappy home with her third husband, their two children, and two children from two previous marriages, Joan confided that she was waiting for a separation arrangement to come through. Pearl had sung Joan's praises as an interesting and clever person who once used the dog door to sneak in and out of her house and avoid the beeping alarm system at night. I never discovered if that was true, or just one of Pearl's tempting nuggets of information to pique my interest, but Joan was much too intriguing to pass up. I continued to meet her for dinners and lunches when time permitted. As Jack Benny's daughter, she was a special person in the Hollywood culture; she represented Hollywood as a product. Growing up in a Beverly Hills mansion with her own three-bedroom suite, a maid, butler and chauffeur, Joan wanted to follow her friends to Beverly Hills High School, but Gracie Allen and Mary Benny enrolled their daughters at Chadwick Boarding School on the top of the Palos Verdes Peninsula after which Joan went off to Stanford. Uncle Ronnie was Ronald Reagan; in fact, she called half the male movie stars Uncle. She was pretty typical of kids raised in the rarified air of the industry's rich and famous. As my shrink, Dr. Rosengarten, used to say, "If it weren't for fancy schools like Chadwick and Beverly Hills High School, I wouldn't have a practice."

Joan knew a lot about music, but her knowledge came from years of private piano lessons with impressive teachers and from attending concerts, not from knowing the music business. She was accomplished in many areas of study and history but knew little about the lives of ordinary people. She looked right at me when she spoke and was kind of intense, but when she told stories, she had timing and a sense of humor. I got the idea that men fell all over themselves for her. That behavior had less to do with her and lots to do with her father. Since I didn't give her that attention and treated her like a regular person, I probably appealed to her. After her divorce came through, we spent a lot of time together, talked endlessly, and had a comfortable relationship over the next four years.

Like others, I was impressed by her father's celebrity status, and though I admired talent and skill, I didn't worship it. I'd grown up in an economic environment far removed from Joan's world. Sometimes I felt like an analyst trying to understand Joan's circumstances and the pressure she'd grown up under, but I was surprised she couldn't understand anything about my life. When we talked about where I grew up, I described my family's house with five adults using the bathroom upstairs, and she asked, "Where were the other bathrooms?"

"There weren't any others," I said.

She looked at me blankly and said, "Oh."

Her father seemed like a humble guy. When we'd all go to dinner, he'd ask me to figure out the tip and insist it be large. Tips included the doorman, busboy and headwaiter. Jack was forever generous. He had his own way of making fun of his fame. When Joan and I were together at her house, Jack would call, and if I answered, he'd say, "Hi Artie, this is Jack Benny. Is Joan there?" Here was a voice I knew, that I'd grown up listening to on the radio and that most of the country would recognize. He knew my voice, but he'd announce himself as if I wouldn't know who was calling.

I handed her the phone one time and said, "I find it strange that he announces himself to me like we've never met."

"You don't know Daddy. You don't understand his sense of humor. Call him back and if he answers the phone, say, 'Hi Jack, this is Artie Kane,' and see what happens."

"No," I said. "He's famous. Everyone recognizes his voice. That's why it's odd."

"Just call him up," she insisted.

Finally, I called and said, "Hi Jack, this is Artie Kane." Jack broke up laughing; he knew I was making fun of his quirks.

He was a very nice and funny-thinking man. Even small, everyday behaviors were humorous to him, and common things were always "the most" or "the best." Give him a glass of water and he'd say, "This is the greatest water I've ever tasted," or "That was the best steak I can remember eating." A master comic and performer with the timing of a trapeze artist, he was disappointed that he wasn't a better violinist. He took three lessons a week and practiced the instrument in earnest. He had no interest in me as a musician and didn't care where I was from, but he'd say to me, "I have a serious question for you, Artie. Now don't be a wise guy, but could you tell me why when I practice my violin in my bathroom, it sounds so much better than it does on stage?"

Jack was devoted to his wife, Mary Livingstone, but she was a complicated person who, at times, treated him dismissively, like a member of the staff. She could carve the meat off your bones with just a few words, so the first time I was invited to a big fancy dinner for twelve notables at the Benny home, my nerves were on high alert because it was Mary's birthday. Uncomfortable, and seated between Mary and Joan, I faced a vast array of silver utensils lined up on either side of my plate. I watched Joan and made a game deciding which to use with each course. After an appetizer of finger foods came what I thought was a tureen of soup. I reached for my soup spoon and Joan's foot clamped down on mine as she demonstrated washing her hands in the finger bowl. She was damn lucky I didn't try to drink it. On the way home, she bawled me out, claiming her mother gave her a look when she noticed I didn't know the rules about working the flatware from the outside in.

I was in no mood and said something unkind, especially after witnessing Mary's poor manners to her husband upon receiving a stunning piece of jewelry he'd bought her.

Relegated to the opposite end of the table, Jack called out, "Happy birthday, doll face," his endearing name for Mary, dating from their television show together. "Do you like your present?"

"Oh yes, Jack. It's the same thing you got me last year," she said, bored.

Eventually I understood the reason Jack had asked me about the sound of his violin in his bathroom. It was the only place Mary allowed him to practice. She hated the sound of his playing, and apparently the sound of his sleeping as well, since his room and bath were in another wing, a block away.

I never understood Mary's attitude toward Joan either. When Joan was growing up, Mary rarely missed an opportunity to remind her she was adopted and could be sent back to the orphanage if she didn't behave. It hurt Joan's feelings. Mary (Sadie Marks) was a high-strung person. She knew Joan adored her father, but Mary had to discipline her. It was weird because Mary had picked her out in the orphanage even though Jack had questioned the choice of adopting a "funny-looking thing like that one." I suspect Jack had never seen a newborn before and didn't know most babies look funny at first. But after two days, and for the rest of his life, he was nuts about his little girl.

As a recognized star and personality, Mary probably forgot where she came from. Reportedly, she had been a salesclerk in the lingerie department of a May Company store. Some of Mary's attitude must have rubbed off on Joan because her greatest issue was her own ranking in the Hollywood caste system. All social events have an A list (dinner), a B list (dessert only), a C list (usually just drinks) and even a D list, although the only person I know of on the D list is Kathy Griffin, a well-known comedian who wears her rating like a badge of honor. Until I started dating Joan, I wasn't on any list. These designations document Hollywood's pseudo-sophisticated behavior, but Mary Livingstone had mastered them all. She played by the rules that set her amongst the royalty, and she made sure she and her husband were at the top of all the lists. Another of her rules precluded her grandchildren from calling her "grandmother." They were trained to call her Miss Mary.

Getting to know Joan's kids was a challenge. I'd been around youngsters up to five years of age, but not older children. Joan's seventeen-year-old boy, Michael, was introspective and stayed to himself. He wasn't around much when I was there. He went off to college and eventually became an emergency room doctor. He was a bright and sensitive kid. Her daughter, Maria, was smart too, and we got along well. Long talks about life, school, friends and even her relationship with her mother were common subjects. Maria was precocious and attended an all-girls' school with plenty of activities. She would wait around to ask her mother about some event and Joan, who spent an inordinate amount of time on the phone with her girlfriends, would wave her away. Once, I stood in front of Joan and said, "Could you get off the phone and give Maria an answer so she can make her plans?" Maria liked that and thought I was her defender, but she learned I was equally protective of her mother.

That lesson came one day when Maria (unlike her mother) wanted to go with me to a recording date. On the way to the studio, driving down Santa Monica Boulevard in my burgundy Alpha Romeo, we were talking about parenting and discipline. I told her I didn't believe in hitting a child and thought there was always another way to handle a situation. Maria agreed and said, "If Mom ever hit me, I'd smack her right back."

I slammed on the brakes and skidded to a stop against the curb, turned to her and said, "Don't even think about it."

Her eyes were big as she shrank back against the door. She knew

I was serious and that I would defend and side with her mother in most circumstances. Still, Maria and I always got along because I listened to her. She knew I liked and respected her.

Years later when I was with JoAnn, Maria came to our house a couple times, once because her mother wanted to sell me Jack's piano.

"Mom wants to know if you'd like Granddad's piano. She says you can have it for $10,000 cash."

"You're kidding. It's worth four times that."

"She knows, but she'd like you to have it, and she needs the cash right now."

This was more than two years after Miss Mary's death. Everything was being held in probate. Provisions hadn't been set out in the wills, and Joan's life was on hold while she navigated her parents' estate through the courts.

Always outspoken, Maria sat in our living room chatting about the years I'd spent with her mother, and in front of JoAnn she said, "Boy! I remember when you were with Mom, and you two used to fuck like rabbits." She covered her mouth and turned crimson.

"Don't worry, Maria. JoAnn's heard just about everything, and she still likes me. She's even got a scrapbook with photos of all my ex-wives and girlfriends."

I treat children based on my own memories of being a child. I remember liking adults who left me alone while I sized them up, so I ignore children and let them come to me when they are ready. I avoid telling them how cute or sweet they are and never grill them for responses. Joan's children from her third marriage—Bobby, age nine, and Joanna, age eight—were well behaved and bright. They came to me in their own ways, and we got along well. One afternoon, Maria called her mother at my apartment and said she'd better get home because both kids were fighting. I went over with Joan.

Bobby was in trouble for hitting Joanna, but with a few questions, I learned Joanna had hit him first. I explained to Bobby that it is never okay for a guy to hit a girl because guys are stronger. I then went to Joanna's room and told her I could see the mark on Bobby's face where she'd hit him.

She looked at the floor for a long time and admitted she'd started it.

"So it's not fair that only Bobby gets blamed, is it?"

"No."

"Good, now if you both apologize, you'll both be smarter next time."

I wasn't involved in their daily lives, but I enjoyed Joan's children and liked my intermittent role as a friend of the family.

Marriage never came up between Joan and me. I don't know if I was in love with her, and was never sure of her feelings toward me, but we had good times. She introduced me to her famous friends; we attended many events and were fond of each other. Joan called me years later and thanked me for being a positive influence on her kids.

Through her, I experienced parts of Hollywood I would never have imagined. We could talk about any subject and share ideas, philosophies. I'd never been with any woman who had a serious side and was educated in so many subjects. A voracious reader, she inspired me to broaden my reading just to keep up with her. I felt I was growing, maturing, and becoming a well-rounded person. I ordered bookshelves.

Kirk Douglas was a friend of the Benny family. We sometimes stayed at his home in Palm Springs when he wasn't using it. Having dinner at a restaurant there, Joan pointed out an extremely wealthy man who'd recently become a widower. Several of her unmarried girlfriends had made a play for him because he was a good catch. "I don't get that," I said. "You mean just because he's rich?"

"Sure, if I had nerve enough, I'd go after him, too."

We were living together in a way, and that comment stunned me and put me in my place. I realized I would never qualify for Joan without a pedigree or a big bank account. I felt nauseated and wounded by that revelation. Maybe I did love her. I knew Joan was money oriented, but I was learning to what extent.

Her awareness of social status influenced many aspects of her life. Chasen's, a West L.A. superstar restaurant, catered to Hollywood's royalty. It was Jack's favorite place to eat, and he always sat in the "A" booth. Joan told me she didn't care if we ever went there, but if we did, she needed to sit in the "A" booth.

I said, "Don't you know that if I walk in there and give the maître d' a hundred dollar bill, they'll seat me anywhere I want?"

Of course her father commanded respect without the hundred dollars. Jack's generosity contrasted with the TV character he played. Not only was he generous with money, he knew how the system worked and was helpful to other entertainers like Jack Paar and Johnny Carson. He also knew the scene could change as new and bigger talents arrived, their names replacing those on the ever-revolving marquee.

When Jack and Mary went to New York, where Jack was roasted by the Friars Club, Joan and I traveled with them. While in New York, Joan and I had lunch at 21, at the *preferred* table. When the check came, she called the maître d' over and said, "I'd like Mr. Kane to sign the check."

I certainly didn't have an account there, but he said, "Oh yes, Ms. Benny."

So I signed. It was on Joan's account. It was her money. I didn't understand what she was doing, but she told me once that her goal in life was to be *Mrs. Somebody*. She wanted status and recognition—not necessarily on her own merit, but as someone's partner.

Some of the elite were gracious and kind to me when I accompanied Joan in their world. Filmmaker Billy Wilder's wife, Audrey, often saved my life by paying attention to me at the parties she and Billy hosted in their fabulous Malibu home. Audrey had been a band singer with

Tommy Dorsey and appreciated musicians. When Joan and I walked into the parties, her people would whisk her away and leave me standing in a crowd of stars who had no interest in me. One night, I stood looking at the longest sectional couch I'd ever seen, and I had a clear view of every comedian in the business: Jack Benny, Milton Berle, George Burns, Johnny Carson, Jack Lemmon, Walter Matthau, and so on. I stared, like a kid looking through a candy store window. Jack didn't say, "Hey Artie, over here." Joan didn't wave at me to join her group, but Audrey showed up, slipped her arm through mine, and whispered a lewd remark that broke me up. Without her, I'd have drowned.

That night, my Valium wasn't working in spite of Audrey's attention. She wanted me to play the piano so she could sing, but I hesitated and Jack Lemmon got up, spilled a glass of red wine on the white shag carpet, and stumbled to the piano to play for her. When Joan and I left, I said, "I'm never going there again." Joan cried. She was upset and said, "I've never been part of the 'A' list. I've always been invited to dessert, never dinner. We were here tonight because of you."

"What?" I said, clueless.

"Audrey likes you. That's why we were invited."

I was dumbfounded. For a minute, in this crowd, Joan thought I was her "A" list ticket, and she seemed devastated that I didn't want to hang out in that collection of stars.

Joan was more accepted in the art circles. She always had access to symphony tickets. We often attended concerts—another place where she deserted me and entered the throng of sycophantic patrons waiting to be greeted by the conductor or hoping to shake hands with that night's gifted performer. Zubin Mehta, who never remembered my name even though we had met several times, always grabbed my date for a tête-à-tête. He became music director of the L.A. Philharmonic 1962-1978 through a management blunder that named him assistant conductor without first consulting the principal conductor, Sir George Solti. Solti resigned over the slight. Joan told me I was naive about the symphony and opera world and claimed Zubin was the best PR any orchestra could have because he was attentive to all the society women, implying that was also part of his obligations.

"It's as much about raising money as it is about the music," she said.

Society knew Zubin as the "Darling of the Matrons." I referred to him as Cornel Wilde, in reference to a dashingly good-looking actor known for his Olympic-qualifying fencing skills. Zubin's conducting and baton work often looked like a fencing match between him and his orchestra. I was also a bit jealous of him because he paid lots of attention to Joan, who accused me of being disrespectful about the symphony world.

"You don't know about the arts and what it takes to keep these organizations afloat. Wealthy patrons give millions of dollars in support. The ballet, the opera and the great symphony orchestras can't exist without them, and part of Zubin's job is to encourage their sponsorship."

Here I was getting an education, learning a whole different side of the music business and hoping to maintain a good relationship with a woman I respected and probably loved. With scarce hope of a permanent arrangement, I was content to be her friend and lover.

Joan and Jack Benny

SEVENTEEN

High Society

These social engagements with their potholes and lessons served me well and knocked some of the rough edges off my prickly personality. With Joan's help, I learned to get along with people and to soften my approach during conversations, which saved me from arguments. I respected Joan's view and thought processes, so I was willing to compromise my black-and-white outlook to discover gray areas of agreement. With Joan, I was more forgiving than I'd been in my marriages and with my own family. I recall a lecture from my mother, "If Aunt Sadie asks you how you liked dinner, you don't have to say the meat was tough. You could say you especially liked the carrots or dessert and spare her feelings." She was right.

When Joan bought a home in Beverly Hills, I maintained my own apartment, but she did pick out a room in her house that served as my office/studio. It was a nice arrangement that allowed us to spend more time together by giving me a place to work on my composing assignments. Pleasant as it was, the arrangement underscored our ambiguous relationship. I was never quite sure what I meant to her, or, for that matter, what my feelings were for her. Did I love her? Maybe. One day when she was not booked for a lunch or meeting, I invited her to come to the Fox scoring stage to hear me play in the orchestra for a film session.

Joan thought for a moment and said, "I'll come when you are the composer and conductor."

I didn't know at the time that Joan was parroting the opinion her mother expressed when told her daughter was dating a pianist named Artie Kane.

"Joan, dear ... Mrs. Henry Mancini. Yes. Mrs. Artie Kane. No!"

I believe Joan appreciated my musical talent and was impressed with my achievements, but I didn't like her snobby attitude. After all, I had the position of *first call* in several studios and was busy as ever with session work for television and motion pictures. Yet, her comment prodded me further into studying composition, and I spent my free time learning the process of how the composer, music editor and director decide where to add music in a film to elevate the audience's emotional response.

In addition to Joan's not-so-subtle nudging, I was interested in exploring new, creative musical endeavors, such as composing for film, because I felt I'd achieved everything I could as a studio pianist. This was the same drive that had led me to quit the ice show in New York; people were just as skeptical then as now. A well-known composer/arranger in the business told me, "Artie, you can't take up the pencil at forty-four; you've got to do that when you're a teenager and can develop skills. You can't start a composing career at your age."

Some people always say, "You can't do that NOW ... you should have thought of that twenty years ago." But I'd been studying with two outstanding teachers for several years, and I had twelve years on-the-job training playing piano for film scores. I decided I had a good background for pursuing a career as a film composer.

After the dear professor Tedesco died, I was fortunate to continue my studies with another wonderful teacher, Dr. Albert Harris, who had also studied with the master. At my first meeting with Al, I told him I'd once overheard Tedesco discussing an assignment turned in by a well-known record producer and arranger, Buddy Bregman. Evidently,

Buddy had gotten Al Harris to do his orchestration assignment, and Tedesco commented, "Oh, oh, I see Albert is making his same mistakes on your assignments, Mr. Bregman."

At that point, I was thoroughly into orchestration and composition, thanks to my Italian professor. Al Harris helped me refine my skills, and in 1974 I got a chance to compose and orchestrate music for a horror film known by several titles: *It Lives by Night, Bat People* and *It's Alive.* The director, Jerry Jameson, someone I'd previously worked for, recommended me. No money was available for an orchestra or recording session—only a $15,000 fee for the composer. I didn't care. It was a chance to compose.

I got an agent, Alvin Bart, who referred to me as a *mercy hump* because he usually worked only with big talents, like Elmer Bernstein and Hank Mancini. Al liked to hang around their sessions, so when I was playing piano for Hank, Al and I would sometimes meet for breakfast. He's another one who told me not to give up my day job, that I was too old to become a composer. In return, I called Al a leech and reminded him that he couldn't eat if Hank didn't work.

"You'll make a couple meals off me, too," I said. "You don't have to do anything; I already have the job." Good natured and salty, Al agreed to represent me as a favor and for his 15 percent.

There was never a question of doing the horror film project nonunion as Al had suggested. I've been a member of the American Federation of Musicians (AFM) since I was thirteen and never strayed, even when I was starving in New York. Consequently, I knew I'd have to chip in plenty to pay for the musicians, recording engineer and studio, plus hire a union payroll company to run the job. I wasn't expecting anything back from the film, which had a frightful plot about a doctor who is bitten by a bat while camping with his wife. He's transformed into a vampire bat, and it goes downhill from there.

I wrote a good main title song, hired my friend, studio singer Sally

Stevens, and a good orchestra, and filled the picture with music. I was nervous conducting my own music, but the musicians were all friends and colleagues. Theater reviews claimed the film performed poorly at the box office. As I was walking out of the screening, I overheard the director and producer say the print had too much green in it, which made it dark. I remember thinking it wasn't dark enough because you could still see the picture. It didn't matter. I'd gotten my chance and scored a film. I was ecstatic!

At the time, I was also playing piano for *Wonder Woman,* a TV show based on a comic book character. The series had wall-to-wall music like a cartoon. The show's composer, Charlie Fox, had also written themes and scores for *The Joan Rivers Show* and *Love American Style.* I had previously received a thank you note from him for my work on his film *The Stranger Within.* His score was exceptionally beautiful and I was lucky to have worked on it.

One weekend, Charlie called. "Artie, I broke my wrist playing baseball, so I'm out of the composing game for now."

Charlie knew I wanted to write. He told the producer I was his pianist on the show and the only person he knew who would write the music in the same style.

These are the kind of breaks (Charlie would love the pun) that are life altering. For me it was like winning the lottery. I would get a chance at my dream, to try out the skills I'd been learning and studying the last eight years. I couldn't thank him enough, but I felt awful about his wrist. Charlie was matter of fact about it. He knew it wasn't going to ruin his career. He went on to compose themes and underscore for *The Love Boat* and the film *Other Side of the Mountain.* He wrote the hit song "Killing Me Softly with His Song," and the theme song and other compositions for *Happy Days, Laverne and Shirley* and numerous other shows. A mighty talent for sure.

Each *Wonder Woman* show had thirty minutes of music and recorded once a week. It didn't matter that some film projects gave composers three months to write the same amount of music. Television, geared to the network schedule, allows no flexibility. When they say they want it by eleven o'clock the next day, that's what they mean, and if you can't do it, they find someone who can. It would cost the production company (in this case Warner Brothers) a million dollars to miss a network deadline.

For the first show, I put in long days writing and rewriting. I was still up at two in the morning the day of recording. Nearly in tears, I couldn't think of a single note to put down for the last two music cues. If I don't go to bed now, I thought, I won't make the morning recording. Finally, I said, "Screw it." I did what I could and let it go.

I put the music in the back seat of my car in the driveway and left the door unlocked so the copyist could pick up my scores at four thirty to prepare the parts for the orchestra to play by the 8:00 a.m. downbeat.

One of the two missing cues was a dramatic scene I'd sketched out but hadn't orchestrated. Though I had indicated strings here, flutes there and a horn entrance, I hadn't fully written the cue for the copyists to prepare the orchestra parts. Looking at it, I thought it resembled the piano parts Professor Tedesco used to give me where he'd scratch in the instrument names for my homework. The other cue was a march. I showed up at the studio in a panic thinking this was the start and end of my career. The music editor and copyist were on stage, so I went to them and confessed, "I'm sorry guys, I just couldn't finish."

"What's the trouble?" the copyist asked.

I handed over my two unfinished sketches. "That's all I've done."

The copyist looked at them and said, "No problem. I have an orchestrator who can hammer it out for you in an hour. We'll record it at the end of the session, and I'll track the march from another show."

Artie and Charlie Fox

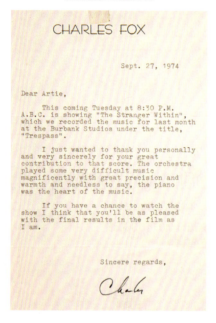

I could breathe again. Every music department has talented people capable of jumping in and saving the day.

That experience expanded into a new career for me, in part because Charlie never came back to the show; he had other projects going on. I stayed with *Wonder Woman* and slowly got over the initial fear of a blank page and a deadline. I began to enjoy my new career composing music for television shows.

Meanwhile, I hadn't found the nerve to ask Joan to a session where I'd written the music. I was waiting for the right project—maybe a motion picture—to come along.

A three-week hiatus in production for *Wonder Woman* left an opportunity for Joan and me to travel again. I hoped this vacation would be better than our New York trip where I had felt out of place and outclassed at the restaurant 21, or our Washington, DC trip, where Joan had thrown a tantrum in our hotel room because she wanted a private tour of the White House. This time, we decided to go to Hawaii. I'd been there once in the early sixties, to Oahu, to play and conduct for the *Andy Williams Show*. I wasn't impressed because Oahu was so commercialized. This time, Joan arranged for us to bypass Oahu and hop over to the Big Island where we had reservations at the Mauna Kea Beach Hotel, a resort and championship golf course for the rich and famous—and there were plenty of them, all letting down their guard and enjoying time away from the industry. Our suite opened onto the beach, a short walk along tropical gardens and out to the water. What a difference from my first trip when I stayed in Honolulu, which reminded me of any southern California city, only set in a humid climate with armies of palm trees. In contrast, the lush landscape and luxurious accommodations of the Mauna Kea Beach Hotel called out to me later in life and coaxed me to return a couple more times.

About the time Joan and I returned from Hawaii, Frank Sinatra was planning a party for Jack's eightieth birthday. Joan wasn't invited. I could tell it was killing her. She really loved her father and couldn't imagine not sharing in his birthday celebration. Frustrated, she admitted to me that her mother was in charge of the list.

"You'd better get on the phone and call her," I said. "Tell her in no uncertain terms that you and I are expecting engraved invitations for dinner, not just for dessert."

Mary swore she didn't make out the list.

Joan said, "I don't give a damn who made the list. I know you have the power to fix it. Just make sure we get *the invitation.*"

We did, and I was proud Joan stood up to her mother. Who knows how my life might have changed if Jinx had showed such courage with Louise?

Joan and I drove to Palm Springs and checked into our hotel. I think Jack and Miss Mary were staying at the Sinatra compound. Before the party, Jack called and asked Joan to ask me if I had brought an extra set of cuff links because he had forgotten his. That's what life's all about. Don't give me that star stuff … it's about who's got some spare cuff links. As it happened, I did.

I never told Joan I'd played on Sinatra recordings. It saved me from discomfort in case he'd forgotten.

Sinatra had a compound that bewildered my imagination. A couple hundred people attended, along with the California highway patrol and security detail for Governor Reagan. The first time I had met Ronald Reagan was at Jack Benny's house. Reagan had just spilled spaghetti sauce on his suit jacket. I was a wise guy and made light of his accident by joking: If I get a speeding ticket, can I call you? He looked at me like I was an ant and changed the subject.

If Reagan remembered that embarrassing moment, he didn't let on. We had an interesting chat about studio financing. Reagan loved to talk about the industry and had an inside track with his friend, Lew Wasserman, head of Universal/MCA. According to Reagan, Lew received a call from his production manager warning him their new film was a hundred thousand dollars over budget because they were going to have to build a special set with a ticket price of $100,000. Lew called the director, who was new in Hollywood. The director said he didn't need the set and had told the production manager to cut it from the budget.

"Good, now you are only $40,000 over budget," Lew told the befuddled director, "so here's what you don't understand." He then explained that the studio has carpenters, painters and so forth on salary year-round. Their cost is built into every project. If you don't build the set you save $60,000, but you still have to pay the overhead.

By this time, everyone at our table was listening to the story. The governor was getting a real kick out of explaining how producers were screwed one way or the other. I got a glimpse of how it works the same way in music. Salaries for music department executives are tacked onto the cost of every music project. Executives, whether or not we use them, are paid first. That leaves less money to hire a string quartet, say for a wedding sequence, or to pay for a singer. We hardly get started before the budget is in the hole and I'm told to cut two musicians from my orchestra.

John Wayne and his wife Pilar were also at the Sinatras' home for Jack's party. Joan was friends with them, so we had been to parties at their Newport Beach house and on his boat, *Wild Goose.* The minesweeper was built in Seattle in 1943 and had been decommissioned after the war and converted into what looked like an ocean liner to me. A handmade, round table out of koa wood had been installed on the aft deck for infamous poker games. Like some stars, John matched his screen image; he believed in God, country and apple pie. He made everyone feel welcome and Pilar was charming. Both paid attention to Joan and me and asked if we were enjoying ourselves, probably because I looked uncomfortable. Dressed in a yacht-appropriate jacket, I was the only man who wasn't blonde and blue-eyed. There was no diversity in the Newport Beach crowd.

I almost fit in at his parties, but that day John was holding court and blurted out the N-word like it was an everyday part of his vocabulary. It hit me that he probably used several offensive labels like *kike* and *dago,* along with other racial slurs. I must have flinched because Joan put her hand on my arm. She sensed we'd be leaving. We did, abruptly. You can say hurtful things, make racial remarks and be intolerant, but I don't have to sit at your table and put up with it.

Neither fame nor fortune breeds manners or decent behavior, and certainly, stardom illustrates that truth abundantly. People who don't read and study history, who aren't exposed to different cultures and who don't show respect for all human beings can be guilty of barbaric and hurtful behavior. I know this sounds preachy, but it's my belief, and I was happy Joan felt the same.

So it was as I navigated through a variety of Joan's friends. Some were great people; some were not. Isaac Stern gave a concert with the L.A. Philharmonic. Joan's close friends and big supporters of the symphony, Leah and Larry Superstein, hosted a party for him afterward at their home. Joan knew him well because her father was a huge fan. She introduced me to Isaac backstage, and then we drove him to the party. I was uncomfortable about Isaac's performance because he had played out of tune. He was past his prime, and I think music giants should go out on the right note, so to speak. I tried to be gracious and said I enjoyed the concert.

In the car, Isaac's attention was totally fixed on Joan. At his age, he wasn't attractive; he was overweight and resembled a giant toad. But when a man has fame and money, he believes he has appeal. At the party, Isaac made a show of drinking brandy from a heated snifter while slobbering over two women, hoping to connect with one for the evening. When that didn't happen, he wanted to leave. The host asked me to drive Isaac back to the Hotel Bel-Air. Before we left, Isaac leaned over to me and asked out of the blue, "What do you think of Art Tatum?"

He must have thought I was a jazz pianist, but what could I say to a question like that? "He's dead, I think."

EIGHTEEN

Tradition

Joan's association with Leah and Larry Superstein and her longtime friendship with the Chapros, who were strong supporters of music in Los Angeles, prompted more invitations to attend celebrity gatherings at both homes, including one where Joan introduced me to virtuoso violinist Jascha Heifetz.

After hello, Heifetz made his way to the piano and played a note, then turned to me with a cold stare. Not sure what to do, I said, "B-flat." Then he hit a fistful of notes, so I named them all. He turned to Joan and announced, "He's got it." Joan told me he was irritated that she had a "new friend," especially a pianist with perfect pitch.

A week later, the Supersteins invited me to dinner where Heifetz told fans around the table, "My friends call me Mr. H." Two women were fawning over him, "Mr. H this and Mr. H that." So I joined in to inquire about his violin, "Mr. H …," I said.

His head whipped around, his eyes glared at me, and he snarled, "Yes, Jim? It's Mr. Heifetz."

This kind of awkward behavior culminated in a summer buffet on the patio at Hannah Boorstin's where, following Joan, I filled my plate from an array of fancy platters, and then joined her at the table. I discovered I'd forgotten my salad and circled back, but when I returned Jascha Heifetz had moved my plate of food and was sitting in my chair. I heard Joan say, "Jascha, that's Artie's seat." Heifetz ignored her, so I said in a firm tone, "I was sitting there." Joan pushed her chair back, stood, and said to me, "Honey, we're leaving." She apologized to Hannah and we left. I told Joan I never wanted to see that man again.

Such occasions made me realize you shouldn't get to know the people you idolize; just buy their records and appreciate them from a distance.

Whenever I told my mother about meeting concert artists and superstars, she would ask, "Did you tell any of them what you do?"

"No," I'd answer.

"That's right," she said. "Keep it a secret. Maybe they'll come looking for you."

I explained to her that Heifetz couldn't help me in my career, nor could others in that realm of the music world; however, my connections with studio music departments, such as the head of Fox Music, Lionel Newman, provided opportunities for me.

Lionel stayed at my house when his wife threw him out after catching him at the racetrack. Since I was spending a lot of time at Joan's place and working at the lovely office she'd provided me, I told Lionel he could stay as long as he needed. About a week later, I called and warned him I'd be stopping by to pick up more clothes and some dress items for a black-tie event. He was lying on my queen-size bed, his arms crossed, watching me match up shirts and pants from my closet.

Lionel Newman, head of 20th Century Fox Music Department

"Artie, I know you're with the Benny girl and have to dress up for dinner, but how long are you going to be?"

"Hey, it's my house."

"I know, but could you hurry up?" he grinned.

In addition to inviting me to celebrity parties, Leah Superstein asked me to her house to discuss several songs she had written. She had studied music and piano since childhood and wanted me to record an album of her compositions. I picked eleven songs I thought would record well and then set up a couple of recording dates. Evenings, I worked at my place, jotting down piano arrangements and preparing the material, running each one by Leah for her approval. What I didn't realize at the time was how unhappy Joan had become over this working relationship. Joan and Leah's friendship went way back. Still, Leah was a frightful flirt, and the two friends were always in competition over the attention of artists and stars. I was so obtuse that I didn't notice the flimsy excuses Joan gave for not attending the recordings of her dear friend's songs.

Playing and producing the album for Leah was a torturous experience for me. Larry was a genius businessman with only an appreciation for the arts, but both of them suddenly became music experts. They had countless suggestions during the sessions. Maybe it was payback for the arrogant attitude I'd displayed toward the backers of my first album. In the end, the final version of Leah's album pleased her, and she was genuinely grateful, but during the process, a distance had developed between Joan and me. We'd stopped meeting for dinner because I was often eating at the Supersteins' and writing arrangements at night.

Experiences like these seem to happen in the industry when artists jump from one impassioned project to another, working intently each time with a new personality. They get distracted from everyday life and give their all to the endeavor at hand. Meanwhile, their main relationship or marriage suffers. That's why Jaye P. had wanted me to go with her to all her performances, to ground her and be part of them. While working with Leah, I did notice Joan was becoming less available and that I didn't spend as much time at her house.

Studio work filled the void. My colleague, Ralph Grierson, showed up one day with a bunch of two-piano arrangements of George Gershwin songs and scores. He asked if I'd like to record them with him for Angel Records. There it was, the elusive record album proposition. Should I try again? Ralph's recording contact with Angel Records was solid, as he had recorded three previous albums for them, so we picked six popular songs, three preludes and a twenty-five minute arrangement of *An American in Paris*. I began practicing, seriously practicing, or woodshedding, in musicians' lingo.

It was just before Christmas '74 when I got a call from Joan, who'd returned from a Mammoth Lakes ski trip with her children, telling me her father was in a coma. I met her at her parents' Charing Cross house. Mary looked disheveled, overwhelmed and upset, and for the first time I felt sorry for her. She asked me to answer the door and direct people into the living room, or for very close friends and family, up the stairway to Jack's room. She trusted me to make the right decisions and to send anyone away who did not belong there. I took this assignment to heart and was firm in sorting through the stream of well-wishers. Word of Jack's condition had travelled through the Hollywood community, and his friends poured in to pay their respects to a man they loved. Mary seemed unable to function in her usual social capacity, so Joan took over as hostess.

The gathering turned into a celebration of Jack's life as people told stories and laughed through tears over remembered events. In the foyer, I smiled every time I passed by the fine antique table Joan had sent from Carmel for her father's photos—all autographed to him from luminaries and dignitaries. He had complained to Joan and me months earlier that he wanted them downstairs where his friends could enjoy them instead of in his bedroom where Mary had put them. Joan and I made a special trip up the coast to find the perfect piece for his display. As guests lingered over them, I thought how happy it would have made Jack.

Some of the people were strange. Danny Kaye came to Jack's room to kiss his feet. It was a fetish of his to kiss the feet of the dying. I also saw people admiring and handling photographs, trinkets and collectibles. I watched to be sure that they didn't glom on to items for mementos or keepsakes. I recall speaking with Jack Lemmon's wife, Felicia, when Jack spilled not a glass this time, but a whole bottle of red wine on the white living room carpet. There were gasps, then nervous laughter, then uproarious laughter, prompting more stories and shared memories.

Jack Benny died on December 26, 1974. At the Hillside memorial service three days later, Mary looked stricken. Unsure of herself and shaky, she stood clenching her fists so tight I was sure her long manicured nails would draw blood. She didn't want to talk to people, so I stayed close like a bodyguard while I walked her to and from her assigned vehicle. It was one of the few times she liked me and depended on my help. For once, she forgot I had no status.

By contrast, Joan was greeting everyone, making sure all went as planned. She didn't need my help or my shoulder. She was remarkable and admirable in her role those last four days before his passing and at the memorial. Jack had been the glue between the pages of mother and daughter. With his death, Joan lost the buffer between herself and her mother. She also lost her connections, her entrée, her celebrity and the man she most adored.

At Hillside Memorial Cemetery
December 29, 1974

Photo: Cal Montney
Copyright © 1974. Los Angeles Times.
Reprinted with Permission.

Rehearsals and Recordings: Gershwin Album

The day after Jack's memorial, my calendar showed weeks of rehearsals scheduled in preparation for the Gershwin recording sessions in late March. Ralph Grierson and I practiced at his home studio where he had two grand pianos placed so the curves of each humped into the other so that we faced one another while playing. There, we worked out the complicated arrangements and decided which parts we'd each play. I found it nerve-racking to go over and over the material. I was used to studio jobs where if I noticed a difficult piano part, I worked on it mentally during breaks or on cues when I was tacet. But this recording project required much more than that.

Ralph was nervous, too. He admitted that my ability to sight-read difficult music, learn it quickly, and grasp the essence of a phrase intimidated him. On the other hand, Ralph's practice habits and his approach to learning serious repertoire cowed me. Listening to Ralph talk about his earlier recording experience of playing Stravinsky's *Rite of Spring* with the internationally recognized pianist and conductor Michael Tilson Thomas brought back memories of my ill-prepared concert playing *Rhapsody in Blue* with the Columbus Symphony. I wished I'd had a teacher coaching me. Instead, I had no choice but to learn it on my own in a week. Ralph's study habits were more like that of a concert pianist, woodshedding passages, trying various dynamics and way, way too much discussion.

Shortly before the recording date, we got an offer from Mickey Nadel to perform the Gershwin selections for a live audience at a pub called the Mermaid Tavern in Thousand Oaks. A former symphony bassist, Mickey, and his wife, Ann, turned the place into a popular hangout for musicians. Ralph had played a concert there and thought we would get good feedback from a performance. This prospect of a public performance added a layer of angst to my mounting tension over rehearsals and the upcoming recordings. We decided to break up the piano performances for the tavern with some Gershwin vocals that would add variety to the show. We needed a vocalist.

As my relationship with Joan Benny waned, I occasionally had dinner with Sally Stevens, who was a vocal contractor for recordings and film music, as well as a lyricist for songwriters. Sally was the daughter of Ken Stevens, the manager of Holiday on Ice when I was with the show in the fifties. As I mentioned earlier, I'd hired Sally to write lyrics for my first film assignment, *It Lives by Night*. When Ralph and I approached her to sing Gershwin between our two-piano numbers, she jumped at the chance. I accompanied her. Sally had a classy style, a versatile voice and could have been a recording star in her own right.

The night of our performance, colleagues and friends packed the room and cheered us on. Their support played a big part in my confidence about the upcoming recording sessions scheduled at Capitol Records in Hollywood.

I invited Joan to one of the recording sessions. She agreed to come, but I sensed it was a duty for her rather than an interest in me or the project. I felt I couldn't do much to win her admiration in my profession. I was never going to be a concert artist and though some doors were opening up for a shot at film composing, I would never secure the credentials to be her status symbol and earn her respect. I never knew if she was dating other men, but I assumed our relationship was over, though we still talked occasionally.

During the mixing of the album, I was excited because I thought we'd done a great job, and I was ecstatic with the product. Angel Records and the producers were also pleased—a relief after my prior experience. This time I kept away from the producing team and concentrated on the music, something I knew. Keeping quiet and out of trouble drove me nuts, and I started smoking again after seven years of clean living. Luckily, through Ralph's insistence, all our rehearsing, working out fingering and marking page turns paid off. The end product showcased the work we'd done and the Grammy nomination we'd earned.

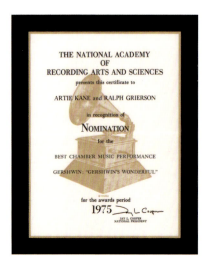

A few weeks later, Sally arranged a surprise party for my forty-sixth birthday at a small restaurant in Studio City. She had invited close friends; the food was good, friends were fawning, I was uncomfortable. It was a nice gesture on Sally's part, but I was drunk and ungrateful because I hate surprise parties and being the center of attention unless I'm performing. Despite my boorish behavior, Sally and I remained friends and maintained a good working relationship.

Sally Stevens and Artie

Life and music were terrific and I was cookin' with work. My composing career moved along in the right direction with better and better projects. The only trouble was I never heard from my agent, Al Bart. He didn't bother to keep in touch with me because I wasn't an important client like Hank Mancini or other celebrities. Therefore, any new television contracts I got came from people I'd worked with before.

I made an appointment with Al. "Why should I pay you 15 percent for doing nothing?" I asked. He was incensed that I'd take him to task for not calling. I fired him on the spot. Al played the hurt card, like a dumped girlfriend, but I was determined to find a new agent.

When Lionel heard I'd dumped my agent, he recommended his brother, Marc Newman. Well connected in the industry, Marc represented an impressive crop of composers from John Williams to Dave Grusin. Marc knew which pictures were in production at each studio. He had personal relationships with the heads of music, had breakfast with the producers and got information even before Al did, who depended on flirting with the secretaries to get the scoop. Marc and Al had a contentious association that stemmed from Al's aggressiveness in stealing clients and his churlish treatment of women. Al fought hard for his clients, but he was brash, whereas Marc was a good salesman with excellent connections through his film dynasty family, the Newmans. Five of Marc's brothers had significant ties to film studios.

Meanwhile, when I was scoring at Warner Brothers, I met Carol Faith, Charlie Fox's agent. Carol had taken over her husband, Peter Faith's composing agency after he died unexpectedly. Carol was smart, had a fabulous sense of humor and an enviable family that seemed caring and close-knit. I always thought she could have been a comedian or written television sit-coms. Her clever repartee amused me, and her foibles were familiar because she had lived on the outskirts of Beverly Hills and had friends around the fringes of the industry. I thought about signing up with Carol, but I went with Marc.

MY MOTHER HAD SERIOUS THYROID PROBLEMS, but Uncle Joe said she was doing well in treatment. I was traveling back and forth from Columbus to see her when Joan and I had our last disagreement. She wanted to go with me to see my mother, but our relationship had not been close for months, and she'd never met or talked with my mother, so I thought her visit would be inappropriate while my mother was unwell. Maybe Joan was offering a shoulder to lean on as payback for my assistance during her father's last days, but she'd been distant before Jack's death, and when she made that reluctant appearance at the Gershwin recordings, I could feel a stiffness had crept in and replaced the comfort we once shared.

During the next few months, Carol's and my relationship evolved into daily communications, meals and meeting her family. We rented a house together on North Beverly Drive, the not so pricey part of Beverly Hills. I got the idea that all my love troubles would be solved

Carol Faith

if I married a nice Jewish girl. On one of my calls home, I said to my mother, "I've got some good news for you." I thought I might cheer her up and make her feel better, or at least get a laugh out of her.

"What is it?" she asked.

"I've met a nice Jewish girl." I held my breath for her response.

My mother never dropped a beat when she replied, "You'll spoil it."

I should have known better, but I said, "What kind of a reaction is that? How will I spoil it?"

"Another skirt will come along," she predicted.

While I always kept in touch with Uncle Joe, I called one day and found Mother was much worse. I got worried. Joe was like the rest of the family; he never wanted to spread bad news—like the time my mother failed to tell me Joe had been hospitalized after suffering a mild heart attack. I yelled at her for not telling me sooner so I could fly in to see him.

Joe finally admitted that my mother had cancer and the treatments had failed. I cancelled all work and flew out again. During the flight, I resolved to apologize for disappointing her. When I got to the house, I went to her room. Propped up with pillows, sitting in a chair, she looked drawn and colorless. I got down on my knees, took her hand and said, "I love you, Mother, and I just want to apologize for not being the son you wanted me to be."

With empty eyes and through clenched teeth, she said, "It's too late."

I couldn't speak. I cried … and cried. Joe tried to comfort me. I've never gotten over it. I left Columbus that night remembering those were her last words to me.

Two weeks later, I drove home from work. Carol stood in the driveway. She put her arms around me and said, "Your mother died this morning. I packed a few clothes and a jacket for you. Your flight leaves in an hour."

I was grateful she didn't garbage it up with "I think you should sit down for this … *blah blah*." She instinctively knew how to treat the situation. No drama, just the necessary information and the means for me to handle it.

Mother died on September 15, 1975. So happens, it was Yom Kippur, the holiest day of the Jewish calendar year—a day reserved for atonement and repentance. By sheer will, my mother was determined to live until that day so I would never forget the significance of her death. What I've never forgotten is the career she gave me, along with her brand of love. She always did what she thought was best for me and aimed all efforts toward my success. I am grateful to her, and I love her for all of it.

Returning from the cemetery to the family home on Plymouth Avenue, I found several cousins in my mother's room rummaging through her dresser drawers and closet. "What are you doing here?" I demanded. They said they were looking for things of hers they'd like to have. I asked if they might wait a few days. Honestly, I thought my family was barbaric, but nine months earlier, I had been through Jack Benny's death and witnessed even stranger behavior.

LIFE WITH CAROL WAS FULL OF HUMOR, FAMILY AND BUSINESS. She had an office in Beverly Hills where she met with clients and made deals. She drew up contracts for several composers who stayed with her when she took over her husband's agency after he died.

I kept a breakneck schedule composing and recording weekly *Wonder Woman* episodes. Unlike other studios and production companies that had a stable of composers revolving around their television shows, I was the only composer on *Wonder Woman*. Consequently, I only accepted studio calls during the show's hiatus. One night I watched an episode to see if I was doing justice to my assignments and was shocked to see the screen credit for the theme and underscore attributed to me. I called Charlie immediately, horrified that my benefactor was being slighted.

"Don't change anything," he said. "I'm getting paid correctly for the theme on the royalty statements, and it's good for you to get the credit."

That's the kind of guy Charlie is, generous and encouraging. I did fix his credit with the studio because I couldn't accept the mistake.

Charlie Fox and Dominic Frontiere helped me join Broadcast Music, Inc. (BMI), a royalty organization that collects performance fees for composers of songs, film music, TV shows, etc. The first year, BMI sent me a stipend, a kind of good faith payment betting that I'd continue working in the industry. The next year, when I got my first check based on performances, I thought they'd made a mistake. I had no idea that in addition to my negotiated fee from the production company, I'd receive a healthy royalty collected quarterly from networks broadcasting over 196 prime-time national and international markets.

I was feeling good about my music composing and financial opportunities, and I had a good relationship with Carol and her parents. Her father, one of the sharpest guys I ever talked with, procured goods for men's clothing companies. Abe was up on every aspect of life and had a well-thought-out opinion on most subjects, including money and politics. We had good discussions. I learned from him and I respected him. Carol's mother, Adele, could have been a stand-in for Gracie Allen. She was unconsciously funny. One afternoon, Abe came home and said, "Adele, the bank called today and claimed you were overdrawn in your checking account."

Adele looked surprised, "That's not possible, Abe, I still have blank checks left in my book."

Abe and Adele were accepting of me. So was Carol's brother, Bob, the inventor. He sold his clever gadgets to companies like Bell and Howell, and Seiko, and then started his own business called Think Outside, Inc. All of us, including her extended family, were together at dinners, get-togethers, events and parties. It was a little too much family for someone like me who'd shunned all that when growing up, but I had a feeling of belonging. The next logical step was for Carol and me to marry. I asked her; she said yes.

We bought a house in Beverly Hills. Its impressive location didn't stop Carol's father from making myriad suggestions. "This is wrong; this needs fixing." He'd call in the morning on weekends with an idea about remodeling, or say, "I've been up all night thinking about the walls." He wanted everything to be wonderful for his daughter, who had been dealt a troubled hand when Peter Faith died so young.

Our wedding was at the renowned Hotel Bel-Air. My dear Uncle Joe, my cousins Phyllis and Marvin and his wife, Sue, all flew in from Ohio. None of my family had ever come to my marital unions before. Friend and benefactor, Dominic, attended with a few other colleagues. This union seemed like the real deal. We had a small ceremony with a rabbi, then a dinner for twenty-five friends and relatives at the hotel.

The Tribe

Yes, we went on our honeymoon to the Mauna Kea hotel on the Big Island of Hawaii. Yes, Carol's parents came along. Truthfully, it was terrific because I really enjoyed her parents. Life seemed settled, and though my mother couldn't be there to rejoice in my newfound happiness, which had all the appearances of normalcy and stability, I felt comfortable. I was a member of a fine tribe of Jews. Oy vey!

Carol and Artie marry at the Hotel Bel-Air

NINETEEN

WHAT KIND OF FOOL AM I?

CAROL'S FATHER ADVISED HER on most everything, but one area where I could help was her agency. After we married, I set up an in-person meeting for her with Lionel Newman and his secretaries at Fox, people she could contact about upcoming projects that held potential for her clients. I did the same at Universal, MGM and a few independent companies where I knew the cast of characters. Soon, she was gleaning information from studio executives and their assistants.

While Carol was busy with her work, I received a call to compose the score for Richard Brook's film, *Looking for Mr. Goodbar,* at Paramount Pictures. As the new guy on Marc's roster, I was cheap but eager.

Richard Brook's writing and directing credits were intimidating: *Blackboard Jungle, Cat on a Hot Tin Roof, Elmer Gantry* and *In Cold Blood.* During my first meeting with him and his music editor, I was so nervous that Richard took me out in the hall and asked, "What's the matter?" I admitted this was my first major motion picture and I was afraid of him. He said, "Do you know anything about baseball?" I nodded. "Well, if you goof up on the first ball, you just have to play the next ball. And that's how this film will go. You'll write what you think, and if I don't like it, you'll write something different the next day." He wasn't so intimidating after that.

Richard wanted to remain independent from studio pressures and did not take advice from Paramount's music department. He had the picture temp-tracked with existing music from the studio's music library. The temp-track serves as a guideline during a film's editing phase to indicate the mood and atmosphere desired by the director. It also provides the composer with the director's concept. A horror film will often be tracked with Bernard Herrmann's *Psycho* music to build tension and fear during early screenings. It's the kiss of death for a composer because producers tend to get attached to the temp track and become prejudiced against the composer's musical approach.

The producer of *Goodbar,* Freddie Fields, wanted Richard to include a song at the beginning of the film. Richard said no, but Freddie wasn't listening. He relayed the gist of the movie's story to lyricist Carol Connors and then sent her to meet with Richard. Carol sang one line of the lyric that she'd conjured up for my opening theme that Richard had approved. She called the song "Don't Ask to Stay Until Tomorrow." Richard was astonished she'd come up with a line that embodied the theme of the film without seeing it. He didn't know Freddie had prompted her.

I wasn't happy that Richard agreed to transform my dark, moody theme into a song. I had to switch gears and sketch out a song with a verse, a bridge, and a chorus so Carol could write lyrics. Her words didn't fit the rhythmic patterns of the melody, but somehow Marlena Shaw recorded it and made it sound okay—just not the hit record or shining example I'd hoped for. The underscore used so many records that my original music seemed incidental to the film. Still, my career tagged along with the success of the picture and gave me a prominent credit as a film composer.

When Doug Cramer became head of production at Spelling Productions, he left *Wonder Woman* and took me with him. I rotated with a couple other composers scoring *Love Boat* and *Vegas* for the Spelling lineup. While working on my first *Love Boat* assignment, I heard from a producer at Lorimar about scoring a movie-for-television starring Tuesday Weld.

Artie Kane, composer

The film, *A Question of Guilt,* triggered sympathy in me for a woman accused of killing her two children. Though she wasn't guilty, she was convicted because she was promiscuous and dressed trashy.

The movie's director, Robert Butler, and producer, Peter Katz, asked me to audition my ideas. I was nervous but remembered Quincy Jones once told me, "If I could play the piano the way you can, I'd have every movie in town." That meant a lot to me and gave me courage. When I played for them the opening vamp and theme I'd written for the film, I could see Robert and Peter nodding and getting into the music.

As I got more deeply involved with the character and the tragedy of how the jury perceived her, I recalled composer Jerry Goldsmith's advice: "If you can find somebody to root for in a script, you'll have the ingredients for a great score." In *A Question of Guilt,* my feelings for the character inspired the score.

I wrote nonstop for a month. The pressure of composing for both *Love Boat* and *A Question of Guilt* was enormous, but it exhilarated me and I thrived on it. The emotion was night and day different in each project. No chance I'd get mixed up musically. Even after finishing that movie, I stayed busy constantly.

While I was home scrambling with my composing projects, Carol would be off pitching one of her clients to some producer over lunch or attending a recording session as a show of client support. She was doing well with her agency. She was happy. She didn't discuss her schedule with me, but sometimes while plotting my next music cue, my mind would wonder who she was out with that day.

We were on separate tracks. I wrote late into the evening unless we had dinner plans with friends or weekend visits with her family. We should have made time together to share our successes and worries, but didn't. Our career decisions were made outside our marital relationship.

Opportunities developed quickly for me under Marc Newman's guidance. He called me about scoring a Columbia picture called *Eyes of Laura Mars,* a Faye Dunaway/Tommy Lee Jones thriller. It was the first film for producer Jon Peters. He and Barbra Streisand lived together. Jon had bought the screenplay with her in mind for the starring role. She didn't take it, but she did record the hit song "Prisoner" for the film's soundtrack. Previously, Jon had been a successful hair stylist married to the talented actress Leslie Ann Warren. My agent, Marc, told me I had to interview with Jon even though I'd met him earlier. Still, I had a frightful reaction to the thought of interviewing with someone who was producing his first picture and had little experience in film scoring.

"I'm terrible at interviews," I pleaded with Marc, "Tell him to hire me or not, but save me from ruining my chances with an interview."

"You've got to meet with him. It will be good practice for you. Jon wants you to join him for lunch at The Beverly Hills Hotel. The food will be great and you'll get the job."

I went to the meeting, and Jon walked in with Barbra, whom I knew from recording sessions. Both greeted me as if we were old friends.

"Hey Artie, you going to do my movie?"

"Sure, I'd love to, Jon, but you have to talk to my agent when it comes to business. I'm just a piano player." Barbra laughed at that.

"Don't worry about the money," he said. "We'll make a deal."

So it was all hugs and old pals stuff. I was uncomfortable during lunch as predicted, but I survived. I went home and called Marc to discuss money.

"Not your problem, Artie. I'll take care of that part," and he did. He got me twice what I'd made for my last movie and more than half what they'd have to pay a major composer at that time.

The next problem was the screening where the timings and placement of music cues are decided. I arrived with my current mentor, composer Earle Hagen of "Harlem Nocturne" fame. We sat in a small theater room at Warner Brothers.

During the running of the film, Jon Peters said, "You know that effing director didn't give me what I asked for. I wanted blood on the screen, and he didn't do it. Artie, you've got to put the blood there with the music."

"Jon, I can't put blood where there isn't any."

"Yes you can. Make it scary."

The only thing scary about the movie was the idea that Jon wanted music to make the film something it wasn't. In the plot, a killer stalks and kills fashion models in New York. The camera acts as the stalker, but it cuts away before the kill, so there's no physical attack on the screen.

Earle, a world-class cynic, told me after we'd left the studio lot, "What this means is that Jon knows a good haircut when he sees one, but he's in foreign territory between music and film."

That's true about many movie people. Steven Spielberg is the exception, and maybe that's because he played clarinet in school. It gave him the sense to hire composer John Williams to enhance the goose bumps and tears in the films.

Earle suggested using a form of music based on the twelve-tone scale instead of the eight-tone scale of music. He thought the dissonance created by that approach would serve the picture well. I hired Earle's orchestrator and began sketching for twelve woodwinds, twelve cellos, twelve violas and so on, having them all work against each other. There was a sensual moment in the film where Faye Dunaway lay on her stomach in a darkened room with Tommy Lee Jones running his fingers gently up her bare back. It screamed for a music cue to carry the whole love scene. I had an idea for a dramatic cue using Barbra Streisand's vocal from the end credits, which I'd already conducted and recorded. I had the music mixer, Danny Wallin, extract her voice track. I built a lush arrangement with strings and woodwinds that framed a whisper of that haunting voice. The mixer and I worked for a couple hours perfecting it.

One day, composer Jerry Goldsmith walked by the transfer room and heard it. He came in to see who had written such a terrific cue. That was enough for me; Jerry's approval was like a gold star. I had told Jerry many times how he influenced my writing and film work and how much I admired his composition. I was fortunate to have been his pianist on many projects.

Jerry Goldsmith and Artie

In the end, a movie-wise friend, who attended the scoring and dubbing sessions, warned me, "You can't have two female stars on the screen at the same time, especially in a love scene."

"What are you talking about?" I asked. "Faye Dunaway's the only woman on the screen."

"You have Barbra's unmistakable voice floating in the background. I'll bet Faye makes you take it out."

After the premiere of the film in Chicago, the director Irv Kershner called me. "You know the love sequence? Faye wants the voice out.

She got permission from the producers to rent a dubbing stage for half a day. Barbra's voice is gone."

Sometimes egos can harm the very product they should be promoting. The scene was marvelous with the barely audible voice and strings, but Faye preferred a weak scene with no goose bumps. The rest of my music worked well, and the film received positive reviews and earned a fine profit.

Not long after this film, Marc Newman was diagnosed with liver cancer. He was very ill. His brothers called Carol for a meeting at the hospital where Marc offered Carol his clients if she would give a percentage of her fees to his family for three years. Marc explained the horrible history he had with Al Bart, begging Carol to take on his composers so none would gravitate to his archenemy. This was a tough situation for Carol, who had a full plate making deals for Peter's clients. Marc's decline was swift. He was thin with a yellow pallor when she met him at Cedars-Sinai, and she couldn't disappoint him, so her stable of clients grew to about forty. Now we were both up to our eyeballs in work, living the good life in Beverly Hills. Moreover, my wife became my agent by default.

When I was scoring *Wonder Woman,* I was required to use the orchestra contractor at Warner Brothers Music Department. Former secretary Patti DeCaro took over that position when her boss, Kurt Wolf, retired.

Patti DeCaro

Patti and I met often to discuss orchestra personnel and special instrumentation I might need. These chats seemed to coincide with a lunch date. As I began working on Warner Brother's *Eyes of Laura Mars,* the calls and discussions multiplied and often steered off topic.

Unhappily married to an unstable drummer, Patti complained of abuse. She was raising their out-of-control teenage daughter and filing for a separation. She called me at home a little more than was necessary for a working relationship. Conversation would begin with some minor detail about the orchestra, and then she'd lapse into her wretched situation with her husband and the juggling of her job and personal troubles.

"You are such a good listener, Artie, and your advice is invaluable to me."

Yes, I offered solutions to her marital problems and her daughter's bad behavior because I had lots of experience.

Carol didn't appreciate the calls and long conversations with Patti any more than I liked the attention Carol showered on her clients. Perhaps I was a little jealous that she didn't need my opinion or ask my advice anymore. We discussed it once. Her answer surprised me.

"When I took over Peter's clients, I was on a bike with trainer wheels and needed help, but now that I have Marc's clients, I've graduated to a two-wheeler, and you need to let go now."

One night as I was hanging up after a long call to Earle about a cue I was suffering over on a television show, Carol stood in my office with her arms folded and said, "I know you're not doing anything wrong, but I think that you're giving too much energy to this woman."

"I was talking to Earle Hagen about the music on a Spelling show."

"Well, you're usually counseling Patti. Pretty soon you'll be asking her how to write your music."

She was right. I had been on my white steed again, at the ready to help a needy woman travel the tangled trails of her life. Why is someone in need so irresistible to me? I must have a savior complex. It's exactly how Rosengarten described me.

I recognized Carol's irritation and understood why she was disturbed about the attention I'd been giving to Patti. I told her I would put an end to the personal side of the conversations, but I still had to use Patti to hire my orchestra for *Wonder Woman* because she was the Warner Brothers contractor. Cutting off the relationship completely wasn't an option in my mind.

Carol wouldn't accept my response. She told me she was frustrated and felt betrayed by the time I wasted giving advice to that woman, and she refused to utter the name. I was shocked to see her trembling with anger. She was so upset she threw something at me—like in the movies—but I was blind to the emotional pain I was causing her. This was not the amusing, smart business agent I'd married. Of course, I could only see my side, my career. I was confident I could keep Patti at arm's length, advise her in her personal life and work with her. I dismissed Carol's feelings though I knew she was right to be concerned about Patti's cunning behavior and duplicitous phone calls.

Carol wanted to have a joint session with my shrink, Dr. Rosengarten, who by this time had been counseling me longer than all my marriages strung together. After hearing our predicament, Rosengarten told Carol, "I can tell you this about Mr. Kane. If he says he'll end the personal side of the relationship, he'll do it. My suggestion is that you let him accomplish the task as he's suggesting because his word is good."

She wouldn't. Or she couldn't. The more pressure Carol put on me, the closer I felt to Patti because I looked forward to seeing someone who wasn't leaning on me. I began sharing my home problems with Patti. In her third miserable marriage, with hints of abuse, she was vamping and taunting me and was happy about the discord between Carol and me.

Over the next couple of months, the frosty atmosphere at my home seeped into every corner of our marriage. I came home around 11:30 one night and discovered Carol had locked me out of our house. I don't remember where I'd been, but that doesn't matter. You can't do that to me. Part of the money that bought that house had come from my mother's estate. I was angry. I called but Carol wouldn't answer. I called Patti who had finally separated from her husband and moved into her own apartment with her daughter, Vicki.

I want to go on record here and admit that I chose the worst possible way to deal with every aspect of the quagmire I'd created with Carol. Not only did I eventually move into that apartment with Patti, I also had to deal with her daughter, Vicki, who drank and drugged. The name-calling and yelling matches between mother and daughter roared through the walls until I thought I was in an asylum. I'd already learned not to interfere with a mother's tactics, though I showed my disapproval.

After the first month at Patti's, I knew I'd made a rash and unhealthy decision. This was not the life I wanted to live. It was like standing on a precipice knowing I was going to jump, but waiting for the start-gun to go off.

Patti pushed her husband for a warp-speed divorce, giving up everything but a monetary settlement. She was on the moon, wanting to buy a house with me and planning for our future.

Carol and I had a few messy meetings about splitting my music royalties until I suggested splitting her agency. A short discussion over that rat's nest settled our differences, and our divorce came through quickly, so quickly that I was suspicious she'd already started seeing someone else. The whole ordeal made me despondent. I liked Carol. I liked her family. I'd screwed up royally. I should never have been with Patti. None of this made sense, and yet I plowed right into the field of manure that enveloped her life.

My emotions were out of control; my behavior was illogical and unmanageable. I was just like Sara Jane, using sex to distract me from my indecent behavior.

Patti and I scoured real estate listings for a house we could buy with our combined settlements. We were like criminals on the run. We purchased and moved into a gated property in Tarzana that had belonged to a rock guitarist with a name band. Since Patti had taken nothing except her personal belongings and a financial settlement from her marriage, I took her shopping for furniture at Ethan Allen, her dream store. We spent money like we'd won it in a monopoly game. Every purchased item had to be delivered immediately as if we were afraid our new house would evaporate like in a cartoon. She was Cinderella remodeling her castle. I leased a brand new BMW for her, her dream car.

Patti's mother was a nice woman who lived in a nasty apartment up two flights of stairs. She wasn't well and had a terrible time with those steps, so I paid friends to move her into a better, safer neighborhood in a ground floor unit and added her rent to my monthly bills. I was convinced I could help Patti's daughter, too, make her feel safe and good about herself. When she turned sixteen, I bought her a car to show I trusted her; she wrecked it. I bought her another, and she wrecked that one, too. She had too many DUIs, so they took her license away. You'd think I'd have learned something from Jaye P.—that doing what drunks swear will make them stop drinking only enables them to drink more. I had my lawyer bail Vicki out of jail. Patti and I bailed her out another time. I met her thug boyfriend in my driveway in the middle of the night with a gun strapped on my leg and scared myself instead. What was I becoming?

Within a year and a half, the relationship between Patti and me had deteriorated to resentment and blame. In her business, she stopped returning composers' calls and avoided her job at the studio. She had piles of overdue paperwork and contracts from her office stacked around the house. She chain-smoked, drank and had debilitating migraine headaches. She had a stream of losers that hung around the house, married girlfriends with lovers on the side, wives with cheating husbands. Patti had warned me at the start that she was a "throw me in the back seat and screw me" kind of girl. I think she said that as a come on, but it stuck in my head. I realized I didn't want to be with someone who had no respect for herself.

I holed up in a small office near the side entrance of the house where I ground out music for *Love Boat, Vegas* and television movies, and then I'd drive off to a studio for a couple days of recording.

My small office at Redwing

Evenings brought special problems. My stomach couldn't handle the spicy Italian food Patti cooked or brought in, and going out to a restaurant was off the menu because she'd drink her dinner, and I was embarrassed to be with her. I lost weight. I doubled up on my scoring assignments and told Rocky Moriana, the music editor and director of music for Spelling, that I'd take on more projects when he had a crunch. Working long into the night, I slept on the couch to avoid scenes in the bedroom.

Patti and I never found contentment living together. Between her daughter, her girlfriends, the hassles of moving and furnishing a house, and Carol's moving on to a new relationship, I felt no peace, no love and no comfort. I do know that Patti and I stopped having meaningful conversations. Before the night that we'd had sex in a seamy motel on Riverside Drive after Carol had locked me out of the house, we used to talk for hours, discussing philosophy, why marriages fail, the musicians' union troubles, the players and who was working for which composer. The film industry and its characters were a hot topic, along with Ronald Reagan's possible run for the presidency, especially since I'd met him a couple times. There was no end to the vast number of subjects we'd covered, but during our divorces and nesting activities in Tarzana, we lost interest in each other's views, and Patti thought I was too strict about every facet of our lives. I couldn't cope with new ideas and was rigid about protecting the property. She seemed as depressed as she'd been when I'd met her. She made fun of my paranoia and mocked my wariness about the world. I think she wanted life to be a constant party. On a stage with musicians hanging around, she sparkled with life, and she loved going out for drinks and dinner after a session. But life couldn't always be like that.

Though I'd updated a security system on the house, I kept a handgun close to the couch in case that lunatic boyfriend of Vicki's returned. On alert and safety minded, I signed up at the Black Karate Federation (BKF) and took a series of lessons with a couple of other composer friends. I also spent an hour a week shooting at a nearby gun range. My instructor, a former state trooper, managed the range and let me in at night after eleven o'clock when the gallery closed. After we finished with regular target practice, he'd open up all the lanes and teach me reflex shooting with moving targets.

My mother would never have understood what I'd done to my life. For once, we were of the same mind; I didn't understand either.

TWENTY

Strike Up the Band

In the spring of 1980 I'd just finished scoring an action/thriller film called *Night of the Juggler* for Columbia Pictures when Rocky Moriana called me for a meeting at the Aaron Spelling offices. The producers' association had notified him that the American Federation of Musicians (AFM) was threatening an industry-wide strike to procure residual payments for reruns of television shows.

"I've got two shows ready for music," Rocky told me. "I need *Love Boat* first and *Vegas* a week after. You'll have to record them before the musicians take a strike vote in July. They'll be the last two shows I can give you until this issue is settled, unless you want to write shows for me to record in London. I have studios there on hold."

I was shocked that there was even talk of a strike. Every musicians' strike I knew

Rocky Moriana, my boss
Aaron Spelling Productions

of resulted in a downturn of work. That was true in New York and Los Angeles. I'd never crossed a union picket line since I'd joined the union as a teenager. I certainly wouldn't cross one now.

Even writing under a recording deadline was unnerving. Constantly distracted by news of the strike, I found it difficult to concentrate on composing. Valium didn't help. A union board member called me to report that routine film negotiations had stalled over television residuals. That news was troubling because residuals had been off the table for years and for good reason.

In the 1970s after Cable Television was deregulated, the motion picture studios found ways to capture additional revenue from films after their initial runs in the movie houses. They sold the products to television networks and cable stations to be featured on programs like *ABC Sunday Night Movie.* They also packaged them for rental or sale to the public. At the time, the industry unions representing writers, directors, actors and musicians negotiated a share of those profits as deferred compensation for their members based on their percentage of work on the film. The change created a major income increase for those recording film music. But musicians were left out of the bargaining when the other three unions went on to negotiate additional payment for television series reruns. It wasn't an accidental slight. Producers had warned the AFM that they would never cave on television residuals for musicians because that would open the floodgates for other ancillary guilds like camera operators, film editors, set builders, costumers, makeup artists, sound engineers, etc. to band together for the same residuals, which would bankrupt the industry.

While investigating the background of our current proposed strike, I was told a group of musicians saw an opportunity to force industry to pay musicians residuals on TV film contracts by riding the coattails of a brewing actors' strike. I contacted a small group of influential musicians who agreed to meet secretly to discuss a strategy for avoiding a strike. As a long-time friend and supporter of the president of L.A.'s Local 47, I agreed to call Max Herman and used a speakerphone so the group could listen.

"Max, you've got to tell the membership the truth. Tell them this is a strike we're going to lose."

"Artie, I know, I know, but this is what the members want," Max insisted. "They're going to go for it, and President Fuentealba is willing to call the strike. He said we had a good chance of winning if we stand together with the actors who are fighting for higher wages in Pay TV."

"What the hell does Victor Fuentealba know about the film industry, Max? He's in New York, for God's sake. I don't give a damn if the members say they want to strike. It's up to you to convince them it will never result in residual payments for TV. Instead, it will cause serious consequences for future negotiations."

Max refused to call a meeting. Our group was convinced Max was being used.

The Los Angeles Local had been a thorn in the side of federation leadership for several years because work dues from West Coast film musicians funded a huge percentage of the Federation's operating costs. Because of our perceived clout, Local 47 made constant demands on the national union to negotiate better contracts with the producers to create an electronic media department, and this year, they demanded their share of television residual payments. Three of us set up a meeting with Victor to discuss the dangers of pursuing an unbelievable goal.

"I don't care if the strike fails," Victor bellowed. "All I know is I'm sick and tired of Local 47 trying to run the Federation. If you want to help your colleagues, get them off my back. Right now, I'm calling for the strike, and Max is supporting me."

There it was—a vendetta against the L.A. Local. Victor was getting even with us for all the demands we'd made on him and the Federation.

Victor, Max and several musicians garnered support from Ed Asner, President of Screen Actors Guild (SAG). The strike date was set to coincide with the screen and television actors' boycott of the Emmy Awards over their fight to increase scales for Pay TV. About 5,000 musicians and 60,000 actors went on strike against the Association of Motion Picture and Television Producers (AMPTP) on July 31, 1980.

After eleven weeks, actors reached their settlement, and with it, their support for musicians waned. SAG forced their membership to cross musician picket lines to avoid "breach of contract" and "secondary boycott" charges from the AMPTP. That's what happens when union members fail to read the small print in their contracts.

In my experience, you can't have a successful strike unless you shut down production at the studios. So, you need other guilds to stand with you, or you have to convince the Teamsters to back you; they've got the muscle to stop everything from moving materials to transporting animals and their trainers. If Teamsters step out, work stops. Various meetings were set up between musicians and Teamster leaders, but in the end, there were too few musicians to command that kind of support.

I had finished writing and recording both television shows for Rocky before the strike vote. When the vote passed, I had a sick feeling in my stomach about the music business. I thought it was a mistake to take on the industry over an issue that served up residuals for a small number of already busy musicians instead of fighting for a principle that would secure more work opportunities for all musicians.

Just as I'd feared, the strike would have far-reaching implications and irreversible consequences. It was a can of worms that affected everyone in the industry and pit musicians against one another. Symphony musicians who also worked the film studios were quick to raise their voices in support of the strike. A friend took issue with a cellist from the

L.A. Philharmonic who was picketing and wanted the union to hold out indefinitely until we got residuals.

"Sure," my friend told the cellist, "you still get your symphony paychecks, but those of us who work only the film studios have no money coming in."

Infighting between factions of the union heated up as the strike dragged on and depleted our strike fund. When the recording studios shut down, ancillary businesses and personnel felt the sting of the strike too. Three cartage companies that delivered musical instruments to sessions faced serious financial problems. Musicians tried to keep their spirits high by donating performances to support the strike. A group called The Striking Harp Band played a concert to raise funds for their cartage company.

I was sad to see a steady line of musicians taking time out from picket lines to fill out loan papers at Local 47's credit union. My business manager sent me an envelope of documents with sticky flags indicating where I should sign to open a line of credit so he could keep up with my expenses. Everyone in the music industry was in trouble. Warner Studios Music Department had closed its doors, and Patti was lurking around the house all day in her nightgown.

During a brainstorming session with our group, I got a message from a friend at the union to call a copyist, JoAnn Johnson, who had a small music service and also worked at Disney Studios. She told me she had discovered where Disney and her composer clients were recording in Europe. She also knew of several nonunion sessions that were being held at night in Los Angeles. Many players had no idea their colleagues were doing scab work; she thought this information might change the course of the strike.

By November, with no further negotiations scheduled between our union and the producers, I talked JoAnn into coming to a Thursday night meeting at the local to inform the officers and board members that our strike was ineffective and had not shut down any film music recordings. She agreed to share her research but asked for protection because she had been labeled a strikebreaker for refusing to go on the picket lines. I told her I'd also refused to picket and that Bob Bornstein, a well-known copyist from Paramount, would be sharing information on Lorimar Productions at the meeting. I promised she'd be safe and that Bob and I would walk her to her car.

What I didn't know until my friend at the union mentioned it was that JoAnn had recently sued Local 47 through the National Labor Relations Board (NLRB) for suspending a member of her staff for nonpayment of work dues. During the fifties, Local 47 had devised a sure way to collect work tax from its members by putting a clause in employer contracts demanding that musicians' earnings be sent to the union. Musicians had to stand in lines at the Hollywood union hall and pay the 4 percent work tax before the union would release their checks. Up to this point, all efforts to change the policy had failed.

JoAnn filed charges against the union for coercing and restraining the rights of musicians under section 7 of the Labor Relations Act. The judge had ruled against the union and ordered it to mail checks to members and bill them monthly for the tax. Because the NLRB had taken her case, JoAnn had access to their law library and help from a lawyer assigned to her to research union regulations and labor practices. While she was there, she also researched cases in which members had compelled union leaders to abandon a strike by calling for interim strike votes. I thought this was gutsy, and I was astonished by the amount of research she'd done and what she'd uncovered.

I told our group that the procedure might work to bypass our union leadership. First though, we'd have to educate our local board and enough union members about the hopelessness of the strike, and then demand a meeting.

On Thursday, I showed up at the union board meeting after a karate session, dressed in torn blue jeans, tennis shoes and a bright blue jacket from the Black Karate Federation with my name on it. Although she didn't say so at the time, JoAnn thought I looked like a thug and walked like a gang member. Luckily, Bob assured her I was okay, and the board members greeted me like an old pal. The three of us identified the companies that were recording in Europe and Los Angeles. The board informed us that actors were now crossing our picket lines and that the New York Musicians' Local 802 had told its members to take all film-recording calls, falsely claiming the strike involved only the West Coast musicians. We were doomed.

The gamble with a strike is that you teach the bosses how to get the product they need from another source. It may not be as good, and it's bloody inconvenient, but each time it gets easier for them, and the product gets better. Our livelihood was on the line, and we risked the possibility of a shutout from producers. As the meeting continued, tension and anger mounted, but the current was shifting as the board grasped the dire situation. I felt we'd reached a turning point that might put us all back to work.

When we left that night about nine thirty, Bob and I flanked JoAnn as we walked her out of the union building. I assured her she was safe. She looked at me like I was nuts, but I pointed to a red van across the street. Two black guys and one white guy got out and walked toward us. They were all off-duty cops who were friends of mine from the karate federation. JoAnn turned to Bob and said, "I guess I can trust Artie Kane's word."

Max finally called a meeting for all members working on film contracts. More than six hundred angry musicians showed up Saturday morning at the union hall. Five of them were my friends from the police department, posing as musicians, prepared to keep the peace. Several people took turns at the microphone, but only one woman spoke. JoAnn was timid but told them what she had discovered.

Then one prominent violinist yelled, "Strike breaker," and a roar shook the room. JoAnn took the microphone off the stand and walked to her accuser. "Would you like to say that into the mic, Paul?"

Silence ruled the room. I took the mic from her and said, "Now let her talk. She's got information that can help us."

JoAnn named the television shows that were recording in New York and Europe, gave the recording dates and identified the studios used. She said she'd been given a list of our own members who were recording nonunion sessions at night in Los Angeles. That shut everybody up. By the time the meeting was over, most everyone wanted to end the strike. JoAnn told them we could demand another vote right then and force our leadership to abandon the strike and that the NLRB would support us.

Victor Fuentealba had successfully taught our local to stay out of his way. He had kept the strike going for five and a half months and claimed it benefited the members by showing producers we were tough. History shows the opposite and remembers the strike as ill-conceived. Subsequent film negotiations saw the end of premium pay for weekend work and lower compensation for longer hours, plus a poor deal for Pay TV. We had no power, and the producers knew it. Somehow, Victor managed to keep his job.

Two years later, Max asked JoAnn to run on his ticket for the local board. She agreed and served two years for the local and two years for the Recording Musician's Association. She learned how to get her point across.

The only good thing about the strike was that I met JoAnn. At the time, I had no inkling of how that meeting would change my life.

By January 15, 1981, we had been without work and pay for 167 days. With the strike over, we scrambled for any work that surfaced, competing for a smaller number of jobs because much of the product had gone overseas and because losers never fully recover from a strike.

TWENTY-ONE

A Time for Love

As studio music departments re-opened for business and musicians began returning to recording sessions, bruises faded and wounds healed. Many projects had been shelved or rescheduled for the next season, but some still had to be finished before the summer hiatus.

Back at Fox Studios, Lionel Newman complained to me about finding a suitable replacement for his longtime librarian who had put in for retirement during the strike. His departure left the library without a supervisor or a music prep office. I had an idea that JoAnn might be interested in the position if she could make the right deal.

"I know someone who could run the department for you," I told him.

"Yeah, and how would you know a librarian?" he asked. "Who is it?"

"JoAnn Johnson."

"I can't have a girl do that kind of work. Do you know how heavy all that paper is? She'd have to carry bundles of it from the library to the stage. Is she even a copyist, and does she know how to notate music?"

JoAnn

"This girl can carry all your bundles of music," I guaranteed. "And yes, she's been a copyist at Disney for five years."

After I gave him JoAnn's qualifications and history, he arranged to interview her. He hired her on the spot.

JoAnn was the best thing that happened to Lionel and his music department. Over the next seven years before he retired, Lionel was her champion, and she built a fine music library for him, unearthing and cataloguing many film scores that otherwise might have been lost. Lionel had made her a deal that included bringing her own clients into the Fox facility. She could hire as many copyists/librarians as she needed as long as Fox Studio shows got first consideration. Her own business flourished and her clientele grew. I couldn't tell if Lionel went the extra mile to make that deal as a favor to me or if he wanted to show up his brother over at Paramount. There was a lot of competition in the Newman family. It turned out JoAnn had done her homework. She asked Lionel for the same deal his brother had made with the librarian at Paramount. JoAnn thanked me for the recommendation, but she got the job on her own credentials and experience. She was well known for her ability to listen to a recording and notate the music. For instance, she had worked on *The Partridge Family* show, writing out the music as David Cassidy and the group made up the songs.

JoAnn's and my relationship was affable but professional. I stopped by the Fox library one day to pick up work she'd done for me. She had a capable and talented staff of copyists and librarians. I noticed their notation had the look of calligraphy, well-spaced and easy for musicians to sight-read. JoAnn's reorganization of the library made everything accessible. After a friendly chat, I knew that my instincts to recommend her to Lionel had been right.

A few months later, I had a root canal that wiped me out. I was at home in a lot of pain, squirming in an uncomfortable wingback chair and holding an ice pack against my cheek. Patti sat across from me, on the couch, badgering me about our relationship. She yapped constantly while I was trying to find a comfortable position and deal with the pain in my mouth. I escaped into my office, looked up JoAnn's number and dialed.

"I don't know where you live," I said when she answered, "but I just had a root canal and need a quiet place to sit with an ice bag. Are you home, and could I come over?"

"Oh sure," she said, and gave me directions to her house.

She lived in a cottage—one of ten around a small park in a dicey area of the San Fernando Valley. An auto body shop and a Norm's Restaurant lined the main street, but down a hidden driveway was a pocket of pulchritude that left the city behind. JoAnn answered the door, took one look at me and guided me to a couch in a wood-paneled living room. She gave me a pillow, an ice bag and a towel, plus a glass of water with a straw. I drifted in and out of sleep over a couple of hours while she worked on music for a client. We talked a little, and when I felt better, I thanked her and left.

As I pulled out of her driveway onto the street, Patti pulled alongside my car. Aghast, I slammed on the brakes. She lowered her window and sneered, "I know where you've been, and I know what you're doing."

In my mind, Patti's and my relationship was over. I drove home and locked myself in my studio for the night.

I could no longer live with Patti and her troubled family: the substance-abusing daughter, the suffering mother, the financially needy brother. I'd been giving money toward all their living expenses to the point that I'd elevated their lifestyles to middle class.

Within a couple of weeks, I rented an apartment nearby, month-to-month, and packed a suitcase with a few clothes and sundries, including my ample supply of Valium and Dilantin. I took music paper, video equipment, an electronic keyboard and anything else I needed for composing with me. I'm not sure how I worked during this time, but the music and drugs kept me going, and I continued to record.

Shortly after I moved out, a neighbor on Redwing tracked me down through the musicians' call service and told me a Mayflower moving van was camped in front of my house, and the crew was loading up furniture. I raced over and discovered an empty house except for my piano, three chairs, a bed and TV, some file cabinets and my desk. I called my attorney, Doug Smithers, who advised that someone had to live in the house for me to retain the insurance. I offered the house to my karate instructor and his wife. They moved in and took care of the place for several months.

Work saved my bank account and me during this time. It provided stability in my life, so I took every project my agent and ex-wife, Carol, found for me.

One day while recording at Fox, I stopped by to have lunch with Lionel, but he had a screening, so I asked if I could take his librarian to lunch.

"No, I don't think that's a good idea. She's a very nice person, and I don't want her corrupted by you," he said, a grin spreading across his face. He called the library and asked JoAnn to come up to his office, and then he sent us off to the executive dining room at the Fox commissary.

Two hours later, I walked JoAnn back to the library. Her crew had gone for the day. She showed me scores she had found wrapped in brown paper packages jammed into shelving too small to hold the sheet music flat. Rodgers and Hammerstein's *State Fair*, *South Pacific*, and *The Sound of Music* were spread across library desks with heavy film cans pressing out the creases in the paper. She had a reverence when handling them, and her eyes sparkled as she explained her new catalogue system. Sitting side by side on a production table, I turned and kissed her. She didn't object or shrink or look shy. She smiled and looked directly into my eyes. It seemed like minutes before we looked away.

I was enthralled. I asked to see her again. She agreed. That afternoon we took a long drive along the Malibu Coast and stopped to watch the waves pound the shore like our hearts pounded as we stood close together.

Over the next six weeks, we lunched at out-of-the-way bistros in Beverly Hills or at the Santa Monica Pier. I borrowed a friend's beach house for lazy afternoons on weekends. One afternoon, I played Johnny Mandel's song "A Time for Love" on a Fender Rhodes keyboard that was in the house. It was the first impromptu piece I had ever played for any woman, but it felt right for JoAnn. Maybe it was because she was a superb musician, and I sensed she would appreciate the way I played the song. Something was different and special about this relationship. I knew it, and I felt it in my heart. The tension and panic I'd suffered with Patti was gone, and I no longer counted the minutes until I could down another pill.

JoAnn loved the ocean and owned a 34-foot Columbia sloop. She was undemanding, understanding and unbothered by my past. She'd never been married, never lived with anyone and had an opinion about everything, which sparked interesting conversations. She was the bright spot in my unsettled life of relationships.

By this time, Carol had forgiven me. She was seriously involved with a nice man, an optometrist with a terrific sense of humor, whom she planned to marry. She was still my agent. We had patched up our professional relationship and our friendship months before. When I told her I was sort of dating JoAnn, Carol's interest in the details was as addictive as her attachment to her daily soap operas.

In September of 1981, JoAnn planned a trip to Minneapolis with her mother and cousin to celebrate her grandmother's ninetieth birthday. I asked if I could go along. I told her I would buy the plane tickets, but she informed me she'd already purchased her three tickets and would have her travel agent get mine. I mentioned I traveled first class. She said her tickets were already first class. I said I'd investigate hotels. She said the party would be held in a private dining room at the Sheraton Ritz, and we should stay there. I said I would take care of it.

I booked a two-bedroom suite for her mother and cousin and the presidential suite for us, which the hotel had created twenty years earlier for President and Mrs. Kennedy, though they never stayed there. The presidential seal remained in the center of the living room carpet, along with a roomful of French antique furniture, plus a Steinway grand piano that I played for JoAnn using the soft pedal. Such elegance seemed possible only in a country villa, but the Sheraton had created the special accommodation on the top floor of the hotel overlooking the city and the Mississippi River. Bedroom suites with separate entrances were situated on either end of the living and dining room—a good show of propriety for JoAnn's mother.

When room service delivered breakfast on our first morning, I got on my knees in front of the seal and asked JoAnn, "Will you marry me?"

"Yes, I will, but I don't cook."

"I'll hire a chef," I promised.

"Okay. When and where shall we plan it?"

"On the way back? We could stop in Vegas."

"No way," she said. "I'm 38; I've never been married. I want something special like a small wedding on a beautiful yacht."

When she told her wise and clever grandmother—the greatest influence in her life—that she had met the right person to marry, the matriarch asked, "What did you catch, my dear?"

"A musical gem," she answered.

She told her steeped-in-Catholicism family that I'd been married before; they had the good manners not to ask how many times.

We picked December 5—enough time to invite family and friends—and we booked a vintage 80-foot yacht for our day. I paid off the lease on my apartment and moved into JoAnn's tiny one bedroom cottage. In spite of her German shepherd and a feisty pet squirrel named Julius, it was the most peaceful place I'd been during the last three years.

FIRST THINGS FIRST: the Redwing house and the leased BMW were costing me a fortune. My lawyer, Doug Smithers, had Patti sign papers to list the house. She argued. He said, "Either allow the property to be listed with a real estate agent, or make the mortgage payments yourself." She signed.

Since Patti had driven off with the BMW, I had to continue paying the lease or cough up $30,000 to buy it. I had to get the car back. Through friends, I discovered where Patti was living and called one of my karate friends to help. We found the car parked on the street in front of her new boyfriend's house. The street was quiet at seven thirty on a Saturday morning. No one noticed my car pull up to the curb across the street. My friend got out, took my set of car keys, ran toward the BMW, unlocked the driver's door and slid behind the wheel. He started the car as the boyfriend's front door swung open. Patti flew out and ran toward the BMW, but it screeched away from the curb and raced down the street. Then she recognized my car and ran toward me. I pulled away and gunned the motor.

It still cost a bundle to pay off the lease early and turn in the car, but it was one more severed tie in that poisonous relationship. Before the Redwing house went on the market, Doug offered Patti double her investment in the house plus half the profits. She wanted more, including all the furniture and appliances I'd bought for the house.

A week after repossessing the BMW, I received a call from my business manager, Harold Plant, to come into his office. When I got there, Harold, the always calm, well-mannered accountant and head of the firm, looked perturbed, and said, in a tone I'd never heard, "Sit down Artie."

He told me that Patti had hired an attorney and filed a palimony suit against me in the Superior Court of California, with thirteen complaints consisting of partition of personal and real property, breach of contract, infliction of emotional stress and fraud. They were seeking damages over $2 million and more to be determined. He handed me the 38-page document of the filing. I think I sat with my mouth open until Harold pointed to the part where she asked for a piece of my performance royalties on the music I'd written during the time we'd lived together. It was then I felt a rage boil up in me.

Harold put his hand on my shoulder, said he'd been researching attorneys for me and had one in mind.

What a load of crap! How could I tell JoAnn about this? She surely wouldn't want to marry me now. Feeling sick and depressed, I arrived later that day at JoAnn's and overheard her on the phone with her mother.

"Mom, please stop crying. The Catholic Church is not going to forbid you to attend your daughter's wedding. This is going to be my day, and no church rules are going to spoil it. There will be a civil ceremony with a superior court judge joining Artie and me in marriage. I want you and Dad to be a part of it, but you must go see a priest about your concerns so you'll be able to enjoy the day and celebrate with us."

After today, I thought, she won't have to worry about her parents coming to our wedding. As soon as she hung up, I told her about the lawsuit. "Are you kidding me?" she asked.

"No honey, it's true. That's what Harold wanted to see me about today."

"Let me see that." She held out her hand for the complaint and paged through it, stopping occasionally to mutter an obscenity or exclaim about the damages sought.

"Let's not worry about this now. After we're married, she'll have two of us to fight. She's not going to get anything more than half the profits from the sale of the house. What she's demanding is utterly ridiculous for a two-year relationship where she worked full time. Michelle Triola didn't work and still didn't get money from Lee Marvin even after their five-year cohabitation."

"Does that mean you'll still marry me?" I asked sheepishly.

"Not only am I going to marry you, I'm going to protect you from that woman."

I grabbed her; we hugged … for a long time.

JoAnn's mother called two days later to share her joy and relief over the good news she'd received while meeting with the priest. JoAnn had gambled that a reasonable member of the clergy would encourage her parents to rejoice in their daughter's marriage. The priest told them their worries were unfounded, that they should support their daughter and enjoy the occasion. We booked a hotel room for them at the marina near the yacht so they wouldn't have to drive back and forth from Orange County in one day.

Marvin Hamlisch, a close friend of JoAnn's since 1971 when she worked for him on Walter Matthau's film *Kotch,* was less than joyful about her plans to marry me. She had called Marvin months earlier and told him, "I've met a great guy. He can afford me. We had lunch and an actual dinner date at a Malibu restaurant. You'd like him, and he's a wonderful musician."

Marvin, as usual, suspicious and protective of her, grilled her with questions. When she hinted that her new friend was a well-known studio pianist, he said, "Not Artie Kane, I hope."

"What do you mean by that?" she challenged.

"Don't you know his history or what he did to my agent, Carol Faith?"

After a brief warning about my past, he cautioned, "You seem determined to continue the relationship, but be careful and just have fun dating him."

As our wedding day neared, I walked in on a tearful phone conversation between JoAnn and Marvin. She said, "Artie makes me happy whenever we're together. It's more happiness than I've had in years and if it only lasts six months, it's worth it to me. Besides, there's no guarantee how long any of us have. I could die next week, but I'll be happy." She was silent for a minute, and then said, "Forget I called. You're uninvited to my wedding." She hung up and melted into tears.

I sat down next to her, held her in my arms, and wondered how did I get so lucky? Nothing stopped this girl from confronting a problem head-on. I wanted to call Marvin and tell him how he'd hurt her, but for once, I knew I should stay out of it. They didn't communicate after that and Marvin stopped using her as his copyist, which hurt her worse. In 1982 Marvin composed the music for *Sophie's Choice,* for which he received an Oscar nomination. JoAnn suffered over the loss of her friend and client even more when he didn't respond to her note of congratulations. However, on the day of our first anniversary, three large boxes arrived from Cartier in New York. They contained sets of the finest crystal water goblets, champagne flutes and hock wine glasses accompanied by Marvin's note of apology and a request for forgiveness.

Although Marvin didn't drink, he suggested, "How about, let's toast to the future?" That gesture renewed his and JoAnn's friendship, and I knew I'd be in trouble with him if I ever hurt her. Kidding on the square, he joked that losing a friend was one thing, but the loss of the only person he trusted to do his music transcriptions was unbearable. Seven years and myriad projects later, he invited music producer Brooks Arthur and his wife and the two of us to dinner at Tony Roma's to meet his bride-to-be and invite us to their wedding. For more than thirty years, Marvin was JoAnn's faithful client and a treasured friend to both of us.

JoAnn is a problem solver. She always finds a way to negotiate her position, leaving the other party smiling. This included a conference she had with my business manager over the pre-nup he advised me to have her sign to protect my assets.

Her meeting with Harold, who was the personification of a continental gentleman, went like this: "Thank you for looking out for me, Mr. Plant," JoAnn said. "I assume this document is for my protection, and though I realize Artie has a risky history, I don't want to start our marriage by not trusting him." She tore the agreement in half and handed it back to him with a check. "Here is payment for my half of the rent on the *Mauretania* yacht and for half the cost of our wedding. I'll let Artie pay the charges for our Hawaiian honeymoon, where I'm sure he plans to take advantage of me." Harold's eyebrows raised and a small smile lifted the corners of his mouth.

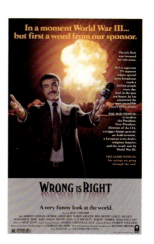

With all this going on, I received a call from Richard Brooks, the director I'd worked for on *Looking for Mr. Goodbar*. He asked if I was available to score *Wrong is Right* starring Katharine Ross and Sean Connery.

Sure, why not, I thought. The music had to record in early December. We couldn't change our wedding date, but we moved our trip to Hawaii to the tenth so I could finish scoring the picture before we left.

Meanwhile, we took Harold's advice and hired David Kagon, Lee Marvin's attorney. Patti had hired the short, man-eating attorney Joan C. Bell. The first order of business was a hearing about the BMW scheduled for

David Kagon,
my fabulous attorney

December, two days before the wedding. Despite the fact that Michelle Triola had failed to win any compensation in her complaint against Lee Marvin, the legal principle of palimony became grounds for many cases of monetary suits involving celebrities and their scorned lovers. David asked me the big question: Had I ever planned to marry Patti?

"David, I've married seven women already. Don't you think I would have married Patti by now if that had been my plan?"

"Point taken," David said. "Now go write the music for your movie, and have a fine wedding and honeymoon. I'll advise Ms. Bell and her client that the BMW has been paid off and sold. We'll get on with the rest of this suit after the holidays when you return and get settled."

In a whirlwind of activity, JoAnn sold her boat. We bought a new, bigger boat and named it *Noteworthy*. We rented a house, and, the day before our wedding, I stopped at Lionel Newman's office at Fox Studio and gave him a pass so he and his wife could drive into the marina and park next to the wedding yacht.

Noteworthy, 47-foot cutter-rigged sloop

With a sly look in his eye, Lionel said, "I have something for your car, too, and I'll bring extras to give out at your wedding tomorrow."

He handed me a bumper sticker that read: "Honk if you've been married to Artie Kane."

"You can't do this," I objected. "JoAnn has a great sense of humor, but her parents will be there, and they have no idea how many times I've been married."

Thwarted yet determined, Lionel distributed the bumper stickers later to friends and colleagues who remind me about them even today.

JoAnn and I married on December 5 and were celebrated by forty friends as we sailed on the *Mauretania* around Marina Del Rey. At the breakwater, morning fog lifted as we pledged our love to each other. When nerves drained the color from my face, my friend Mason steadied me with his hand, but JoAnn's smile gave me a strength and resolve I'd never known. That evening we had dinner with her mom and dad and dropped them at their hotel.

On December 5th, 1981, I married JoAnn

Our wedding yacht: the *Mauretania*

Even though we'd been living together for more than a month, the excitement of our wedding night was not lost on me. I waited in bed for what seemed a long time. I called out to ask if she was all right. She said she was fine. I'd already discovered she didn't wear makeup and was thrilled she looked the same in the morning as she did the night before.

There was no painting on or removing a plaster disguise. She didn't wear pajamas either. So what could be taking so long, I wondered. When the bathroom door opened, JoAnn entered the room like Loretta Young in a long, white gown and a beautiful smile.

"Uh … What is that?" I hesitated.

"It's my wedding negligee," she announced. I bought it at Neiman Marcus just for tonight. It's hand painted silk."

"It … it's beautiful," I stammered, "but please take it off, honey; I hardly recognize you."

She didn't take it along on our honeymoon, but she made me pay for it. She takes it out occasionally to remind me how boorish I was on that sacred night.

Monday, it was back to work for both of us. I finished the recordings for Richard's movie. JoAnn made sure her office would function while we were away. Then, we set off for Hawaii, unaware that my seventh wife and her new husband would be joining us.

TWENTY-TWO

Blue Hawaii

Checking bags at the airport, I heard a familiar voice call my name. When I looked up, Carol, my ex-wife but still agent, was walking toward JoAnn and me.

"What are you doing here?" I asked.

"We're going to Hawaii for our honeymoon," she said before introducing her new husband, Norman Tetef.

We all shook hands and shifted back and forth on our feet until a glint in Carol's eye foretold of some amusement she was about to impart.

"When Norm and I first caught sight of you," she said, "I told him, 'Don't worry, honey; we won't have to talk to them on the flight. They'll be in first class.'" Carol had lost none of her wit and was quick as ever with the barbs.

JoAnn and I were flabbergasted when we discovered they were on our same flight to Oahu, our same flight to the Big Island, and were staying at our same resort for the same number of days.

"I thought you got married a few months ago," I accused.

"We did, but we couldn't get away until now. Norman's an optometrist, remember? He had months of appointments booked in advance. This was our first chance to leave."

"Why didn't you say something at the recording sessions last week when I told you I had to finish the film before JoAnn and I could leave on our honeymoon?"

"You didn't mention a date," she countered, "and why would I think you'd take JoAnn to the same resort you took me to for our honeymoon?"

"Ouch." We had a good gallows laugh, and it was obvious we'd be having an interesting ten days in Hawaii.

While Norman and JoAnn got to know each other in the airport lounge, Carol took me aside to ask about the threats against JoAnn I had heard about and previously shared with Carol.

"JoAnn doesn't know about those," I explained, "but she did hear the rumor that Patti and her boyfriend had a party and burned a blonde doll in a wedding dress in effigy."

Shaking her head and dropping her voice in a rare serious moment for Carol, she asked, "What's the matter with those people?"

"I don't know, but I arranged for three cops to be at the wedding, and two of them are here at the airport with us now, but JoAnn doesn't know that."

Carol wanted to know how I had learned about the threats, so I explained that my friend Steve Cowdrey had been setting up my old sound system for Patti when he overheard her talking with her new boyfriend. Apparently, the boyfriend had connections to unsavory types from Las Vegas who could be hired to scare people. After that information had leaked out, I wrote a letter to my attorney naming people to investigate if anything happened to JoAnn and me.

It seemed surreal to be talking with my ex-wife about my ex-girlfriend while embarking on my honeymoon with my new wife.

As we rejoined our mates in the lounge, Carol said, "Well, you won't have to worry about it once we're at the Mauna Kea. Let's at least have dinner. And by the way, my parents are coming over to spend a few days with us."

"Geeze," I exclaimed, dreading the thought of seeing them. "Do they hate me?"

"Oh no, not at all. They are so happy to have you out of the family. They love Norman."

So it went. We shared our limo to the resort, had dinner together, and promised to meet on the beach the next day. On the third morning, after JoAnn and I had our favorite breakfast of papayas, spinach omelets and coffee, JoAnn answered a knock at our door. There stood Abe, Carol's father, with his ear on a glass pressed against our door. His wife, Adele, stood a few steps back laughing into a handkerchief.

Abe put out his hand and said, "I hope I didn't disturb you newlyweds. I'm Carol's father, and you must be JoAnn."

Carol and Norman appeared from behind a potted palm tree on the veranda near our door, and then we all laughed until tears ran down JoAnn's cheeks. Later, on the beach, Carol motioned for me to come over to their cabana. She showed me a syndicated cartoon drawing that ran in many daily newspapers. Titled "Love is …" The caption read: "Love is … telling her she's the eighth wonder of the world."

All excited, Carol said, "JoAnn's such a good sport. Don't you think this would be a great personalized license plate for her car? You know … your eighth wife?" she winked. Carol seemed to find humor in most every circumstance.

I took the paper back to JoAnn and told her Carol's idea, which she loved. Thirty-five years later, her license still reads "8TH1DER."

Surprisingly, I was calm and relaxed on our honeymoon, and

A shared honeymoon on the Big Island: JoAnn, Artie, Norm and Carol

I enjoyed touring the Big Island and showing JoAnn the sights. The friendship we began with my seventh ex-wife, her husband, and her parents endured for many years. Carol's father always referred to JoAnn as his adopted daughter-in-law.

Our time away from Los Angeles was a welcome break from work schedules and decisions about the palimony suit, which we thought would gradually fade away. We were in better emotional health when we returned and moved into our rental house—a dated, large family home in a nice neighborhood, surrounded by overgrown gardens. It had a writing room that suited my desk, video equipment and studio piano. My red Doberman and JoAnn's German shepherd got along famously, and Julius, her pet squirrel, loved his sunny spot on the garden patio. We never listed our home address anywhere, and we never used the post office. All mail—checks, bills, etc.—was sent to our business office, Plant-Cohen. We never invited anyone over except JoAnn's parents. Since I no longer heard talk about threats, I felt comfortable on the property. The location was convenient to Fox Studios where JoAnn kept a grueling schedule between the demands of Lionel's music department and her own clients.

Often, she would get up early to make a 4:30 a.m. music pickup. One of her clients would leave his music for her to pick up in his backyard barbecue. The first time I learned of this arrangement, I followed JoAnn in my car to be sure she was all right. I worried about her sneaking around on someone's patio in the dark, but she assured me she'd been doing the same thing for two other clients for years. Music composers are notorious for waiting until the last minute, so after the pickup, JoAnn would assemble a crew of ten copyists who would extract, transpose and write out the orchestra parts for each instrument, print it all up and deliver it for a 9:00 a.m. recording session.

After the holidays, we turned our attention to our new sailboat.

JoAnn had learned to sail as a kid on lakes in Minnesota. She made me sign up for sailing lessons at the California Yacht Club on a 27-foot Soling that had a centerboard keel. She said nothing was better for learning about wind direction than a center-boarder. Although she was an experienced sailor, she went through the course with me. If I was going to be the captain and helmsman of *Noteworthy,* our forty-seven-foot cutter-rigged sailboat, she said I had to start on a small boat that didn't take twenty minutes to come about. Navigation was her bailiwick, which spared me learning algebra and geometry, subjects I had skipped in school. The best lesson I ever learned during the course was the man overboard procedure: If a man goes overboard, you never go in after him because then you have two men overboard.

"Stay in the boat," the instructor repeated ad nauseam. I wish I'd known this earlier in life. It would have spared me from trying to rescue every beautiful woman I met who suffered from depression, divorce, drinking or some other problem.

April approached, and as depositions for the lawsuit were scheduled, sailing took a back seat. I was the first to give my deposition, and I went reluctantly and nervously. In that small room with the rectangular table and hard wooden chairs, I felt like a condemned man, but for once, I followed my lawyer's advice. I sat stone-faced and answered Patti's lawyer, Ms. Bell's questions, with a yes, no or I don't recall; I didn't elaborate. Despite an extra Valium, my insides crawled with anger, yet outside I showed little emotion, which I knew gnawed at Ms. Bell.

Short and stubby, she belabored the issues: Did I promise to marry the plaintiff? Did I tell her we would share everything as if we were married? Did I require the plaintiff to use my business managers to manage her assets and income and place them in joint accounts? Did I buy her a car for her birthday and then take it away? On and on she went. My answers to all of these questions were negative.

Ms. Bell spent a long time trying to establish that I had controlled Patti's income and comingled our funds. This was so far-fetched that for a moment, I thought she was joking. Somehow, I maintained an affectless demeanor, which irritated Ms. Bell, so she adopted a sarcastic tone, yammered on about my intentional infliction of emotional distress on Patti and accused me of fraud. In the end, when she claimed I owed half of my music royalties to Patti, sweat began to dribble down my sideburns.

It was demeaning and degrading to hear someone accuse me of lying, stealing and inflicting pain and co-opting Patti's funds for my own purposes; however, I was certain that my business manager, Harold Plant, would set the record straight during his deposition. His reputation for recordkeeping was spotless.

Three days later, Patti had her turn in the hot seat. I thought it would provide me a measure of retaliation. It didn't. Instead, I felt dirty, as if I were in a mud bath without a rinse cycle. My lawyer, David Kagon, pulled no punches. His questions were direct, and he asked them until he got the answer he wanted. It took two days for her to claim I'd proposed to her on her thirty-eighth birthday and told her we would get married on her fortieth birthday.

I've never waited two years for anything except a divorce.

At my business manager's deposition in May, Harold produced his accounting ledgers as evidence, confirming the complete separation of funds between Patti and me. The financial statements indicated I'd paid 95 percent of all the bills for the house and furniture, plus all our living expenses, including those related to her daughter's arrests and legal troubles. Harold highlighted moving costs and monthly rent that I'd paid for her mother's new apartment. He showed loans I'd made to Patti's brother that he never repaid. He produced doctors' bills for Patti and her daughter that I'd paid with funds from my mother's estate. Meanwhile, for the two years we lived together, Patti's money was held in interest-bearing money market accounts, in her name only.

Never satisfied, Ms. Joan Bell demanded a continuation of Harold's deposition into June so that her tax attorneys could examine two years of my tax returns, pension investments and financial records, including my residual and royalty payments. Patti wanted a share in my royalties. She claimed that during our relationship her contacts in the industry and recommendations at Warner Brothers had advanced my career.

A week prior to the deposition, Ms. Bell hired two accountants and a tax attorney to camp out at the Plant-Cohen offices where they ransacked my tax returns and monthly statements. Some of JoAnn's business files were housed in the same file cabinets. Our very precise and protective bookkeeper, Bea Miller, caught Patti paging through some of JoAnn's records and had a fit. Ms. Bell quickly ushered her client into the waiting room, but the offense had been committed. We didn't know it at the time, but that purposeful blunder became important later in the case.

I continued to worry that the lawsuit would ruin JoAnn's and my relationship, but somehow we didn't dwell on the case. We were too busy, working and sailing, to let it bog us down. Admittedly, though, a big weight lifted when an offer came in on the Redwing house. It sold for half again its worth, and a sizable chunk of change was put into interest-bearing trust accounts, set up per the attorneys' insistence, including accounts for themselves. Cha-ching, cha-ching, cha-ching went the cash register, but as long as the palimony suit dragged on, we couldn't touch any of it.

We consoled ourselves on our sailboat. Our sailing guru, Bobby Harris, who took care of *Noteworthy*, introduced us to a shipwright who remodeled the forward cabin to a half berth and created an alcove where I could work and compose music for my television show assignments. A master woodworker, he built Honduras mahogany cabinets to hold my VHS player and monitor, a lift-top desk to store all my equipment and paper safely, plus a pull-out shelf that held my electronic, four-octave keyboard. When he finished, the interior looked as if it had always been fitted that way.

Most Wednesdays, during the summer hiatus in television, JoAnn could sneak out of the studio early. We'd struggle through rush hour traffic to Marina Del Rey where *Noteworthy* took up a fifty-foot slip on the main channel. We'd have an evening sail followed by dinner at the Captain's Table. The rest of the week, we'd work like crazy until the weekend when friends would join us sailing and for great meals at the Lobster House or other fine eateries at the marina. After a few months, though, battling the traffic got old. The 405 freeway morphed into a parking lot no matter which direction or day of the week we traveled. We began a search for a house closer to the boat.

The line producer on *Love Boat,* Henry Coleman, owned a home and other properties in the Venice Canals five minutes from our boat. He arranged showings of newly built homes for us to tour. Henry wanted to see a rebirth of the original charm of the man-made waterways built during the early 1900s. Dotted with super high-end, two-and-a-half story, beautifully landscaped beach dwellings, the canals showed promise for a serious restoration project. We were enthralled with the designs and construction of the homes as well as the serenity of living on the waterways. With the palimony suit looming, however, our finances were as tight as a close-hauled jib; our house hunting was a pipe dream.

In August, our attorney, David Kagon, notified us that a settlement offer had arrived. Because the depositions disclosed that funds and earnings had been kept separate, we were confident Patti's wings had been clipped. We also thought Patti would want to settle the lawsuit and gain access to her share of the trust accounts so she and her new boyfriend could get on with their lives. Not so.

I sat in David's office and listened to Patti's new demands. She wanted half of the proceeds from the sale of the house and half the interest from the trust accounts, with no consideration of the amounts put down by either party. I was to pay all taxes on the proceeds of the sale as well as Patti's individual taxes and penalties because she had been too distraught to pay them when due. The Compromise and Settlement Agreement stated that Patti would keep all furnishings and appliances from the Redwing house, which were currently in storage under her control. I was to pay for a new BMW and deliver it to her with her personalized license plate.

When I heard her final demand, my equilibrium slipped, and for the first time I thought I could become violent—not with Patti, but her lawyer. As nuts as Patti was, I knew it was Ms. Bell who had convinced her that I'd purposely inflicted pain and emotional distress on her. How? By buying all that furniture to make her feel guilty? By financially supporting her family members, causing her a feeling of helplessness? By giving her gifts to make her feel beholden to me so I could destroy her with my generosity? They wanted another $100,000 plus legal fees just for the emotional damage I'd supposedly caused this woman. That's a lot of money now, even more so back then in 1982.

I could feel heat rising in my neck. I felt nauseated. My ears burned. I realized I was holding my breath.

David looked alarmed. "Artie, are you all right? Your face is beet red."

I heard David's voice, but I couldn't answer him until I exhaled. I thought my head would burst open. My heart was thumping and my lunch was backing up.

"David, I want this lawsuit settled and I don't care what it costs as long as JoAnn and I are rid of these lowlifes. Make them a counter offer, and tell them Patti can have half of all the proceeds from the house sale. I will indemnify her against all tax consequences and pay her taxes. She can have all the furniture and appliances after I see the Mayflower inventory, but I want my personal papers and files returned. I will pay all her legal fees, but I will not pay one cent for her self-inflicted emotional distress. Nor will I pay for a car, or one dime of her support. And, if she goes after my royalties, I'll bury her."

"Artie, you don't have to make a counter offer," David interjected. "We don't even have to answer them."

"I can't listen to the lies anymore. I want it over."

David tried to talk me down from my surrender. He said they were posturing and that he could negotiate a much better deal for me, but I told him no. If they will settle for money, they can have it. His secretary drew up the offer; I signed it and left.

JoAnn was waiting for me at home. When I told her Joan Bell's settlement demands and showed her what I'd had drawn up in response, I saw a crack in the strong, unflappable girl I'd married. The color drained from her cheeks. She didn't say anything. She could see how upset I was, so she put her arms around me and asked, "What's the deadline on your counter offer, honey?"

I didn't understand what she was asking, so she asked again.

"Did David give them a deadline to accept your offer?"

"I don't think we talked about that," I admitted.

"Call David and tell him to give Patti and her lawyer the shortest amount of time allowed by the court to answer your counter—like a week or ten days, if possible."

I didn't know what was in her mind, but I did what she said. David amended the offer with a termination date of September 30. JoAnn also called David later and asked him to advise me not to attend any more meetings with the enemy. She said she would represent my interests going forward. David argued that she couldn't do that, but she insisted his law firm research the matter. Because Patti and her lawyers had gone through the accounting files for JoAnn Kane Music Service, JoAnn believed she had the right to be at all future meetings, depositions and settlement conferences. She made a good point, and David listened to her arguments.

"They're gloating over Artie's reactions to their accusations and demands," JoAnn told him. "Patti knows injustices drive Artie crazy. The outrageous settlement they proposed caused him to lose objectivity and give away the store in his counter offer. They've been banking on that chink in his armor."

David researched JoAnn's premise and found case law backing her request to represent me in the future. And thank goodness we put the earliest possible date on my counter offer because they blew it. Yes! Time ran out; they didn't respond; they fumbled the ball; they missed the deadline, so we withdrew the offer and probably saved ourselves from bankruptcy. I remember JoAnn pacing through the house during the last two days of the month before the deadline, hoping the phone wouldn't ring. By that time, I knew what a terrible risk I'd taken. People say I'm volatile, that I take an instant dislike to someone to save time. The truth is I do make snap decisions. I overreact, which is just what Patti knew I'd do when pushed too hard. In this case, I had someone watching my back who jumped into action to save us both. I think JoAnn and I had a special dinner celebration over their blunder. I know David called to congratulate us, "That was a close call," he admitted.

We didn't think about the lawsuit for a while after that. David wrote a stinging letter to Joan Bell in October, stating that in spite of his reminders and warnings to her about the fast approaching termination date of our offer, she had not responded or acted in time and that our offer was no longer valid. David wrote yet another letter of demand for my personal papers and for the inventory of the stored items from the house. He left nothing hanging. He followed with one more response, pointing out the misinformation and incorrect figures contained in their previous settlement offer. We let things settle, especially my nerves.

We had better things to think about. I had two shows to write, and JoAnn's office was busy. All the while, interest on the trust accounts continued to accrue.

By November, we had to consider signing another year's lease or buying a house. Harold Plant encouraged us to buy something rather than throw money away on a rental. When we told him we had found a house in the Venice Canals, he looked skeptical, and when we told him the price, he looked stricken.

"There's no way I can make that work for you," he said. "You have to find something for a lot less. What's the matter with Sherman Oaks where you're living now? It's a lovely part of The Valley with reasonably priced homes."

"It's too far from the marina and our boat," I complained. It takes us an hour to drive to the water, longer in rush hour. We found a perfect place, but it's on Sherman Canal, not in Sherman Oaks."

The stern look on Harold's face remained, but by the end of our meeting, he could see we were hooked on the canal house and the neighborhood. He straightened his tie, which I took as a signal that he would get to work ferreting out financing for us by using his numerous bank connections. We had met the architect and the builder of our dream house who told us if we made a deal soon, we could pick out tile, carpet and all the finishing touches.

JoAnn and I celebrated our second Christmas together by sailing to Malibu on a blustery December 25 and returning to our new house on Sherman Canal for Christmas dinner with friends. JoAnn, the one who doesn't cook, had been taking gourmet classes, and they were paying off. The following week we planned another sail for New Year's Day. The weather was perfect, but I woke up in a cold sweat. A severe and debilitating panic attack gripped me for most of the day. Hours and another ten milligrams of Valium later, I stared at the canal from our deck and felt a calm wash over me. Ducks paddled around leaving a trailing v-wake; water lapped against the rocks. JoAnn handed me a pad and pencil and told me to write down everything I could remember about the panic attack and how it had subsided. She nagged me, lovingly, to keep a daily record of how I felt for the next couple of weeks so I could discuss it with my psychiatrist, Dr. Rosengarten, as well as with my internist, Dr. Uhley. A reversal of roles shocked me. For once, I was following orders from someone who cared about me, someone in my corner, someone who had my back. Instead of my usual role of rescuer-in-chief, I listened to my wife who didn't need rescuing; she needed a healthy husband.

Captain Artie

Home on Sherman Canal

Below deck

Under sail to Malibu

TWENTY-THREE

Take the "AA" Train

Rocky Moriana telephoned for a meeting just as I was leaving to have breakfast with our boat broker, Max Hardoniere, who'd become a friend and told fascinating stories about his life in the French Underground. I dreaded getting Rocky's call for a new show so soon after recording and delivering the previous week's assignment. He had approached me about alternating between *Love Boat* and yet another television series for the Aaron Spelling Company. I'd settled into a comfortable routine scoring *Dynasty* and *Love Boat* and was used to the hour-long drama of jealousy and mean-spirited antics between Linda Evans and Joan Collins, and the three segments on Captain Stubing's ship, the last one always ending with an emotional payoff and soaring music.

That afternoon, I found Rocky in his music editor's hat, ready for a spotting session—mapping out scenes and timings of

Artie and Max at breakfast on the boat

music cues—for the new series, *Matt Houston*. The show starred Lee Horsley playing an outrageously wealthy Texan dabbling in detective work while overseeing his oil-drilling rigs off the coast of California. During the screening, we discussed a different flavor of music for the new show, segueing from a slow-moving ship cruising the high seas with happy passengers to a bustling city with curvy roads, car chases and crooks.

The next day, Rocky, who guarded the company's wealth like it was his own, spent the money to messenger the music notes to me so, as he put it, I could "get right on it." The show had to record in eight days to make the network's airdate.

Cranking out music for television shows every twelve days, and sometimes sooner, left no time for worries about the palimony suit or for anything else except my weekly visit to my shrink, Dr. Rosengarten. JoAnn thought it was important to continue those sessions and the discussions I had with him about my nervous system and the trouble I was experiencing with Valium. Any free time JoAnn and I managed to find, we spent on our sailboat. On weekends, we'd pick up deli sandwiches at a nearby shop and eat lunch on the aft deck while watching heavy boat traffic maneuver through Marina Del Rey. Carol and Norm, some music colleagues and JoAnn's folks joined us often, and when time allowed, we'd jockey our way into the parade of boats, exiting the breakwater for a dash up the coast.

One weekday, I was laboring over a two-part *Love Boat* when David Kagon, my palimony attorney, called to set up a meeting. I liked David, but as kind and classy as he was, every time I heard his voice on the phone, I felt anxiety creep over me. This time was no exception. My body tensed as he informed me the enemy camp had sent over sixty-six interrogatories, detailed questions covering all aspects of the timeframe of Patti's and my relationship, to be fully answered in writing and under oath within thirty days. Here we go again.

I cancelled my session with Dr. Rosengarten that afternoon to meet with David instead. Recently, I'd become apprehensive about leaving the house. It took several tries, but I made it to my attorney's office, though I was an hour late. David sat me down and told me to stay calm. Another wave of anxiety swept over me.

"Now Artie, I want you to listen carefully. I've read this document twice," he said, waving a thick report at me, "and I can tell you every word of it is meant to anger you and drive you over the edge. There is no way any of this would be considered by a judge if the case ever made it to trial, but we're going to play their game and get all this information on the record."

"You mean we're going to answer all these questions?"

"Yes, every one of them, in writing. Since Joan Bell now realizes how badly she bungled your settlement offer last August, she is making a last ditch effort to find something to use as leverage to make their case. We're going to deprive them of that chance."

Even with David's warnings and assurances, I worried if I'd survive this new assault. Patti and her lawyer treated the breakup of Patti's and my relationship as though we'd been married twenty years when all we'd had was a two-year fling. They asked for three years support and a portion of my music royalties in perpetuity. I could feel the heat rise from my gut to the top of my head where sweat collected and spilled down into my shirt collar.

"Calm down, Artie," David repeated. "Think of it as a game."

These latest probes into my life were all about money—money I'd received between June 1978, when Patti and I had our first cup of coffee together, and September 1981, well after I'd rented an apartment to get away from her.

The interrogatories asked about my inheritance from my mother's will. They wanted a list of all the music I'd been hired to write during that period, the project airdates and the fees, royalties and investments I'd made. They asked for addresses of any real estate I may have purchased with monies earned while I'd been living with Patti. They demanded names, addresses and contact information for my friend who retrieved the BMW and for the couple who moved into the abandoned house so I could keep my insurance policies current. Finally, they wanted a list of all people with whom I'd discussed the lawsuit. This last request was a veiled threat to depose music and industry colleagues. The thought of dragging more people into the legal proceedings made me sick.

I turned down the next show from Rocky and scheduled several more appointments with David. During the musicians' strike of 1980, I'd been agitated and distracted trying to compose, but that paled by comparison to my ranting and pacing over this lawsuit and Patti's miserable attorney. Mentally, I was composing murder mystery music with the attorney as the victim while I was supposed to be answering her accusations and lies.

JoAnn kept reminding me, "She's not after money; she's trying to hurt you. Every time she sees you, honey, she gets pleasure from the anger you project."

JoAnn wasn't the only one leery of Patti's motives. A colleague of mine, Marty Berman, called my ex-wife and still agent, Carol, and told her she ought to get to know Patti because, "She's really a nice girl."

"So why the palimony suit if she's so nice?" Carol asked, scribbling notes.

"As payback for the six or seven women he's left before."

According to Marty, Patti felt bad about the raw deal Carol got and thought she should have received royalties from the music I wrote while we were together. Patti swore she was going to get something from all this. Maybe it was too late for Carol, but somehow Patti's lawsuit was supposed to prevent JoAnn from getting hurt so bad when I left her.

When Carol told me this, she remarked, "How bloody altruistic of her. I had no idea she was so concerned about me." I didn't believe

Carol until she sent me the notes she'd taken during the conversation. Meanwhile, three musician friends called complaining they'd been subpoenaed for depositions.

"Not by me," I told them.

Between strategy meetings and answering the interrogatories, I felt myself losing control and called my internist about upping my Valium dose. The month before, I had reported having dizzy spells and numbness in my arms and hands. My doctor seemed unconcerned about my complaints, but said he was taking me off Valium. He'd had several conversations with the neurologist who had diagnosed my brain seizures in 1967, and they agreed to leave me on Dilantin for the seizures but to try decreasing the Valium. Two weeks later, I was completely off the drug. I was feeling raw, unable to control my emotions. I often felt weepy. And the lawsuit made it worse.

It was tax season, and Patti's attorney threatened that if we didn't get a settlement soon I'd be paying huge tax penalties for Patti. Apparently, she hadn't paid her taxes and blamed her omission on my unwillingness to give her the money she was owed. Christ, it was her own damned lawyer who wanted all funds kept and monitored in three interest-paying trust accounts.

Though David assured me this tax ploy was nonsense, I couldn't stop beating myself up, worrying about JoAnn's reactions and her ability to tolerate me and all the baggage I'd brought to our marriage. I asked David to schedule another settlement conference with the hope of getting rid of this albatross. JoAnn had to give a presentation to the union board the day of the conference and couldn't join us at the start, but promised to arrive soon after.

FIVE OF US MET IN A SMALL DEPOSITION ROOM adjacent to Joan Bell's office. The court reporter sat poised over her machine at one end of the table. David pulled out a chair for me to squeeze into across from Ms. Bell and Patti. I could feel their eyes watching me. Patti whispered something, then, still eying me, Bell directed a question to my attorney.

"Mr. Kagon, is your client feeling all right? Does he want something to drink?"

She sounded like my rotten uncle, Dave, who made fun of me when I was a kid, "What's the matter? Is the little boy feeling sick again?"

I was feeling shaky and didn't want to start the meeting until JoAnn arrived. David put his hand on my shoulder and looked concerned. I realized what a mistake it was to come off Valium so fast. I couldn't breathe and gasped to get some air.

I stood up. The chair crashed behind me. I stumbled over it on my way to the door. I heard David calling my name, coming after me, but I didn't stop. I ran to find my car, and with my heart racing, I drove away breathing into a paper bag.

At home, I sat at my piano. I wanted to play something, anything, but my hands trembled. My whole body was quaking. I heard JoAnn come in from the garage calling my name. I hollered to her. "Honey, I'm sick. Something's wrong. I can't get my hands down to the keys. I can't feel my arms."

She ran in, stood behind me, hugging me until I calmed down. Later she told me I was swaying like Ray Charles. She said she'd been terrified when David told her I'd run out of the meeting.

My symptoms got worse. I was in the bathroom every ten minutes. JoAnn stayed up with me all night, walking me through the house, soaking me in a warm tub, massaging my back and neck. The next day she stayed home with me. By afternoon, I'd had two more episodes of panic and shaking.

"Artie, you have to see a different set of doctors," JoAnn cautioned. "You are going through drug withdrawal, and these clowns don't know what to do for you. You can't keep breathing into a paper bag the rest of your life."

I couldn't stop crying or shaking.

"Please let me call Dr. Rosengarten and get him to recommend someone. You still trust him, don't you?"

"I don't know who to trust, except you," I told her. "Do what you think is best. I'll try anything to stop these feelings."

My squeaky wheel of a wife badgered both my doctors until she got a referral for us to see a specialist at Cedars Sinai Medical Facility. A neurologist, Dr. Ron Fisk, who specialized in brain disorders, agreed to see us that evening. JoAnn drove me to the medical wing at the hospital where we waited two hours before Dr. Fisk called us into his office. Even in my condition, I liked Dr. Fisk. He listened to me, to everything I said. He didn't dismiss any of my complaints or crazy thoughts. He was kind. He addressed every worry.

Three and a half hours and several tests later, JoAnn backed out of the hospital lot to drive us home. It was almost midnight. She couldn't see the tears streaming down my face.

Still using the paper bag, I sniffled and said, "Honey, my right arm is going numb again."

JoAnn drove to the curb, took my right hand and gently pulled my arm off the open window frame, massaging it until the tingling stopped. She explained that I'd stopped the blood flow by crunching my brachial artery on the edge of the window. She saw I was crying and put her hand on my cheek. She said, "It's going to be all right. You'll get through this; we'll get through all of it."

After evaluating the tests, Dr. Fisk assured me I didn't have a temporal lobe syndrome, or seizures, that I didn't need to be on either Valium or

Dilantin, that I could get over all this and have a nice life with serious exercise and without drugs. He said it would be a long haul and told me to find an AA meeting close to home. He booked an appointment the following afternoon with another doctor, Dave Murphy, a drug withdrawal specialist, himself a recovering prescription junkie and the most unforgettable character I've ever met.

Doctor Dave was thin, scruffy, wild haired and a chain smoker. He didn't get up when I entered his office. He sat behind his desk, looked me up and down and said, "I hear your doctors put you on Valium for a lot of years—probably to keep you quiet. I'll bet you were a complainer."

I was afraid to say anything. I didn't want to stare at him, so I looked around and noticed an electric wheel chair and a pair of crutches next to his desk. I waited. He continued. "Well, complaining is a good thing because it got you to Ron Fisk and me. We're going to get you well with a lot of hard work on your part."

I learned that Dave was both a gastroenterologist and an endocrinologist who'd been in a life-altering car accident that crushed his legs, hips and pelvis. Doctors put him back together with pins and metal shafts, taught him to walk using crutches and gave him drugs for the pain. Unable to cope without the drugs, he became hooked. He understood what I was going through. Caring and sympathetic, he asked me if I'd ever been to an AA meeting.

I couldn't answer at first because I had a huge lump in my throat. I tried swallowing, which made the lump bigger, but when I took in a deep breath I calmed down. The urge to cry lessened and anger emerged. "Why don't these fucking doctors know what they're doing? Ron Fisk said I didn't have seizures and didn't need anti-seizure drugs."

On a rollercoaster of emotions, I finally answered Dave's question, "I don't need an AA meeting. I'm not an alcoholic. AA is for drunks."

Dave smiled and nodded to a chair opposite his wheel chair. "Sit down

Artie. You have a right to be angry about what's happened to you, but the special part of you is what has brought you here for help. AA is for drunks, but it's also for people with addictions—addictions to love, to drugs, to adoring fans. People who think they are special and need feedback from others, forgiveness for their unchecked behavior. These are the types of people who need to learn and practice the principles of AA."

Dave was well connected to the program and preached a sermon about its benefits. At Brotman Medical Center where he practiced, he had a drug and alcohol program that funneled patients into meetings in the area.

"Artie, you need to try a few different meetings and pick one that suits you. I go to one for doctors. There are meetings for priests, for CEOs, and in Hollywood there are meetings for artists and stars who can't cope with life and are dependent on substances to make it through a day. They're called drunks in specialized fields."

I have never met anyone so broken and in such significant pain with such a positive attitude as Dave Murphy. He dealt with his condition through pain management techniques without drugs. He told me stories of people who came within minutes of ending their lives but who were brought back from the abyss through AA. As a salesman, he could have sold snow to Alaskans in the winter.

It took me two weeks to find the right group. JoAnn went with me to some rough gatherings attended by gang members and derelicts. I was afraid of everyone. I sat at the back of the hall near the bathroom, clutching my pouch, inside which JoAnn had sewn a holster to conceal the gun I'd started carrying two years earlier. For an hour, I listened to horror stories and near death experiences of recovering addicts. When I found the meeting that gave me some measure of comfort, and where the crowd seemed less hostile, I chose a sponsor whom I'd heard speak at the opening of the meeting. A businessman who had lost his family because of his drinking, he spent time with me through the first months and kept me on track. I called him whenever I was in trouble, every day at first. Just knowing that other people had the same doubts, fears, insane ideas and paranoia helped me.

Paranoid and agoraphobic as I was, I never missed a doctor's visit or my 6:30 a.m. AA meeting in Marina Del Rey. Hearing stories of people who'd lost everything—businesses, careers, wives, children—and of people who had spent time in lockups—made a deep impression. I used to think I was special and had a right to my crazy behavior because I was an artist. Garbage! Spoiled and enabled would be a better description. We were all so full of ourselves—absorbed with our own feelings and accomplishments. I could always spot a new member. Excuses filled every sentence. I heard myself say, with a straight face, "My wives didn't understand me," never imagining it might be the other way around.

What we all needed was a kick in the ass. With support from AA, with healing and maturity, the stories slowly changed and the truth emerged. Over time, I heard many say, "If one more person had forgiven me, or been kind to me, I'd be dead."

At every meeting, each person would say, "Hi, I'm Ralph. I'm a recovering alcoholic." The group would say, "Hi Ralph." Whether we were drug abusers, doctors' junkies or drinkers, we all called ourselves alcoholics, though some smart guys would say, "I'm a recovering Catholic."

In addition to my AA meetings, I visited patients at Brotman Hospital twice a week to listen to others in worse shape. What a shock to see someone absolutely nuts and drugged out, or drunk and hung over, half dressed, throwing tantrums, screaming for a drink or shaking uncontrollably. Such tense scenes added a new perspective to my life.

Dr. Fisk, the neurologist who referred me to Dr. Dave Murphy, explained that Valium lives in the fat cells, so JoAnn changed our diets. Sandwiches had yogurt instead of mayo, and fish, drizzled with olive oil, sizzled on the grill. Desserts were ignored and fresh veggies and fruits filled the refrigerator. Fisk said I had to get on a serious exercise program for at least a year and then decrease it to moderate for the rest of my life. We bought bicycles. I rode mine four miles up and down the new Venice Beach path every morning after sleeping aboard our finely crafted sailboat—the merciful vessel that finally rocked me into dreamland after a month of sleepless nights.

During this siege, I couldn't accept work assignments on my television shows because I couldn't focus enough to compose music. Going through Valium withdrawal was just like in the books and movies—the shakes, tantrums, hysteria, anger. It was impossible to recover without AA and acres of help. My bosses at the studios just moved on to the next name when I turned down assignments. Everything I'd worked for was on the line because the jobs went to the person who was available when the offer was made. Success happens when preparation meets opportunity, and I was blowing off every opportunity.

The palimony suit threatened to wipe us out financially. We'd surely have to sell the boat. Panic attacks came in swarms, and I continued to carry brown paper bags. But as the weeks passed and then three months went by, I could feel improvement. I was constantly worried JoAnn would give up on me and leave. She didn't need my problems in her life. She was a sturdy Norwegian (I know that's redundant) but I wasn't sure she could handle a palimony suit, the possibility of financial ruin, drug withdrawal, plus the tangled elements of my sordid history.

JoAnn attended Joan Bell's depositions of my three friends plus one we had called. The first three transcripts contained pages of "I don't recall," or "I don't know anything about that." My music colleagues were completely unsupportive of Patti's position and were unable to confirm her assertion that I had promised to marry her. Nor did they know anything about her car or how monies were handled. Ralph Grierson even forgot he and I had argued on a recording stage the prior year about who was on whose side. But the fourth deposition of Steve Cowdrey cinched the case for us.

Steve, my sound system genius and friend, has a phenomenal memory. He easily recalls situations and can repeat conversations with amazing accuracy. He had been working or hanging out at the Redwing house at least three days a week. Under David's question-ing, Steve's testimony confirmed the troubled nature of Patti's and my relationship and living arrangement, due in part to her daughter's drug and alcohol abuse, the girl's unsavory boyfriend, Patti's mother whom I provided for despite her interference in our lives, Patti's ferocious headaches, and on and on. He testified that at no time in his presence did I ever say anything about marrying Patti, nor did she mention it while he was around. During the news coverage of the Lee Marvin palimony suit, Patti had told Steve she disagreed with Michelle Triola's position. She said a woman should leave with no more than what she brought into a relationship.

Captain Steve Cowdrey

The line of questioning grew even more personal. Steve revealed that Patti had told him I hadn't touched her during the eight or nine months before the relationship ended. According to JoAnn, at that moment, Patti turned ashen. Recognizing an opportunity, JoAnn contacted her after the final deposition to arrange a lunch meeting. Patti accepted. In preparation, JoAnn researched palimony cases and made copies of their results and settlements.

JoAnn said Patti was nervous and hadn't wanted anything to eat or drink. Patti said she never wanted things to go this far. She confessed that her lawyer convinced her she could get a good settlement and a couple years of support while teaching me a lesson that I couldn't keep leaving and blaming all the women I took to bed.

JoAnn had a frank exchange of views with her about lawyers and their motives. She showed her case after case where no money or support had been awarded to the plaintiffs in palimony suits to date. Then she presented an offer to Patti. We would give her half the profits from the Redwing property and indemnify her tax situation. She could keep the furniture but had to return all my personal papers—and my Italian wall clock—or as JoAnn later referred to it, her trophy for getting rid of the lawsuit.

It all came down to a two-hour evening meeting at Joan Bell's offices in Beverly Hills where Patti; Joan Bell and her secretary; two of Bell's tax attorneys; an accountant; my attorney, David Kagon; my wife, JoAnn; and a court reporter sat around a table hammering out a deal. My Uncle Joe was visiting us from Florida, so he and I had dinner with Carol and Norm at their Beverly Hills condo. Uncle Joe couldn't believe what good friends we were with Carol and Norm. After all, he had attended Carol's and my wedding. He thought it was all so civilized. On the other hand, Joe referred to Patti as "the bum." He was completely against her, first for breaking up my marriage to Carol, then for messing up my life with JoAnn. Joe would never admit that some of it might have been my fault.

JoAnn refused to allow me into the *situation room* as she named it. When she called Carol to say, "Send them over," Joe and I drove into the underground garage where JoAnn met us and ushered us up the elevator into an anteroom. There we waited for her to bring papers back and forth for my signature and initials. Joe was astonished at how we were handling the whole thing, a cloak and dagger routine that spared me from ever having to see those people again. In the end, Patti got plenty of money and so did we, but there were no emotional abuse payments or any admissions I had to make.

David Kagon's letter accompanying the Settlement Agreement contained a special paragraph thanking JoAnn for negotiating a ceasefire with Patti when no one else could. He went on to say, "We may be changing the name of our firm to Goldman, Kagon & Kane."

TWENTY-FOUR

It's a New World

Shadows of the lawsuit disappeared as the drugs drained from my system. I felt stronger, had more energy and pushed myself to ride further on the bike trails at Venice Beach. Addictive personalities glom onto new activities to fill the void left by drugs, gambling or alcohol. In my case, exercise was the key. I used to loathe working out when I took karate lessons, but Dr. Fisk was right. It was the best replacement therapy and mind-clearing tool. Exercise, and knowing I didn't have a brain disorder, made me feel healthy and invincible. All I needed was a film to score.

I called Rocky to announce my availability, and he put me on the schedule for Aaron Spelling Productions new show, *Hotel.* My agent, Carol, contacted other producers I'd worked with, and my calendar filled with composing assignments.

JoAnn's business blossomed into nonstop music production for Glen Larson television shows and 20th Century Fox films and productions. Her independent work also expanded to include the Boston Pops, the Academy Awards presentations, and the 1986 Liberty Weekend celebration in New York City.

We were busy. For the next two years, our sailboat at Marina Del Rey served as our recreational playground and refuge. Whenever we could

Avalon on Catalina

find a few days, we escaped to Catalina Island or ran up to the Channel Islands. Hiding out for a couple of nights on the boat, with the landline disconnected, brought us pleasure and renewed strength to deal with tight schedules. We managed to slide in a fifteen-day cruise on the Baltic, which we would have booked again, back-to-back, if we could have afforded it. We were definitely addicted to the sea with its beneficial side effects!

Because of a growing divide between property owners regarding the marina in Los Angeles, JoAnn and I sold our house in the Venice Canals and moved to Bel Air. There, music colleague, friend and pianist Stewart Levin, built a studio setup with keyboard

Baltic Sea Cruise

racks for synthesizers and 24-track recording capability in our new home. Stewart is clever; he rewired the house, integrated all my new equipment, and coached me how to use it.

Stewart Levin

My Bel Air Studio

This setup enabled me to assign instruments to my orchestrations and play them back while watching the film, which let me see how well my compositions worked with the script before I leaped into recording sessions. When I began composing for films in 1974, I would sketch out themes and the music underscore, and then orchestrate each composition the way I'd learned from my teachers Marion Evans, Professor Tedesco and Al Harris. In 1983 I had the opportunity to work with an orchestrator. It was the best time of my composing career because it gave me the freedom to watch scenes repeatedly until I thoroughly understood the mood and then could compose music that fully conveyed the emotion relevant to the scene.

John Neufeld

This period of collaboration began when virtuoso clarinetist John Neufeld called to see if I might try him as an orchestrator. Nerve damage in his right hand had forced him to change music careers. He had a vast knowledge of orchestration that he'd gained from his studies and through experience. I made a deal with my boss, Rocky Moriana, that when John orchestrated cues on my shows, he would receive union scale, and when he composed cues, he would receive royalties—neither of which he'd received working for other composers.

John and I had a good working relationship that developed into a close friendship. We discussed every aspect of the score, and I observed how he used the sections of the orchestra to color the music and give it variety. As a result, my writing for the orchestra improved. Each instrument brings its own personality to the mix, and John, who played all the woodwinds, voiced my music in ways I hadn't imagined.

We discovered we had a lot in common. During projects, we shared stories about the traumas of being child prodigies and pleasing our parents. Our hyperactive nervous systems had been nursed along with an assortment of substances from which we continue to recover.

Fortunately for John, but not me, JoAnn recommended him to her client, John Williams, after his long-time orchestrator died. It was a perfect opportunity for my friend and colleague, who worked with Williams on many films, including *Accidental Tourist, Home Alone,* and *Schindler's List.* I wished him well. We have remained good friends, but I've missed working with him.

Later, when I was doing some of my best composition work on *Matlock* and movies for television, such as *Gunsmoke* and *The Chinatown Murders,* I was lucky to have Eddie Karam orchestrate for me. He was so used to turning out music for deadlines that he could work anywhere—a stage floor,

Eddie Karam

a kitchen counter, or in my case, on our dining room table.

With both our careers in high gear, JoAnn and I found little time to enjoy *Noteworthy*. The long commute to the marina played a big part in our decision to sell our beloved sailboat, but we'd become attached to the quiet beauty of our new neighborhood and set out on a four-year remodel of our house to make it worthy of the 1.2-acre property we'd bought in Bel Air.

PART OF JOANN'S SUCCESS IN HER MUSIC BUSINESS stemmed from her insistence on proofreading every piece of music before it left her office. She was first to have a dedicated staff of proofers, and she convinced producers that the cost was minimal compared to having an orchestra on stage with pencils in hand, making corrections in their music as the time and money clock ticked away. Her company was well known for speed, accuracy and its calligraphic script. Therefore, it was no surprise in 1988 when Marty Burlingame, orchestra librarian for the Boston Symphony and Pops, put out a call for her office to prepare the music for a four-day gala celebration of Leonard Bernstein's seventieth birthday at Tanglewood, the summer home of the symphony. The job included onsite assistance with every aspect of the music for six days of rehearsals and four days of performances. JoAnn found it daunting, but felt honored to have been selected for the job.

Her office staff of copyists, proofreaders and librarians worked most of July preparing orchestra parts for guest artists plus a set of ten variations by ten composers on "New York, New York" (it's a helluva town) from Bernstein's 1940 Broadway Musical *On the Town*. These clever compositions, written in his honor by his colleagues, were daunting in their complexity and first up for rehearsal. Since I was on hiatus for television's summer season, I joined the proofing staff to give a final look before the music was packed for shipping.

We arrived in Tanglewood a week ahead of the first rehearsal to augment a staff of symphony librarians. Putting in long hours each day, four or five of us often rushed out to dinner at 10:30 p.m., hoping the restaurant was serving more than just bar snacks.

I continued to proofread music that dribbled in from participants in the last-minute group, making damn sure the music performances would come off without a hitch.

The night before the first orchestra rehearsal, JoAnn was nursing a splitting headache when Yo-Yo Ma came into the library with a special piece, "For Lenny," that he had composed and would play at the event. He asked if anyone could handwrite the cello part on parchment paper so he could present it to Maestro Bernstein on stage. JoAnn pulled out her calligraphy pens and wrote out the piece while the rest of us went to eat and left her alone to concentrate. When I returned, I offered to proof it, and there wasn't one mistake. It was a beautiful manuscript, and I was proud of my wife.

In the morning, one hundred musicians from the Boston Symphony Orchestra assembled for rehearsal on the enormous stage of the Koussevitzky music shed, a five-thousand-seat open-air pavilion, surrounded by a vast lawn accommodating another thirteen thousand listeners. Several staff members filed in with us to hear the rehearsal. Maestro Seiji Ozawa stood on the raised podium and cued the timpanist, who played the famous first four notes of "New York, New York," except the last note was WRONG!

I whispered to JoAnn, who had gone pale, "Doesn't he know the song? Can't the guy read music?"

Maestro Ozawa stopped the orchestra and called out the correction. I watched the timpanist take a pencil and mark his music. My mind raced; then I raced to the library and asked Marty to get the music as soon as they finished rehearsing it. I paced the backstage halls. Finally, Marty brought the timpani part. There it was glaring back at me. The wrong note! I had missed the mistake. I felt mortified and incompetent.

Despite my embarrassing moment, participating in these events with such enormously talented and distinguished people was enriching. The ease of collaboration between JoAnn and me renewed my faith in partnerships after the combative atmosphere I experienced with previous wives. Our bond highlighted generosity toward each other instead of competition. We've returned several times to hear the orchestra at Boston's Symphony Hall and to Tanglewood for summer festivals. Of course, we have remained friends with Marty and his wife, Aline, who is a clarinetist in the Boston Pops Esplanade Orchestra.

FAITHFUL TO THE AA PROGRAM and careful not to sabotage my relationship with JoAnn, I continued to attend meetings and work through the twelve steps. When I wrote out my moral inventory, I labored over it for a month, revisiting situations where I was clearly to blame. I have a quick temper, but the anger fades fast, and I don't carry a grudge. I'm always willing to forgive or admit I'm wrong if the other person is willing to listen. Listing the people I had harmed was one thing, but the ninth step called for a direct meeting, which took courage. I had started by asking for forgiveness from Carol even though I'd already admitted my mistakes in the marriage and apologized for them prior to becoming her client. Patti's name came up next.

When I asked JoAnn if I should arrange a lunch to apologize for my role in that destructive relationship, she was all for it, and said, "It's a good idea because Patti and I continue to work together and share clients."

Patti and I met at a dimly lit restaurant where neither of us ordered lunch, just Coke for me and water for her. I didn't know how to start. The silence between us drove me nuts.

Finally, I began. "I'm sorry—sorry for everything I did that hurt you.

I have no excuses. I understand my actions caused you pain and created turmoil between us."

Patti seemed hostile and said, "You're sorry now, but why did you lock yourself up in your office? Why did you stop talking to me? You drove me into a fierce depression. How was I supposed to get out of it if you wouldn't communicate?"

I was guilty. Period. I admitted I was angry about all the problems with the people around her, and I admitted I was wrong in trying to solve everything with money. I apologized, gave no excuses and was non-judgmental about every issue she mentioned. She said she resented that I made all the decisions and didn't discuss things with her. I agreed I was unreasonable. After three and a half hours, we both agreed to let it all pass. And it did. After that, we saw each other occasionally when I worked at Warner Brothers Studios and we even had lunch a few times.

A year later, Patti married Bob Zimmitti, a superb studio percussionist and drummer. They invited JoAnn and me to the wedding reception at their favorite Italian restaurant and gave us credit as the catalyst for their relationship. You should have seen the other musicians' jaws drop as they noticed us sitting near the bride and groom's table. Several years later, JoAnn and Patti worked together on two Barbra Streisand tours and several Vegas shows. They continued serving the needs of their clients in common. Patti recommended me as a conductor for her client Danny Elfman, and over time, the musicians forgot there was ever a problem between us.

In the fall of 2000, Bobby and Patti, who was battling lung cancer, stayed with us on Whidbey. We took them sightseeing at Deception Pass and toured the island. Patti loved walking through our woods and looking out over Puget Sound.

I still had others on my list for making amends. My AA sponsor asked about my mother. She was on my list, but I didn't know how I could make amends since she had died ten years earlier. "Write her a letter," he said, so I did and forgave her for her last words to me.

I recognized how my mother's fears and outlook on life had caused strife between us. I accused her of being a bigot because she looked down on gentiles and threatened me when I married out of the tribe. I used to tell her to go back to the old country so she could feel persecuted and carry on the tradition of being one of God's suffering, chosen people. My comments exasperated her.

Once she said, "You're not like any of us. I think they gave me the wrong baby at the hospital."

"Well I think they might have given me to the wrong mother," I said.

"That's a terrible thing to say about your mother," she hollered back.

Uncle Joe and Artie

Artie and Uncle Joe on *Noteworthy*

Now I just wish I could thank her and the family for what they gave me: a profession, an education, traditions and humor—all good material for the retelling.

I didn't owe Uncle Dave a thing, but several years ago, I had taken him to lunch during a stopover, and though he never apologized or even mentioned the beating, I forgave him in my heart and chalked up the onslaught to his grisly experiences in the war. God knows I barely survived my short stint in boot camp.

In contrast, my love and thanks always go to Uncle Joe who visited us every year until 9/11 and always claimed my mother would have loved JoAnn.

Other factions of the tribe have come

to see us regularly. Marvin Katz and his wife Sue joined us on cruises to the Baltic. Cousin Phyllis Katz Golden's son, Jeff, lived with us and managed the property during our first year of commuting to L.A. In turn, we traveled east for Joe's eighty-fifth birthday, a Bar Mitzvah or two and various other celebrations. I'm even crazy about JoAnn's family and have always welcomed their visits. It turns out, I do like close ties with many of our relatives. I miss those who are gone from both sides.

One part of the amends that I've never dealt with is my failure with my three sons. Though I have good relationships with David and Adam now, I've never had a serious talk with them to apologize or discuss my absence in their lives. I must address this soon because I can no longer blame their mothers or ignore my responsibility to them.

During high school, David did come to Hollywood to attend recording sessions with me and to see how I earned a living. I could see he was suspicious and angry. His visit didn't solve those feelings, but he must have decided I wasn't as terrible as he'd been led to believe, because he returned when I invited him back. He made the trip again the first year of my marriage to JoAnn. She had a discussion with him explaining that it would take time and effort to build a relationship between us. David agreed it would be worthwhile, but that construction project didn't begin until he married and brought his adorable wife, Joyce, to meet us. Between Joyce and JoAnn, David and I have forged a pretty good relationship for which I am incredibly grateful. They visit us once a year and we keep in touch by email. He is my son and I'm proud of him. He's smart, a fine athlete and a terrific person. He's also good-looking because of his mother. David's dedication to excelling in his studies

Joyce and David

Artie and Bryson

Artie and Coleman

extended to his determination on the basketball court where he was an all-star player throughout school.

As a father to my two grandsons, Bryson and Coleman, David is a loving disciplinarian. When they were growing up, he used the same standards he's always lived by.

Mowing with Papa Artie

A good sales representative with lots of business acumen, he was a top executive at GlaxoSmithKline until he retired. I refer to him affectionately as my drug dealer because two medications patented by his company saved my life a few years ago, and I still take them. Now David is doing what he loves—coaching basketball.

David, a fine basketball coach and referee

Artie and David

I am also proud of my son Adam, who lives three hours away and visits often when his busy schedule as a film director and producer allows. He graduated from NYU's Tisch School of the Arts and earned a Master's Degree from American Film Institute. His industry credits are

Adam and Artie lunching on *Noteworthy*

Adam on the set   Adam and Artie

long and impressive. We've had a few good talks and I've tried to answer some of his questions about our short time living together during his early childhood, but there are a lot of admissions I should make about not being there for him as he grew up.

I've had no contact with Paul in the last twenty years. JoAnn got him a job at Fox Studios in the early nineties that didn't work out well. I used to call or send greetings on his birthday and at Christmas, nothing that would sustain a relationship. My loss, for sure.

I'VE MADE MANY MISTAKES IN LIFE BUT MUSIC HAS SUSTAINED ME. In the late eighties, after scoring a few episodes of *Jake and the Fatman* for Viacom, I became one of a rotating group of composers on a popular spinoff show called *Matlock,* starring Andy Griffith. It was a semi-steady engagement over seven years that allowed me to take other projects between my assignments. One was a series called *Wolf* for CBS where I composed the main title music and scored the entire first season. However, new leadership emerged in that company, and the show was dropped though the ratings were good. Three two-hour *Gunsmoke* television movies also came my way during the same period and offered me a chance to stretch out musically, trying out new approaches to scenes.

A surprise offer came to conduct for composer Marc Shaiman. A third career began to open up for me because many young film composers either didn't conduct or preferred to be in the recording booth with the mixers and producers and not in front of a symphony-sized orchestra.

All three stages of my career—pianist, composer, conductor—hold wonderful memories, but conducting was the most enjoyable with the least pressure. I experienced more camaraderie with the players and distanced myself from giving opinions or making delicate decisions unless asked.

Between lunches at the studio commissaries with colleagues and meetings with composers and their crews, I liked my new position. I was still in the business, still making a living while contributing to an industry that has been good to me. Many clients for whom I conducted used JoAnn's copying office to prepare their music, which meant she often attended the sessions. That was even better.

Working with JoAnn at Fox

On a four-day call for a Danny Elfman picture at Sony Studios in Culver City, I had lunch with the usual suspects: Richard Grant, inventor of the Auricle recording mixer; Dennis Sands; Patti, my ex-girlfriend and the contractor who recommended me; and a few players from the orchestra. Some guy at the table told a risqué joke, and the harpist, Katie Kirkpatrick, remarked, "You guys should try it with handcuffs sometime." Our waitress blushed and the table erupted in laughter.

After the session broke for the day, I headed to Santa Monica Boulevard and stopped at the Pleasure Chest, a well-known sex toy store, thinking to myself, I'll show Katie. I asked the clerk if he had handcuffs. He pointed to an entire wall of them and suggested a fur-lined set as a starter. I bought a white fluffy set, had him wrap them in a gift bag, and the next morning, I set them on Katie's harp chair before the sessions resumed. When I mounted the podium, I looked out at the orchestra and saw Katie cuffed to her harp. All the players around her were watching. She winked at me and said, "Is this how you want me, Artie?"

Katie Kirkpatrick
Photo by DanGoldwasser/
ScoringSessions.com

That's when I learned "If you can't catch, don't pitch."

Nearly all of my conducting had been for live performances or films, but a special call came in to conduct a Natalie Cole record date. Her father, Nat King Cole, was one of my heroes. His distinctive voice told a story that could break your heart or make your day, but he was first known as a jazz pianist like no other.

As a teenager on the staff at WBNS, I was allowed back stage at the Palace Theater in Columbus where the Nat King Cole Trio often played.

Profoundly influenced by his jazz style and piano accompaniments of his own vocals, I imitated his elegant phrasing and imaginative piano fills whenever I could incorporate them into a song I was playing at the radio station. When Natalie and I met, I told her I had idolized her father, watching him through the side curtain at the Palace Theater, and that I felt privileged to conduct for her.

My memories of soaking up musical techniques from Nat King Cole dredge up memories of playing organ on Frank Sinatra's recordings for Nelson Riddle, the man who wrote hit arrangements for Nat as well as for Frank and Natalie. I valued every chance I got to work for Nelson, including his film and television projects.

FEW THINGS CAN MATCH THE EXCITEMENT OR NERVOUSNESS of recording with Frank Sinatra, but in March of 1993, I answered an early morning call from film composer John Williams.

"Hello RT" (a nickname). "Are you working today?"

At first, I thought John was making small talk with me before asking to speak with my wife, his copyist, who had already been at her office since 6 a.m. But no, John said he was having some issues with his back and asked if I could come to the Sony scoring stage to stand by for him. Because of JoAnn, I knew music for *Jurassic Park* was to begin recording that morning, so I asked, "Would you like me to be at Sony at ten o'clock today?"

"That would be great, thank you."

I showered, grabbed a snack and headed for the studio. I called JoAnn's office to obtain a parking spot near the stage but still had to negotiate with security as I drove to the gate. I gave my name to the guard who checked up and down his list.

"Sir, are you a musician? Because the musicians' parking lot is on the west side at the Overland gate."

"No. I'm here for John Williams."

He checked his list again.

"Do you know JoAnn Kane?" he asked.

"Yes, she's my wife."

"Isn't this her car?"

"No it's mine, but sometimes I let her drive it."

"Well then, if you know JoAnn, you can go in."

That was my first realization that my wife had more clout than I had.

It wasn't the only time I was caught unawares that day. Later, as I walked toward the stage, I saw an army of musicians milling around drinking coffee and noshing on breakfast rolls and pastries provided by the studio. Just getting through the stage door, stepping around chairs and instruments and dodging microphone cords and music stands was daunting.

I made my way to the booth where Ken Wannberg, John's forever music editor and my close friend, greeted me, "Hi kid. You got a hundred and six piece orchestra to play with today."

Kenny at work

Ken Wannberg — best sense of humor

"Hi Kenny. So where's the boss?"

"Steven? He's in Poland filming *Schindler's List*."

"No, no. I mean, where's John?"

"John? He can't even get out of bed. He's not coming."

"What do you mean?" I panicked. "He asked me to stand by for him."

"Don't worry, you'll be great kid."

I don't know why he calls me kid. I'm two years older than he is. I've always loved Kenny. He was a film composer who scored several films, including *Mother Lode*, *The Amateur* and *Blame it on Rio*. He didn't fall into any of the Hollywood categories and didn't worry about impressing others, but he was a magician as a music editor. He could cut and patch music and film together better than anyone in the business as long as he had a razor blade and a splicer.

I stood there quaking, terrified of conducting a John Williams score I'd never seen before.

Kenny, unperturbed and always upbeat, said, "Aw, if anything's wrong, we'll fix it in the dub."

I mounted the podium and pulled out the first score. It was black with notes.

A viola player practicing a difficult passage of music, exclaimed, "Gawd, I've never seen so many notes!"

"You should see what I'm looking at," I responded.

Sight-reading a full score of dinosaur chase music at breakneck speed is like running a gauntlet—one misstep and you're toast. The orchestra musicians had their heads buried in the music while glimpsing my conductor's baton out of their peripheral vision. I felt like a traffic cop waving them through an intersection of roadblocks. Just whipping over one page at a time, while conducting with the other arm, took considerable dexterity. During one cue, I mistakenly turned two pages and was lost for several bars of music. Thank goodness the orchestra plowed ahead.

Moments like that make you grateful for good relationships. A conductor must always treat the players with the utmost respect because one day they'll save your ass when it counts.

During a break after recording the first cue, I went into the booth for a playback and noticed seven dark-suited executives standing like security guards behind the console. I asked Kenny who they were.

"Lawyers and department heads from Universal," he said. "They're here to decide if the studio needs to file a claim against its artist insurance policy on John Williams, in case the recordings you're conducting aren't usable."

Queasy, I could feel the color drain from my face. My whole career passed before me as I considered that I was in over my head and not up to the job.

"Well, what do you think, Kenny? Can they use what we've done?"

"I've already told them we'll be able to use everything. John's been listening over the phone, and he's happy."

I think the entire room heard me sigh in relief.

Three days and fifteen hours of recording later, John showed up for the afternoon session, thanked me, took the baton and called up the next cue number as though he'd never missed a beat.

What I didn't know until later was that every night, Kenny had taken the recordings to John's house and played the music with the picture for his approval.

Artie and John Williams

IT'S INTOXICATING TO PLAY KEYBOARD FOR THE BIG STARS or to conduct for film's best-known composers, but sometimes the most rewarding moments are not about the famous. When JoAnn celebrated her fiftieth birthday, John Neufeld presented her with an audio cassette of *Variations on Happy Birthday* that he had written and produced using synthesized instruments. It was an inventive and exciting rendition of the piece, with a soaring finish that brought tears to her eyes. I begged John to orchestrate it so I could record it with a full orchestra sometime.

A year later, Marc Shaiman called me to conduct another film. On the final day of recording, he was in the booth with the film's producers going over last minute changes from the director. JoAnn and her office had prepared all the music for the sessions and she was there to make changes or additions as needed. It happened to be her fifty-first birthday.

John Neufeld had secretly employed JoAnn's office to copy out orchestra parts of his "Happy Birthday" variations. Her assistant furtively placed

MARC SHAIMAN
GOLDEN SCORE AWARD
COMPOSER

Jan. 29. 1999   7:08PM   SHAIMAN/WITTMAN   No. 6400   P. 1

Artie!

    I am SO sorry it has taken me this long to respond to your letter. I know you understand how crazed things get here, but there is no good excuse for not writing back right away. I apologize.

    So, you old fuck, you're deserting the sinking ship known as my career, huh?

    Can't blame ya.

    I am jealous of the thought of quiet serenity, and the chance to share it with the most lovely woman on earth. I won't tell JoAnn.

    Pete has been doing a good job, but there are things he will never know that only your 3000 years in the business can teach a person. I will do my best to show him a thing or two.

    I will ALWAYS be grateful for the lessons I learned working (RIGHT) alongside you. You are an endlessly fascinating man and musician, and I will TRULY miss your input and guidance. I know I speak for countless musicians and composers (they are not necessarily one and the same) when I say you have always been an inspiration to us (and I hardly *really* know you or your inner music, I was just catching up).

    So, I will just have to make due now with the stories and legends, and hope to see you at SOME point. Will you never come visit us at a session, just to taunt us?

    Please?

With the highest respect and love,

the score—titled HBV-11 to look like a movie cue—on my podium and the parts on each players' music stand.

When Marc exited the recording booth and saw my conductor score, he said, "Artie, is that from this movie? You know we're not supposed to record anything outside of the film score. The executives are still here." He paused a minute before adding, "But I'll think of something to get rid of them."

Mensch that he was, Marc announced to the execs that he intended to re-record some of the music and encouraged them to take an early lunch. Kirsten Smith, manager of Todd-AO Studios and a friend of ours, helped usher the producers and director off the stage and told her staff to go ahead and record.

Soon after, long-time friend and orchestra contractor Sandy DeCrescent called the orchestra to assemble and whispered to me, "Go ahead, Artie. The top brass have left the building."

On the podium, I apologized to the musicians for interrupting their break. Then, I called up HBV-11 and said, "Just do the best you can."

Sound engineer Dennis Sands sensed the situation and opened all the mics without turning on the red recording light. I gave the downbeat, and the next five minutes were electrifying. JoAnn looked up from her work and saw Kirsten, Sandy, Marc and all the recording stagehands standing around watching her. Then she recognized John's arrangement. Through smiles and tears, she realized I was conducting a symphony-sized orchestra playing "Happy Birthday" just for her.

TWENTY-FIVE

Our Love Is Here to Stay

Music is how I connect with people. Yet when I'm asked to play the piano, if I don't get a good reaction to my performance, I feel inadequate, as if I've failed to communicate with my audience. This probably stems from my childhood when judges loomed over my shoulder criticizing my fingering, listening for a mistake instead of giving their approval.

Many people don't realize a musician or artist puts his soul on the line when performing. Audiences know how to clap, but often they don't know what to say afterwards. My favorite is the mother who remarked nervously, after hearing me play a Chopin waltz, "My twelve-year-old daughter plays that piece."

Some people are uneasy and start to talk to each other as soon as I begin to play, but regardless of the circumstances, whether at a party, a restaurant, or an impromptu concert, it's bad manners even if they are talking about how good I am.

Michel Legrand, composer of more than two hundred film and television scores, told me that when he's asked to play, he plays for himself, not for the group that is listening, and he never takes requests. He says, "Among musicians there is an understanding and a profound appreciation for the language of music that not everyone can share."

For me, music is emotional and deep-seated. No matter what is going on in my life, the piano is the gift that has given me my greatest joy and emotional stability. When musicians play together in an orchestra, a band or even in a small group, all that emotion morphs into something greater, where the individual musicians draw on each other to create a performance that moves the soul. Synergy. That's what I experienced throughout my musical career.

Some talented musicians don't get the opportunity to pursue a career in music. Some fine players and composers don't have the people skills or the drive to sell their wares. It takes a combination of events, an aligning of the stars, or the help of a pushy mother or a benevolent but strict Uncle Joe to make it happen. I am the luckiest guy to have made a living in the world of music. To do what I love and to have survived on it is a blessing like none other.

I ALWAYS WANTED TO LEAVE THE BUSINESS BEFORE IT LEFT ME. So many musicians I've known never planned for life after the band. They'd get angry when new players came to town and their own work calls declined. I reminded them we'd all replaced someone when we arrived on the recording scene.

A wise friend told me, "Get a hobby. Make new friends, surround yourself with young people, and never stop learning."

I first felt the pangs of overstaying my time in Hollywood while walking to a studio cafeteria with a couple of musicians. "Did you know Harry died last night?" I asked.

One guy said, "Aw, that's sad. He was one great player, but he was getting up there."

The other one said, "I wonder what's on the lunch special today?"

In this country, little value is placed on people as they age, whereas in Asian cultures, elders are venerated for their wisdom and experience. Because of my unemployment experience in New York, I wanted to be prepared for the time when the phone would stop ringing, or as I call it, Life, Part Three. I didn't want to die with my boots on.

So JoAnn and I began a two-year search for property away from Los Angeles but close enough for occasional commuting. We found Whidbey Island, twenty-nine miles northwest of Seattle and a two-hour flight from L.A. It took us a few years to build a house and organize the move, but it was an exciting time, and in the summer of '94, a Bekins moving van squeezed down our narrow, gravel driveway on the Island, carrying all our belongings from five storage rooms of an L.A. warehouse.

I'd just received the music editor's notes and video for the final two-hour *Matlock* show of the seven-season series. I had one month to write and record the show, and I needed my studio piano, hydraulic desk, television monitor, synthesizer rack and recording equipment to do it. So JoAnn hired friends and family to move us in, starting with my studio. I composed music all day. Each night, I was astonished to see our new home taking shape. Although our schedules rarely coincided, we kept a condo in Los Angeles and commuted from Whidbey for seven years, working in the film and music industry.

I KNEW *MATLOCK* WAS THE END OF MY COMPOSING CAREER. The business was changing. Many shows were using smaller orchestras. Composers were producing music with synthesizers in their home studios and delivering finished music scores to producers without recording them with an orchestra in a studio. Although I augmented my orchestras with synthesizers for special sounds and effects, I was not interested in delivering a finished product from my home studio. I surrendered my pencil and score paper.

Soon afterward, my baton took the spotlight. Marc Shaiman called me to conduct his score for *City Slickers II* starring Billy Crystal, who often attended the recording sessions. Marc had written a clever clarinet solo as part of the theme, a standout section of the piece with a fast tempo that was no small matter to play or conduct. The orchestra always begged Billy to tell a joke or two, but one day he had other plans. He'd played clarinet in school and wanted to try playing the solo part. Since Billy was the producer and star of the film, the orchestra, in a rare moment, was more than willing to make room for him in the clarinet section. He borrowed the first clarinetist's instrument and took his seat. I called up the cue, checked that Billy's part matched the main title theme we were recording and gave the downbeat for the orchestra. When the clarinet solo came up, I cued Billy, but he missed his entrance, so I stopped the orchestra and said, "Billy, you'll hear the French horns come in four bars before your solo. Just watch me, and this time I'll give you a better cue for your entrance."

Billy looked up at me, frowned and said, "And you are … ?"

If I inserted pins on a personal map of all the places I'd played or conducted, the map would show I'd worked at nearly every recording facility in Los Angeles, several in New York and even one or two in Europe. Of these, a few venues stand out from the rest for their history and some for their luxurious amenities.

"Wait for my downbeat"

Most enjoyable were my conducting experiences at George Lucas' Skywalker Ranch. The accommodations and working facilities there were so comfortable that I felt I should have paid the studio for the

TTG Studio, Hollywood

Skywalker Ranch

experience. Mr. Lucas had built a state-of-the-art recording studio along with superb post-production facilities, a fully equipped gym and a spectacular pool, plus screening rooms. Bicycles stood ready for our transportation between buildings. When compared with Hollywood studios, which looked like run-down factories, Skywalker was an easy choice for producers who liked comfort. Editors, composers, sound engineers and conductors moved into ranch houses to enjoy grand fireplaces, soft leather furnishings, community kitchens and guest rooms with every amenity. Lunches were served for orchestras and production workers. Music editor Kenny Wannberg, orchestrator John Neufeld and I shared many meals when we worked together on films at Skywalker. I wish I'd recorded the priceless stories we shared about our industry experiences.

Another famed studio, Air Lyndhurst in Hampstead, London, is where I conducted a film score for James Newton Howard's 1995 film *Restoration,* a seventeenth century historical drama filmed in Wales. I had last traveled

Sony Studios

Air Lyndhurst

Artie in character conducting James Newton Howard's score for the film *Outbreak* at Todd-AO Scoring Stage

20th Century Fox

Warner Bros. Studio

to Europe in 1950 when I played and conducted ice shows. This time I flew first class on British Airways where flight attendants made sure I felt like royalty. Baroque in flavor, the score referenced the music of Henry Purcell. Because James was working on two other projects, he could not make the trip to London, so he left all decisions to his recording engineer Shawn Murphy, his orchestrator Brad Dechter, and his conductor, me.

I was miserable when JoAnn couldn't travel with me and share the experience, but as I opened my suitcase, out popped her small, stuffed bear that she'd crammed into my suitcase to keep me company. Brad and Shawn also looked after me since I was out of practice being on the road. They humored me at meals and made sure I got to and from the studio through five days of recordings. Every night when I returned to my hotel, the housekeepers had placed that furry little beast on the pillow to greet me after a demanding day.

In 1997 another conducting offer from Marc Shaiman took me to New York City thirty-seven years after my last engagement there. We recorded Marc's music for *In and Out,* starring Kevin Klein and Tom Selleck, at the dreadful Sony Studios where the orchestra was down the hall from the recording booth, an arrangement that thwarted communications between the two. The worst part of the job was the summer heat, from July 1 through July 15, in New York City. We had only five days of recordings scheduled, but we had two days off after each session. Again, JoAnn could not make the trip, this time because she and her office were busy making necessary changes to the music and emailing them to us at the end of each day before the next session.

I didn't know what to do with myself during all those free days. I don't go to museums, performances or shows, and I hate sightseeing alone. None of my former colleagues was around, and I had no friends in the city. After the first week, I discovered a connection with the flutist who was a friend of a friend. However, she wouldn't have lunch or dinner with me because I was married. JoAnn had to fax a note to her that said, "Liz, please have lunch and or dinner with my lonely husband who needs a friend in a foreign land." Indeed, New York City was like a foreign land to me. That was the longest time JoAnn and I had been apart, and I swore I'd never let that happen again.

In all, I conducted more than sixty film scores for Marc Shaiman, James Newton Howard, Danny Elfman, Michael Convertino, Steve Porcaro and John Frizzell.

Then 9/11 happened. JoAnn was in her L.A. office that early Tuesday morning when she received calls from worried staff members, so she turned on a small TV and watched as the second plane hit the World Trade Center.

I was stuck on Whidbey Island, beside myself with worry. No planes were flying; no trains were running. I didn't want JoAnn driving a rental car back to the Northwest alone. The only way I could bring her home was to beg two drivers from our long-time limo company to drive her the twelve hundred miles to Whidbey. The earliest they could start was the morning of September 19. She arrived home the night of the twentieth. I hated every minute away from her, and the thought of passing each other in planes headed in opposite directions was unacceptable. I decided to retire.

After the world descended into a realm of fear and distrust, JoAnn cut back her work trips to twice a month at her L.A. office. The rest of the time, she managed her business from home. We settled into a less hectic existence, becoming more involved in the island community, nurturing friendships, and hosting guests who loved exploring the Northwest and appreciated camping out in our guesthouses.

I'm grateful to have experienced Hollywood at a time when accomplished composers were hired to score films. I played piano for some of the best, including Alfred Newman, the godfather of film music and the head of the Newman dynasty; Franz Waxman, who composed his first film score in 1933 after his exodus from Germany; and Alex North, student at the Moscow Conservatory where he was the first American to study composition. His jazz score for *Streetcar Named Desire* was a first in Hollywood, and his love theme for *Spartacus* is a classic. I had the pleasure of conducting Alex's film score for *Good Morning, Vietnam.*

Artie and Alex North

From the beginning, Hollywood hired virtuosos, such as Erich Korngold, or my old mentor, Russian pianist and composer, Dimitri Tiomkin, who wrote a host of scores for films and specialized in westerns. I played in the orchestra for luminaries such as American composer Bernard Hermann, who wrote the unforgettably scary theme for *Psycho,* and for Hugo Friedhoffer, a fine cellist who scored the films *An Affair to Remember* and *The Young Lions* and won an Oscar for *The Best Years of My Life.* Johnny Green, winner of an Academy Award for adapting Gershwin's *An American in Paris* for the screen, hired me for several television shows and films he scored.

Next generation composers I worked for were equally talented and prolific with a lifetime of achievements. I probably soaked up the most information about the craft of film scoring from playing on Jerry Goldsmith's sessions. At age sixteen, Jerry was studying theory and counterpoint from the beloved Italian composer Mario Castelnuovo-Tedesco and went on to compose music for more films and television series than anyone to date. It was a thrill to play Johnny Mandel's songs "The Shadow of Your Smile" and "Emily" for his film scores, and a kick to work on Jerry Fielding's dissonant and intricate recordings for Sam Peckinpah's movies.

David Raksin gave the entire orchestra pause with his complicated and beautiful scores for *Laura* and *The Bad and the Beautiful.* He once told me he thought it was his duty as a composer to "test the mettle of the orchestra." Irv Kostal, who worked a lot for Disney Studios, won an academy award for adapting music from Broadway's *The Sound of Music* for the film. Playing for Dominic Frontiere projects was an honor, and I'll be forever grateful to him for paving my way into the music business in Los Angeles. Frank DeVol was first to hire me for a motion picture. I worked on several of his scores, including *The Dirty Dozen.*

It was a privilege to play "Windmills of Your Mind" for Michel Legrand's *Thomas Crown Affair* and to record for Quincy's *In Cold Blood* score. I was even around to play and marvel at the talents of Marvin Hamlisch and Randy Newman when they began their careers in the film industry. Then there is John Williams, who wrote plenty of challenging piano parts that I had good reason to worry about during his sessions. Of course, my long association with Dave Grusin, who I think is the finest all-around musician I've ever known, is a constant source of happy memories, except during the time I was married to his ex-wife.

Artie and Dave Grusin

For thirty years of my career in Hollywood, talented musicians who had a history of film scoring experience headed the music departments. All were unforgettable characters: the very funny Lionel Newman at Fox Music, Bobby Armbruster at MGM Music, Ray Heindorf at Warner

Music, and Stanley Wilson at Universal. It still astonishes me to think I had the good fortune of working with this litany of creative talent.

Music is the final piece of filmmaking—the essential element that pulls emotion from an audience and puts the goosebumps on the screen. If the emotion is missing, the audience is left with a void, and the full intensity of the setting, action and inner thoughts of the characters goes unrealized. Music is a necessary partner in telling the story, an accomplice to the plot, an honest broker for the film's intent. Music is the vehicle that drives home the point, unleashes the tears, and intensifies the rage. The right music can throw an audience into grief, despair and hopelessness, but it can also energize desire, joy and ecstasy. Within the film industry, the composer's role is to tell a story through music that sends chills up your spine or tugs at your heartstrings.

MUSIC BRINGS OUT ALL KINDS OF EMOTIONS AND ATTITUDES. When I met JoAnn, I had a bad attitude about girl singers. I'm not talking about Barbra Streisand's perfect voice singing through my headphones while I accompanied her on piano. Nor did I have a problem with Julie Andrews' clear, charming soprano while I rehearsed her for production numbers or played Lenny Hayton's score for the 1968 film *Star*. Some of the female singers I'd worked with though, in clubs and at the Roxy, were temperamental. Worse, my fifth and sixth wives were talented singers but difficult to live with. Then one day, sixteen years into our marriage, JoAnn admitted to me that not only had

Julie Andrews with Artie on "Star"

she majored in opera and sung many recitals, she had also put herself through school singing in churches and nightclubs around Minneapolis. What's more, she wanted to study voice again and had found seasoned performer Nancy Zylstra, who has a reputation as a gifted teacher, to coach her. This was a shock.

"What took you so long to tell me? I thought you majored in organ," I said.

"I did, my first year at the university."

Worse, JoAnn wanted me to play for her lessons and performances.

She was studying the *art song*. I had no idea what that was but soon learned it was a lyric song, a poem set to music, usually for a trained voice with piano accompaniment. JoAnn insisted I learn the poems, the stories behind the words. She expected me to understand what she sang so that together we could create and convey the meaning of the pieces we worked on and performed. Usually she sang in French, sometimes German and Italian. Occasionally, I'd get lucky and she'd sing in English.

The complexity of the collaboration required between a classical singer and her accompanist amazed me, and the difficulty of Debussy, Strauss, Poulenc, and other classical composers' piano parts surprised me. They were compositions in their own right.

I worried my piano chops might have suffered because I hadn't played much for the sixteen years I'd been composing music, but the skills were embedded in me, developed from years of practicing scales, arpeggios, and playing the classics.

Over the years, we prepared more than two hundred pieces of music for lessons, masterclasses, recitals and one concert. Now I'm disappointed because she refuses to sing. She says voices have a short shelf life and most sopranos don't sing after sixty-five, but I loved that we shared music this way, and it brought both of us pleasure.

I GOT ANOTHER JOLT WHEN VIOLINIST ELIZABETH PITCAIRN came to Whidbey Island in 2006, and I overheard JoAnn volunteer me to accompany her for house concerts and to conduct an orchestra for her performances at the Island's Center for the Arts.

Rehearsal with Elizabeth Pitcairn

My wise wife requested Elizabeth's music be sent ahead so I could look it over in advance. When I received it, I noticed the music had not been marked with her performance requirements. It brought back memories of Andy Williams' unmarked music. But as we rehearsed the flashy repertoire she plays so well, our tempos and phrasing locked into place during those finger-buster rehearsals and performances.

Audiences can tell when something clicks, and when it does, they are with you all the way through the performance. I have an appreciation

for Elizabeth's virtuosity and for her musicianship. She also tells a fine story with a good punch line. We became friends and later, when her schedule permitted, she would visit us for a Whidbey fix.

Performances with Elizabeth Pitcairn

My mother's idea of success for me would have been just what the Boston fortune-teller had told her: my name up in lights for playing concertos with symphony orchestras or for conducting Broadway shows. Mother got a taste of that and liked it when the ice show featured me playing Gershwin and when Carl Reiner told her how proud she should be of her son.

My idea of success has little to do with fame. I just wanted to know if I could play with the best musicians in the business. The exhilaration of performing or recording at the piano, the gratification of creating music with pencil on manuscript paper, and the excitement of conducting an acre of musicians in an orchestra flood my memories and satisfy my soul. Those thrills, plus the colleagues and friendships I've forged along the way, are my measures of a successful career.

JoAnn and I will celebrate our thirty-sixth wedding anniversary this year. Go ahead and gasp. I do every day when I thank the higher power that shepherded me through an incredible career in music, drug withdrawal, lawsuits, health problems and seven previous wives. I don't waste time feeling guilty for having a good life after making so many poor choices because it all got me to a place where I can accept, enjoy and share every day with the person I love. Of course, I had to go through AA and discover it wasn't my job to control the universe and that the sun didn't rise and set on

A man of many talents!

my talent. Maybe I had to go through all that strife to recognize what I found with JoAnn—a real partnership of love and respect where each of us has the other's best interest in mind, and neither of us expects anything but love in return. We're satisfied to share our lives and grow old together.

We live on twenty-five acres above Puget Sound. Our landscape is a mix of wetlands and manicured grounds, and every day I treasure it and the harmony of our lives together. I can't envision a place I'd rather be. More than anything, though, I want to be with JoAnn. If she wants to live in Alaska, I'll just buy a warmer coat—and bring my piano.

Acknowledgements

Huddled in the pages of my memoir are interesting characters and events that have played significant roles throughout my eighty-eight ongoing years. They reveal the unplanned and unpredictable path I traveled to pursue my dreams. I hope my journey encourages others to hang on to their aspirations, because upon reflection, no one can know how their adventure will be shaped. I wouldn't change one step of mine, because each one took me closer to the contentment I now enjoy.

In spite of a rocky relationship with my mother, I learned to understand her humor, and I certainly know she loved me and wanted only the best for me in life. I am indebted to her for steering me to music and the piano, which became the core of my life.

For Uncle Joe's daily attention to my musical career, I am grateful from the bottom of my soul. He never judged me; he always supported me and taught me diligence, which served me well.

Cousin Marvin and the rest of the family have nurtured and put up with me now for eight decades. I love them all for their patience and tolerance. Marvin Katz, Nachama Katz, Marc Schwartz, Arlene Hirsh, and Robert Goodof shared their interviews, videos and research, helping to fill in and confirm the family history.

My many partners helped make me who I am. Because my wife, JoAnn, accepts and loves me despite the baggage I carried to her doorstep, I thank them all for their varied handiwork in shaping me into a compatible, loving partner who finally found his true love.

To those companions, colleagues and heroes who have left before me, I feel honored to have known them and traveled in their company.

Long-cherished friends: Tommy, Kenny, John, Katie, Dave and Nan, Stewart, Ralph, Mike, Steve, Jacques, Herb, Florrie, Sally, Al, Trudy, Carol and Joan have enriched my journey and made it interesting and enjoyable.

New-treasured friends and neighbors like Norm, Noel, Robin and many others are a constant source of pleasure and good conversation over dinners, lunches, Saturday breakfasts, and gatherings.

Dr. Thomas Oliver, Dr. James Douglas, and Cathy Robinson, PAC, deserve special thanks for giving me time to write this volume.

I am grateful that Marian Blue agreed to interview me and to capture the stories that have become the foundation of this tome.

A heartfelt thanks to Ken Wannberg for the title of my book, for his cartoons that always keep me laughing and for nudging me to get on with this project. Thanks to Marty Burlingame for the book's subtitle and for his proofreading.

I'm indebted to the team of writers and editors: Candace Allen, Greta D'Amico, Dan Pedersen, Chris Spencer, Dave Anderson, Regina Hugo, Susan Balint, Patricia LeVan, whose comments and suggestions have made the book a reality. Your encouragement and your brilliant critiques made my story come to life.

Special thanks go to Candace who gently urged me to reflect on the rationale behind my life decisions and to include those assessments in these pages.

Michael Stadler's magical restoration techniques on photos and clippings, and his marvelous knack for snapping the perfect shot, have enhanced the book markedly.

David Malony's and Kirk Francis' patience in recording my music and stories have enriched this account of my life, as has Bob Richardson's research of my family history. A huge thanks goes to Steve Cowdrey for recording the audio book.

I'm grateful to the community of merchants, restauranteurs, artists, builders, and writers whose friendship we enjoy on Whidbey Island.

JoAnn receives my enduring love and gratitude. She still enjoys my stories and is a devoted fan of my pianistic endeavors. She encouraged me to relate how my obsession with music afforded me a career as a musician and how my quest for love rewarded me with our thirty-five-plus years of marital bliss.

PHOTOGRAPHIC CREDITS

Cover photo: Phil Teele, Bass Trombonist/Photographer

From the Berman Family collection—pages 4-12, 14, 17, 18, 20, 24, 43, 44, 48, 55, 57, 59, 60, 75, 138, 139.

Walter Neuron photo—page 17 and 23.

From the Kane Family collection—pages 121, 127, 128, 145, 158, 159, 187, 206, 208, 224, 230, 238, 242, 243, 254, 250, 257, 265, 281, 291, 292, 307, 308, 309, 314, 315, 316, 317, 318, 319, 320, 323, 331-336.

From the New York Public Library scans and permissions—pages 134-135.

Courtesy, Holiday on Ice Collection, Tom Collins—pages 65, 68, 70, 73, 99, 102, 103, 104, 105.

From the Collins Family collection—pages 110, 111, 113.

Columbus Dispatch—page 37.

From South High School's Lens Yearbook, Courtesy Gloria Mertz—pages 34, 36.

photo © Robert Balcomb—page 345.

Balint Family collection—pages 182, 190, 193.

Joel Franklin photography—back cover, title page and page 250.

Norman Tetef, photographer—page 281.

George Fields/Photography—pages 201 and 202.

Steve Davis Photography—pages 147, 172, 276, 277.

Matt Johnson Photography—pages 343, 344.

Dan Goldwasser/*ScoringSessions.com* – Katie Kirkpatrick, Harp—page 321.

Photograph by Cal Montney, *Los Angeles Times,* December 30, 1974. Reprinted with permission—page 233.

Two "screen grabs" from Frank Sinatra's *A Man and his Music Part II,* Warner Reprise Video, now owned by Eagle Rock, Universal

Music Group. Permission granted from Frank Sinatra Enterprises—pages 180 and 181.

Two-Piano recording session photos by Ken Veeder, Capitol Records in-house photographer—page 234.

RMS Caronia photo by Oscar J. Johanson—page 81.

Bruno of Hollywood—page 132.

Maurice Seymour, Photographer, Chicago—Page 54.

PUBLICATION & SOURCE REFERENCES

For the Record, Jon Burlingame

Frank Sinatra, An American Legend, Nancy Sinatra

September in the Rain, The Life of Nelson Riddle, Peter J. Levinson

No Minor Chords, André Previn

Sunday Nights at Seven, The Jack Benny Story, Joan Benny

NEWSPAPER CLIPPINGS & SOURCES

Columbus Dispatch and Evening Dispatch—page 37.

Columbus Citizen, Citizen Magazine—page 16.

Columbus Sunday Star—page 13, 32.

Ohio State Journal—page 51.

Wheeling New Register—pages 18 and 19.

Wall Street Journal—page 181.

Los Angeles Times—page 233.

JOURNALISTS

Norman Nadel (On the Aisle, Column)—page 53.

Dorothy Todd Foster—page 37.

Beatrice Butler—page 33.

Art Robinson, *Columbus Citizen*—page 32.

Marc Myers, *Wall Street Journal*—page 181.

INDEX

Adams, Chaplain Roland C., 86-90
Adams, Edie, 166
Agudas Achim (temple), 11
Alcoholics Anonymous (AA),
　90, 299-302, 312-313, 344
Alliance of Motion Picture and
　Television Producers (AMPTP), 260
Alpert, Herb, 202-203
American Boychoir School,
　19-24, 26, 33, 49, 51, 106
American Federation of Musicians
　(AFM), 117, 122, 221, 257-260
Andrews, Julie, 341
Arden, Donn, 95
Asner, Ed, 260

Bain, Bob, 198-200
Bart, Alvin (Al), 221, 237, 250
Barzman, Alan, 199
Beard, Marshall, 104-106, 108-109, 195
Belarus, viii, 6
Bell, Joan, 275-276, 283-285,
　287-289, 294, 297, 302, 304
Benny, Jack, 208-212, 214, 216-218,
　225-227, 232-234, 238, 240
Benny, Joan, 46, 208-220, 222, 224-225,
　227-233, 235-236, 238, 275, 285,
　288, 289, 292, 294, 297, 302, 304
Bentley, Muriel, 95-96
Berkman, John, 141-142

Berman, Cousin Aaron, ix, 165
Berman, Uncle Dave, viii, 8, 11, 13,
　19, 21, 26, 44-45, 55-56, 297, 314
Berman, Uncle Joe, viii, 6, 8-13, 17,
　19, 23-26, 38, 42, 44-45, 48, 53,
　56, 85-87, 101, 116, 139, 163-164,
　238-239, 242, 304, 314, 329
Berman, Uncle Oscar, viii, 6-8, 45
Bernstein, Elmer, 69, 221
Bern, Switzerland, 82
BMW, 254, 271, 275-276, 287, 295
Boucher, Bob, 129, 132-133, 135, 142
Boxell, Earl, 68
brain seizures, 164, 296, 298-299
Broadcast Music, Inc. (BMI), 241
Broad Street Presbyterian Church,
　19-20, 106
Broner, Bill, 38-39, 42
Brooks, Richard, 275
Brotman Hospital, 300-301
Brown, Ray, 201, 205
Brussels, Belgium, 75-77, 107
Bunker, Larry, 70, 202
Burke, Sonny, 180

Caesar, Sid, 159-162
Calhoun, Miss, 43, 45
Camp Wilson, YMCA, 24
Capitol Records, 236
Carle, Frankie, 37

Carlson, Frankie, 152
Castelnuovo-Tedesco, Mario, 150-151, 177-178, 220-221, 223, 308, 339
Catalina Island, 307
Chalfen, Morris, 70-72, 79, 96, 110, 112-113, 117, 120-121, 124
Cheadle, Jean, ix, 104-110, 195
The Chinatown Murders, 309
City Slickers II, 331
Clark, Jinx, ix, 73-78, 80-82, 86, 91-99, 101, 104-107, 110, 118, 163, 195, 225
Clark, Louise, 74-81, 91-97, 195, 225
Club Gloria, 48-49, 51, 54, 56
Cohen, Nathan (Father), viii, 7-9, 42, 58
Cohen, Sarah Berman (Mother), viii, 5-8, 11-15, 17-18, 22, 25, 27-32, 34-35, 37-47, 50, 54-56, 58-59, 66, 83, 91-92, 94, 101, 116, 125, 138-140, 149, 162-167, 171, 203, 219, 230, 238-240, 243, 252, 285, 294, 313-314, 324, 344
Coleman, Henry, 286
Collins, Tommy, 110-111
Columbus Boychoir School, *See American Boychoir School*
Columbus Symphony, 17, 50, 99, 235
Conservatory of Music (Cinncinati), 25, 51
copyists, 156, 223, 261-262, 265-266, 274, 282, 310, 322
Cowdrey, Steve, 280, 303
Cramer, Doug, 246
Crystal, Billy, 331

Davis, Bette, 163
Davyd-Horodok, viii, 5, 9
Dayas, Karin, 25
DeCaro, Patti, 1-3, 250-255, 261, 267, 269, 271-272, 275-276, 280, 283-289, 293-297, 302-305, 312-313, 321
Deposition, 1, 283-285, 297, 303
DeVito, Tony, 121, 125-127, 136, 139
DeVol, Frank, 155, 163, 340
DiCenzo, Richie, 48, 55
Dilantin, 3, 164, 267, 296, 299

Disney Studios, 261, 340
Dunaway, Faye, 247, 249-250
Durgom, Bullets, 142, 146, 150, 162
Durselen, Roland, 76
Dworkin, Leo, 48, 55
Dynasty, 292

Edwards, Miss Alva (Principal), 34, 46-48
Elfman, Danny, 313, 321, 338
Elliott, Bobbi, 159, 161-163, 170, 172, 182-183
Elliott, Jack, 159-163, 165, 170-172, 176, 182-183, 199-200
Esther (housekeeper), 207
Evans, Marion, 119, 130, 177, 308
Eyes of Laura Mars, 247, 250

Faith, Carol, ix, 238-246, 250-255, 268-269, 273, 279-282, 293, 295-296, 304, 306, 312
Finley, John, 64-65
Fisk, Dr. Ron, 298-299, 301-302, 306
Fort Hayes, 82
Fort Meade, 83, 85
Fox, Charlie, 222, 224, 238, 240-241
Frontiere, Dominic, 125, 148, 153, 155, 177-178, 241-242, 340
Frumanski, Dr., 164
Fuentealba, Victor, 259-260, 264

Gershwin, George, 26, 51, 99-100, 232, 234-235, 238, 339, 344
Gilbert, Matt, 21, 58
Gluskin, Lud, 174-175
Goldsmith, Jerry, 150, 246, 249, 339-340
Good Morning, Vietnam, 339
Grammy nomination, 236
Greystone Hotel, 26, 30
Grierson, Ralph, 204-205, 231-232, 234-236, 302
Griffith Park, 188-189
Grotrian-Steinweg, 169, 171, 178

Grusin, Dave, 170-171, 176-177, 181-187, 195-196, 200, 202, 237, 340
Grusin, Michael, 184-187, 191-194, 196-197
Gunsmoke, 309, 320
Guys and Dolls, 148
Gypsy Rose Lee, 60, 63

Hamlisch, Marvin, 273-274, 340
HAP (half-assed principal), 97-98
Hardoniere, Max, 292
Harris, Bobby, 285
Harris, Dr. Albert, 220-221, 308
Heifetz, Jascha, 229-230
Heindorf, Ray, 176, 340
Helfer, Bobby, 199
Henie, Sonja, 66, 104, 112-114, 116-120, 143
Herman, Max, 259
Herz, Madame, 26-27, 31-33, 61
High School of Music and Art, 27
Holiday on Ice, 64-65, 70-72, 76, 82, 89, 99-100, 104, 110-113, 119-121, 141, 163, 235
Holly, Joy, ix, 56-63, 66-68, 68, 75, 77, 81, 118, 195
Hotel, 306
Hyman, Dick, 119

In and Out, 337
interrogatories, 293-294, 296

Jake and the Fatman, 320
Jarkey, Harry, 48, 53-57
Jobim, Antonio Carlos, 170-171
Johnson, Bobby, 66-67, 79
Johnson, JoAnn, ix, 126, 166, 214, 261-283, 285-291, 293, 295-298, 300-307, 309-315, 319-320, 322-323, 326-327, 330, 337-338, 341-345
Jones, Quincy, 200-202, 246, 340
Jones, Tommy Lee, 247, 249
Jurassic Park, 322
juvenile court, 38-39

Kagon, David, 1-2, 275-276, 284, 286-289, 293-297, 297, 303-305
Kane, Adam, ix, 190-197, 207, 315, 318-319
Kane, Paul Steven, ix, 158, 162, 164, 167-168, 171, 173, 177, 179, 194-197, 207, 319
Ka-Sees, 61-62
Katz, Aunt Flora, viii, 7-10, 12-13, 15
Katz, Cousin Marvin, ix, 12, 13, 25, 242, 315
Katz Golden, Cousin Phyllis, ix, 242, 315
Kaufman, Pearl, 208
Kaufman, Ronnie, 170
Kester, Howard, 28
Klein, Bob, 199, 202, 203
Klein, John, 20-24

Lava, Bill, 164
Lazarus, Dr. Maury, 147, 171, 190
Legrand, Michel, 168, 200, 204-205, 328, 340
Levinson, Peter J., 180
Livingstone, Mary, 209, 211-214, 220, 225, 232-233
Local 47, 148, 152, 259, 261-262
Looking for Mr. Goodbar, 244-245, 275
The Love Boat, 222, 246, 255, 286, 292-293

making amends, 313-315
Mancini, Henry, 150, 205-206, 220-221, 237
Manne, Shelly, 202, 205
Marina Del Rey, 277, 286, 293, 301, 306
Martin Hotel, 107-108
Marvin, Lee, 273, 275-276, 303
Matlock, 309, 320, 330
Matt Houston, 293
Mattiazzi, Count Carlo, 133-134
Mauna Kea Beach Hotel, 225, 243, 280
Mauretania, 275, 277
Memorial Hall, 51-52
Mendoza, Alfredo, 98

Mermaid Tavern, 235
Mertz, Gloria, 36-40,
    43-44, 50-51, 74, 92
Mexico City, 112-114
Midlick, Jimmy, 48, 55
Miller, Bea, 285
Miltown, 145, 147, 149, 151, 163
Mitchell, Red, 152
Morgan, Jaye P., ix, 117, 142-150,
    155-159, 161-164, 167-168, 170-173,
    177-178, 183, 194-195, 231, 254
Moriana, Rocky, 255, 257, 260,
    292-293, 295, 306, 309
Morris, Tug, 55
Murphy, Dr. David, 299-301
musicians' strike, 257-265, 295
music royalties, 44, 253, 272,
    284-285, 288, 294-295, 309
Myers, Marc, 181

Nadel, Norman, 53
Nappo, Carmen, 65, 71
NBC, 116-117, 119, 160, 176
Nero, Peter, 156-157, 203
Newman, Lionel, 198, 230, 237, 244,
    265-266, 268, 276, 282, 340
Newman, Marc, 237-238,
    244, 247-248, 250-251
Night of the Juggler, 257
Noteworthy, 276, 283, 285-286, 290-293,
    302, 306-307, 310, 314, 319

Ohio Federation of Music Clubs, 14
Olodort, Abe, 241-243, 281-282
Olodort, Adele, 241-243, 281-282

Palace Theater, 37, 321-322
palimony, 1, 272, 276, 282,
    285-286, 293, 295, 302-304
Pallet, Dolores, 67-68, 99, 120-121
Parkinson, Geer, 34-35, 42
Perches, Joe, 169
Peters, Jon, 247-248
Pichinson, Rose, 28, 30-31

Pitcairn, Elizabeth, 343
Plant, Harold, 271-272,
    275, 284-285, 290
Playboy, 126-127, 137, 198
Poncho, 94, 97-98, 111
Posey, Lou, 49
Previn, André, 152, 166-167

A Question of Guilt, 246

Reagan, Ronald, 209, 226, 255
Reiner, Carl, 165-166, 344
Restoration, 334
Rhapsody in Blue, 51-52,
    99-100, 102-103, 235
Riddle, Nelson, 179-180, 322
RMS Caronia, 81
Rosengarden, Bobby, 119
Rosengarten, Dr. Leonard, 128,
    172, 184, 186, 196, 209, 251,
    252, 291, 293-294, 298
Roxy Theater, 129-136, 138,
    141-142, 152, 341
Russell, Bryson Kane, ix, 316-317
Russell, Coleman, ix, 316-317
Russell, David, 120-122, 124, 126-129,
    136, 138-140, 158, 196-197, 315-316, 318
Russell, Joyce, ix, 315
Russia, viii, 6-11, 101, 174, 339

Saturday's Rhythm, 49
Schiff, Joan, 46-47
Screen Actors Guild (SAG), 260
Shaiman, Marc, 320,
    326-327, 331, 337-338
Shepherd, Tommy, 179
Sheraton Ritz, 270
Sherman Canal, 290-291
Sinatra, Frank, 143, 177, 179-181,
    205, 225-226, 322
Smithers, Doug, 268, 271
Snook Neal band, 32, 35
Solomon, Izler, 50-52
Sonja Henie's Holiday On Ice, 116

Sosnik, Harry, 120
South High School, 32, 32-34, 36
Spam, 77-78
Stabler, Ben, 100
Staniloff, Midge, 28-31, 37, 66, 92
Stern, Isaac, 227
Stevens, Sally, 221-222, 235-237
Stine, Bill, 73-74
Streisand, Barbra, 143, 168-169, 247-250, 313, 341
Sukman, Harry, 157
Summers & Son, 36
Summey, Paul, 69
Superstein, Leah & Larry, 227-231
'S Wonderful, 232, 234-236

Tail of the Cock, 161
Tallman, Sara Jane, ix, 176, 181-197, 253
Tallman, Susan, 181-184, 195-196
Tanglewood, 310-312
Taylor, Judge Genevieve, 38-43
Teitelbaum, Cousin Jeff, 315
temporal lobe disorder, 164, 298
Tetef, Norman, 279-281
Thomas, Bob, 79
Thompson, Wayne, 119
Tiomkin, Dimitri, 174-175, 339
Tomlinson, Jerry, 142-143, 145
Town Hall, 26
Turner, Ray, 153, 155-156
Tyson, George, 71-72, 99

Uhley, Dr. Milton, 147, 163, 291
USS George Washington, 7

Valium, 3, 5, 164, 179, 217, 258, 267, 283, 291, 293, 296-302
Vegas, 246, 255, 257
Venice Canals, 286, 290, 307

Walters, Cathy, 189, 198
Wayne, John, 227
WBNS radio station, 33-38, 42-44, 46, 49-52, 64, 321-322
Wells, Sherry, ix, 111-122, 124, 126-129, 136-142, 158, 195
Wenona Beach Casino, 54-57
Whelan, Mickey, 153, 155-156
Where's Poppa?, 165
Wild, Earl, 160
Wilkinson, Captain, 85-86, 88-90
Williams, Andy, 159, 176-177, 224, 343
Williams, John, 150, 200, 237, 248, 309, 322-325, 340
Wolf, 320
Wolf, Kurt, 204, 250
Wonder Woman, 222-224, 240, 246, 250-251
World War II, 26, 29, 172
Wright, Agnes, 5, 10, 14, 16-17, 23, 25-26, 33, 51, 63
Wrong is Right, 275

Yom Kippur, 240
Yorkin, Bud, 185

Zager, Belle, viii, 6
Zager, Leib, viii, 6
Zimmitti, Bob, 313
Zylstra, Nancy, 342